Vedic Mathematics
For Schools

Vedic Mathematics For Schools

JAMES T. GLOVER

Preface of

H.E. DR. L.M. SINGHVI

Formerly High Commissioner for India in the UK

BOOK 2

MOTILAL BANARSIDASS PUBLISHERS
PRIVATE LIMITED ● DELHI

: *Delhi, 1999*
001, 2003, 2004, 2005

LOVER

ISBN: 81-208-1670-6

MOTILAL BANARSIDASS

41 U.A. Bungalow Road, Jawahar Nagar, Delhi 110 007
8 Mahalaxmi Chamber, 22 Bhulabhai Desai Road, Mumbai 400 026
236, 9th Main III Block, Jayanagar, Bangalore 560 011
120 Royapettah High Road, Mylapore, Chennai 600 004
Sanas Plaza, 1302 Baji Rao Road, Pune 411 002
8 Camac Street, Kolkata 700 017
Ashok Rajpath, Patna 800 004
Chowk, Varanasi 221 001

Printed in India
BY JAINENDRA PRAKASH JAIN AT SHRI JAINENDRA PRESS,
A-45 NARAINA, PHASE-I, NEW DELHI 110 028
AND PUBLISHED BY NARENDRA PRAKASH JAIN FOR
MOTILAL BANARSIDASS PUBLISHERS PRIVATE LIMITED,
BUNGALOW ROAD, DELHI 110 007

Preface by
His Excellency Dr L.M.Singhvi
High Commissioner for India in the UK

Vedic Mathematics for Schools is an exceptional book. It is not only a sophisticated pedagogic tool but also an introduction to an ancient civilisation. It takes us back to many millennia of India's mathematical heritage. Rooted in the ancient Vedic sources which heralded the dawn of human history and illumined by their erudite exegesis, India's intellectual, scientific and aesthetic vitality blossomed and triumphed not only in philosophy, physics, ecology and performing arts but also in geometry, algebra and arithmetic. Indian mathematicians gave the world the numerals now in universal use. The crowning glory of Indian mathematics was the invention of zero and the introduction of decimal notation without which mathematics as a scientific discipline could not have made much headway. It is noteworthy that the ancient Greeks and Romans did not have the decimal notation and, therefore, did not make much progress in the numerical sciences. The Arabs first learnt the decimal notation from Indians and introduced it into Europe. The renowned Arabic scholar, Alberuni or Abu Raihan, who was born in 973 A.D. and travelled to India, testified that the Indian attainments in mathematics were unrivalled and unsurpassed. In keeping with that ingrained tradition of mathematics in India, S.Ramanujan, "the man who knew infinity", the genius who was one of the greatest mathematicians of our time and the mystic for whom "a mathematical equation had a meaning because it expressed a thought of God", blazed many new mathematical trails in Cambridge University in the second decade of the twentieth century even though he did not himself possess a university degree.

The real contribution of this book, *Vedic Mathematics for Schools*, is to demonstrate that Vedic mathematics belongs not only to an hoary antiquity but is any day as modern as the day after tomorrow. What distinguishes it particularly is that it has been fashioned by British teachers for use at St James Independent Schools in London and other British schools and that it takes its inspiration from the pioneering work of the late Bharati Krishna Tirthaji, a former Sankaracharya of Puri, who reconstructed a unique system on the basis of ancient Indian mathematics. The book is thus a bridge across centuries, civilisations, linguistic barriers and national frontiers.

Vedic mathematics was traditionally taught through aphorisms or *Sutras*. A *Sutra* is a thread of knowledge, a theorem, a ground norm, a repository of proof. It is formulated as a proposition to encapsulate a rule or a principle. A single *Sutra* would generally encompass a wide and varied range of particular applications and may be likened to a programmed chip of our computer age. These aphorisms of Vedic mathematics have much in common with aphorisms which are contained in

Panini's *Ashtadhyayi*, that grand edifice of Sanskrit grammar. Both Vedic mathematics and Sanskrit grammar are built on the foundations of rigorous logic and on a deep understanding of how the human mind works. The methodology of Vedic mathematics and of Sanskrit grammar help to hone the human intellect and to guide and groom the human mind into modes of logical reasoning.

I hope that *Vedic Mathematics for Schools* will prove to be an asset of great value as a pioneering exemplar and will be used and adopted by discerning teachers throughout the world. It is also my prayer and hope that the example of St James Independent Schools in teaching Vedic mathematics and Sanskrit may eventually be emulated in every Indian school.

London
13th March 1995

Introduction

Vedic Mathematics for Schools Book 2 is a text for the first-year at senior school. Book 1 of the series is for primary schools and does not have to be read first since each of the methods in the present work are introduced from their inception. These books are based on the fundamental ancient Hindu system which uses a few simple rules and principles which in Sanskrit are called sutras. The sutras enable fast and easy methods of calculation.

On the discovery and nature of Vedic mathematics

This system of mathematics was recreated by the late Sri Bharati Krishna Tirthaji (1884 - 1960) a brilliant scholar and exponent of the spiritual teachings of the Veda (he held the seat of Sankaracharya of Puri for many years). The Vedas are the ancient scriptural texts of India written in Sanskrit. They are concerned with both the spiritual and secular aspects of life because, in those times, no essential difference was perceived between the two. The Veda deal with many subjects but the texts are frequently difficult to understand. Tirthaji made great efforts to dig out the system of mathematics from these texts and came up with sixteen sutras and about thirteen sub-sutras. A sutra is a pithy statement containing a governing principle, a method or a rule of working and the ones which he discovered relate to mathematics. Not long before he died, Tirthaji wrote an illustrative volume on the subject entitled *Vedic Mathematics* which was published posthumously in 1965 (Motilal Banarsidass, Delhi).

Sri Tirthaji applied the sutras to the mathematics of his day and so in his book we find a good deal of arithmetic and algebra. It has since been shown that the system is equally applicable to more up-to-date aspects of mathematics both at an elementary level as well as in more sophisticated fields. The reason that this is possible relies on the nature of the sutras. They frequently describe how the mind approaches, or deals with, a problem in the easiest way. To take a very simple example, consider finding the sum of 267 and 98. The *blanket* method involves cumbersome arithmetic. Most people would realise that the easiest method is to add 100 and take off 2. The answer of 365 is then found using a *complement*. The Vedic system teaches this sort of approach systematically rather than leaving it to chance and hence we find a number of different possible methods for any particular sum. This is of tremendous use because it enhances variety of strategy. It also enables the subject to be kept alive by directing the attention towards underlying pattern and relationship. Of course, with children, some mastery of the different methods must be accomplished before this more creative approach can be adopted.

The sutras, which are used in translation in this book, provide easily remembered word-formulae for solving problems in arithmetic, algebra, geometry and their various applications. The methods are fast and effective because they rely on mental working. In many applications answers are found in one line and for this reason the mathematics can often appear to be intuitively based. Nevertheless, it is all quite logical and systematic.

Vedic mathematics in education

In the United Kingdom there are growing signs of dissatisfaction with the lack of training in numeracy and the accompanying degeneration of algebraic and other mathematical skills. Some would argue that this is due to misguided educational methods whilst others lay blame on the widespread use of electronic calculating aids. During this century, the treatment of mathematics in education has seen a decline in rigour and, more recently, a move away from the so called 'drudgery' of sums.

Vedic Mathematics for Schools aims at providing a good mathematical training without the necessity of relying on calculating aids. It also aims to relate mathematics to the natural laws expressed in the Vedic sutras.

As with the body, exercise and training are required to develop health, strength, agility and skill, so too with the young mind, training is required for development of knowledge, creativity and the ability to reason. Mathematics and, in particular, the experience of working with number, provide one of the most powerful tools to accomplish this. For this purpose, these Vedic methods are used for basic numerical skills. Not only are they enjoyable, but they also encourage the use of mental arithmetic. For example, there are methods which replace long multiplication and division whereby the answer to any such sum can be obtained in one line. Experience of teaching these methods to children has shown that a high degree of mathematical ability can be attained from an early age while the subject is enjoyed for its own merits.

I have received criticism that Vedic mathematics only provides a few interesting techniques and is not really relevant to a core curriculum. There has also been the comment that children do not understand these methods *which are merely tricks*. None of these comments has ever come from anyone who has studied and practised the system but only from those who seem to be looking at it from the outside and therefore have little understanding themselves. A soup packet has the name, cooking instructions and even a picture printed on the outside. Until the soup has been tasted, however, there is only peripheral knowledge and certainly no basis from which to make a sound judgement.

Nevertheless, in reply to the first criticism it has to be understood that in the Vedic system there are general methods for all calculations and algebraic manipulations, and also short and easy ways for particular cases, for instance in multiplying or dividing numbers close to a power of ten. Where such particular methods are introduced at an early stage it is because they usually relate to more general aspects of the system at a later stage. The current methods of calculating which have been adopted by most schools are 'blanket' methods and no short cut methods, or even intuitive approaches, are systematically used. For example, with division, only one method is taught and, although it will suffice in all cases, it may often be difficult to use. The Vedic system in this book teaches three basic methods for division which are applied to meet the particular case although each could be used for any division sum.

The second criticism raises an important issue in relation to school mathematics. This concerns the use and understanding of set formulae to solve problems. There are many instances in education where the students are required to learn a formula to solve a particular type of problem whilst not understanding the mathematics behind the formula. We could take as an example the well known formula used for solving quadratic equations. When students first learn to use this formula there are few who understand how it has been derived. The usual practice is to gain some familiarity with its application before learning how it arises. Another example which is even more stark concerns the formula for finding the volume of a pyramid with a polygonal base. The formula is Volume equals one third of the base area times the perpendicular height and is learnt quite early on in the school curriculum. But to prove or derive this result the student needs to be adept either in three dimensional geometry or in the calculus. The formula is simple but the derivation requires mathematics of a much more advanced character. Much of school mathematics is like this and there is nothing amiss. When a student is faced with a problem which can be solved using a simple well-known formula then, by all means, it should be used. We accept the validity of such formulae on trust and, that it works is magical. The magic becomes mathematics when the formulae are understood.

Vedic mathematics appears, at first, to have a magical quality. When the methods are understood, particularly in relation to one another, then it is unified mathematics.

On the nature of mathematics

Mathematics is a practical science as it helps us with daily life. It also helps us to understand the mysteries of the universe.

The study of mathematics may be seen as having two directions, an outer and an inner. The outer direction moves us to applying number, order and mathematical relationships in the world around us. It is practical, useful and beneficial. This includes the everyday activities of shopkeepers, accountants, technicians, engineers, scientists, gamblers, etc., etc. In fact our lives, in the ordinary sense, would be very limited were it not for the applicability of number. This carries with it the responsibility of those with some understanding of the structure of mathematics to ensure that institutions are retained which enhance and disseminate mathematics as a structured body of knowledge.

The other direction in mathematics is an inner one. It takes us back to the very foundation blocks upon which the subject stands. Ultimately it reminds us of our origin, the unity, Supreme Self, which is the basis of the entire creation.

Mathematics returns us to unity in a very simple way and this is because it starts at one. The number one is a simple expression of this unity. So too is the idea of equality. We speak, read and write 'equals' so frequently that it is all too easy to pass over its philosophic significance. There is so much in mathematics to remind us of the underlying unity in all forms and creatures.

So these are the two directions but they are not exclusive. It is more the case that the inner direction enhances the understanding of the outer direction. Indeed, without the inner the outer direction becomes lost, trivial and lifeless. It is the Vedic system that enables these two directions to be studied in mutual harmony and this may be accomplished through correct appreciation of the sutras.

It has been found that in India today there is widespread belief that the Vedas are merely historical texts consisting of various hymns and injunctions for the performance of sacrifices, etc. A more accurate understanding of Veda is found in the idea of true knowledge. The nature of knowledge is that it is a living aspect of the human mind. This is the spirit in which these sutras are to be regarded. When you are faced with a problem and the method of solution comes to mind, the law by which the solution is found is expressed in one of the sutras. Thus the sutras have to do with the way the mind works in the present.

About this book

It is assumed that pupils using this book already have a degree of mathematical ability. In particular, the times tables need to be fully established. It should also be stated that regular practice of mental arithmetic is an essential accompaniment to this course.

Each method used for numerical calculations is introduced separately and exercises are carefully graded to enable the distinct developmental steps to be mastered. Each technique is denoted by one or more of the sutras. The text incorporates explanations and worked examples of all the methods used and includes descriptions of how to set out written work.

The structure of the book is such that at the end of each term a bright pupil should be able to complete about eight chapters. There are three revision chapters, the last of which contains practice papers. It is not necessarily intended that teachers rigidly adhere to the order of chapters as presented. Nevertheless, there are certain topics that should be covered before moving on to more advanced work.

The course has been written in conjunction with teaching a group of ten and eleven year-olds. The main emphasis at this stage is on developing numeracy and its principal fields of application, since this is the most essential aspect of mathematics. The text concentrates on these areas of mathematics and treats them as the core curriculum of the subject.

Experience has shown that children benefit most from their own practice and experience rather than being continually provided with explanations of mathematical concepts. The explanations given in this text show the pupil how to practise so that they may develop their own understanding.

It is to be hoped that teachers may provide their own practical 'ways of demonstrating this system or of enabling children to practise and experience the various methods and concepts. Of course, where teachers are unfamiliar with the system themselves they would also have to practise. It is difficult to appreciate the full benefits of Vedic mathematics unless one gets immersed in the techniques, leaving behind all previous personal paradigms and prejudices about mathematics.

J.G. 3rd July 1997

Contents

List of sutras found in the text with their applications

Nikhilam Navataścaraman Daśatah
All from nine and the last from ten

Multiplication, 1ff
Division, 27
Subtraction, 36ff
Converting vinculums, 214

Ūrdhva Tiryagbhyām
Vertically and crosswise

Multiplication, 13ff
Adding fractions, 114
Subtracting fractions, 117
Areas of rectangles, 133
Multiplying with vinculums, 217

Parāvartya Yojayet
Transpose and adjust

Division, 32
Division of fractions, 57
Solving equations, 66
Converting vinculums, 213

Vilokanam
By mere inspection

HCF, 44
Prime factors, 45
LCM, 46
Simple equations, 65
Divisibility for 2, 5 and 10, 106
Ratios, 161
Rectangles in circles, 169
Multiple products, 180

Antyayoreva
Only the last digits

Multiplying by 11, 20
Divisibility by 4, 107
Decimal/fraction conversions, 125
Multiplying decimals, 189

Sopāntyadvayamantyam
The ultimate and twice the penultimate

Multiplying by 12, 21
Divisibility by 4, 107
Divisibility by 8, 107

Pūraṇā Pūraṇābhyām
By completion and non-completion

Adding noughts for division, 26, 193

Lopana Sthāpanābhyām
By elimination and retention

Casting out nines, 101
Divisibility by 3, 109
Multiple products, 180
A Module to find the average, 203
Frequency tables, 209

---

* This appears in different forms in the text because some sutras can be translated in various ways.

Chapter 1 - Multiplying by *All from 9 and the last from 10*

Complements

Number begins at one which is an expression of unity. Just as our lives may become easier and happier by coming under one law so many arithmetic problems are made easier by relating the numbers back to unity or one.

In the number system there are only nine numbers and a zero or nought. With these we can display all multiplicity. In counting, once we are past the number ten then the numbers repeat themselves. The points where the repetitions begin are 10, 100, 1000, etc. These numbers, one with any number of zeros following, also represent the unity from which number begins.

The sutra for relating numbers back to unity is *All from nine and the last from ten* (*All from 9* - for short).

This simple formula relates any number to the next base of ten above. For example, with the number 86, the nearest base of ten which is more than 86 is 100. 86 is 14 less than 100. 14 is called the **complement** of 86.

If we take all from nine and the last from ten we have ,

$$8 \text{ from } 9 = 1$$
$$6 \text{ from } 10 = 4$$

For larger numbers the complement is found by subtracting all the digits from nine and the last from ten.

To obtain the complement of 783 we take each of the digits from 9 and the last from ten.

783
217

7 from 9 = 2
8 from 9 = 1
3 from 10 = 7

The complement is 217.

When there are noughts at the end, the last number is taken from ten (nought is not a number). For example, the complement of 740 is 260, that is, 7 from 9 = 2, 4 from 10 = 6, and the nought is just added at the end. The meaning of the sutra is *All from nine and the last **number** from ten*.

Care must be taken when there are noughts involved.

<u>503700</u>
496300

5 from 9 = 4
0 from 9 = 9
3 from 9 = 6
7 from 10 = 3
The final noughts are brought straight down.

Exercise 1a Write down the complements of the following:

1. 87	**7.** 64	**13.** 903	**19.** 1111	**25.** 5003400
2. 94	**8.** 28	**14.** 1340	**20.** 38730	**26.** 123980
3. 36	**9.** 44	**15.** 3564	**21.** 27463	**27.** 453601
4. 42	**10.** 54	**16.** 8004	**22.** 354600	**28.** 364720
5. 88	**11.** 874	**17.** 30460	**23.** 70603	**29.** 2758407
6. 75	**12.** 426	**18.** 8638	**24.** 99992	**30.** 6666667

Using complements in calculations

The following examples show how complements may be used in simple calculations.

	Mental working
36 + 29 = 65	36 + 30 − 1 = 66 − 1 = 65
735 − 198 = 537	735 − 200 + 2 = 535 + 2 = 537
29 × 6 = 174	30 × 6 − 6 = 180 − 6 = 174
352 ÷ 49 = 7 rem 9	350 ÷ 50 = 7, 350 ÷ 49 = 7 rem 7 and so 352 ÷ 7 = 7 rem 9

Exercise 1b (Oral) Use complements to answer the following:

1. 16 + 9	6. 57 – 9	11. 43 + 19	16. 53 + 29
2. 28 + 9	7. 48 – 9	12. 52 + 19	17. 46 + 39
3. 56 + 9	8. 25 – 9	13. 55 – 19	18. 256 + 99
4. 45 + 9	9. 78 – 9	14. 64 – 19	19. 45 + 39
5. 28 + 9	10. 203 – 9	15. 72 + 29	20. 28 + 59

21. 199 + 9	26. 83 – 29	31. 200 – 99	36. 543 + 298
22. 299 + 56	27. 78 – 29	32. 450 – 298	37. 231 – 97
23. 198 + 72	28. 500 – 298	33. 500 – 397	38. 576 – 69
24. 295 + 45	29. 100 – 68	34. 1000 – 795	39. 708 + 295
25. 597 + 83	30. 380 – 39	35. 664 – 199	40. 900 – 396

41. 39×2	46. 39×3	51. 39×5	56. 199×4
42. 49×2	47. 59×3	52. 19×5	57. 299×3
43. 29×2	48. 19×3	53. 49×5	58. 98×2
44. 19×2	49. 29×3	54. 59×5	59. 198×3
45. 69×2	50. 99×3	55. 29×5	60. 249×4

61. $9\overline{)20}$	64. $99\overline{)100}$	67. $49\overline{)100}$	70. $39\overline{)80}$
62. $9\overline{)30}$	65. $99\overline{)200}$	68. $49\overline{)202}$	71. $199\overline{)401}$
63. $9\overline{)50}$	66. $99\overline{)304}$	69. $29\overline{)90}$	72. $249\overline{)503}$

73. Add together 19, 29 and 39.

74. On one day the temperature changed from 79°F to 102°F. What was the temperature increase?

75. The cost of one window lock is £9.99. Find the cost of 15 of these locks.

76. On average a certain car can travel 29 miles on a gallon of petrol. How many miles can it travel on 8 gallons?

77. Find the cost of six pens at £1.99 each.

78. What is the cost of five notebooks at 99p each?

79. Find the rent for 4 months on a shop at £295 per month.

80. What is the total length of 6 pieces of fence each 1.95 m long?

3

Multiplication using *All from nine and the last from ten*

There are many applications of the *All from nine* sutra, the first of which has to do with multiplying two numbers together.

Suppose we have to multiply 8 by 9.

1. We should take 10 as the base for the calculation, which is the next power of ten above the two numbers.

2. The two numbers are set down as shown and the complements from the base, 10, are written alongside. The minus signs indicate that 8 is 2 less than 10 and 9 is 1 less than 10.

$$
\begin{array}{r}
(10) \\
8-2 \\
\times\ 9-1 \\
\hline
/
\end{array}
$$

3. The answer is obtained in two parts and to distinguish these a diagonal stroke is placed in the middle of the answer line.

4. The right-hand part of the answer is found by multiplying the two complements, that is, $2 \times 1 = 2$.

$$
\begin{array}{r}
(10) \\
8-2 \\
\times\ 9-1 \\
\hline
7\ /\ 2
\end{array}
$$

5. There are four ways to obtain the left-hand part of the answer:
   i) the base (10) minus both complements, $10 - 2 - 1 = 7$,
   ii) the sum of the numbers to be multiplied minus the base, that is, $8 + 9 - 10 = 7$,
   iii) cross-subtract, $8 - 1 = 7$,
   iv) cross-subtract $9 - 2 = 7$

6. The product is thus $8 \times 9 = 72$

   In practice, it will be found that the cross-subtraction method is simpler and more efficient. With cross-subtraction, there is a choice and whichever is easiest should be taken.

This method of multiplication is very old and it is from the cross-subtraction involved that we have our × symbol for multiplication.

Exercise 1c Use *All from nine and the last from ten* to multiply these, taking care to set them out correctly.

1. 5×9	**3.** 9×9	**5.** 9×6	**7.** 7×9
2. 7×8	**4.** 6×8	**6.** 7×7	**8.** 8×8

We can now apply the sutra to numbers which are close to larger bases such as 100 or 1000. The method is exactly the same as before.

The next example is 96 × 72.

1. On applying the *All from 9* rule we obtain the complements for both numbers and these are set down on the right, as before, with minus signs to indicate that the complements are deficiencies from 100.

$$(100)$$
$$96 - 04$$
$$\times\, \underline{72 - 28}$$
$$/$$

2. The four ways to arrive at the left-hand part of the answer are:
   i) $100 - 28 - 04 = 68$ or ii) $96 + 72 - 100 = 68$ or
   iii) $96 - 28 = 68$ or iv) $72 - 4 = 68$
   Evidently the last of these is the easiest and so should be used.

$$(100)$$
$$96 - 04$$
$$\times\, \underline{72 - 28}$$
$$\underline{68\ /\ 12}$$
$$\underline{1}$$
$$69\ /\ 12$$

3. The right-hand part of the answer is the product of the two complements, 28×4, which is found by multiplying 8 by 4 followed by 2×4 and carrying digits to the left in the usual manner.

4. The result of 28×4 is 112 but since there are only two digits in each complement it follows that there can only be two digits in the right-hand part of the answer and so 1 must be carried to the left giving the answer as 6912.

It is to be remembered that the number of digits in the right-hand part of the sum is always equal to the number of noughts in the base. In the previous example, the base, 100, has two noughts and so there are two digits in each complement. So it is that the complement of 96 is 04 and not just 4. The following rhyme helps to remember this:

> *The complement digits in every case,*
> *numbers the same as the noughts in the base.*

Exercise 1d Use *All from nine and the last from ten*

1. 96 × 96	9. 992 × 992	17. 398 × 999	25. 9999 × 9999
2. 95 × 92	10. 777 × 995	18. 994 × 886	26. 9878 × 9998
3. 97 × 76	11. 996 × 456	19. 697 × 994	27. 7865 × 9997
4. 94 × 88	12. 111 × 990	20. 990 × 990	28. 998 × 867
5. 91 × 93	13. 987 × 992	21. 934 × 997	29. 996 × 993
6. 67 × 98	14. 991 × 354	22. 1234 × 9996	30. 9991 × 9465
7. 96 × 87	15. 112 × 992	23. 9993 × 9876	31. 9980 × 9995
8. 37 × 99	16. 994 × 654	24. 9998 × 1010	32. 9995 × 9321

Multiplying numbers above a base

This method for multiplication may be extended to multiplying numbers above the base. Instead of finding the complements of the numbers to be multiplied we find the excess or surplus in relation to the base. The *All from nine* sutra is not actually used to find the surplus; instead this is found by mere inspection.

---

12 × 16

Using a base of 10, the surpluses of 12 and 16, that is +2 and +6, are set down on the right.
Starting from the right, 2 × 6 = 12, but since there is one digit in the surplus we have a 1 to carry to the left.

$$\begin{array}{r} (10) \\ 12 + 2 \\ \times\ \underline{16 + 6} \\ /\,2 \\ 1 \end{array}$$

As before the left-hand part of the answer is obtained in one of four ways:
i) 10 (the base) + 2 + 6 = 18
ii) 12 + 16 − 10 (the base) = 18
iii) by cross-addition, 12 + 6 = 18
iv) also by cross-addition, 16 + 2 = 18
Whichever is found to be the easiest should undoubtedly be used and this is usually the cross-addition. Since there is a 1 to carry the answer is 192.

$$\begin{array}{r} (10) \\ 12 + 2 \\ \times\ \underline{16 + 6} \\ \underline{19\,/\,2} \\ 1 \end{array}$$

Exercise 1e Multiply

1. 15×15	6. 11×17	11. 14×11	16. 11×11
2. 14×16	7. 14×12	12. 13×15	17. 12×12
3. 13×14	8. 13×16	13. 16×16	18. 13×13
4. 11×13	9. 14×14	14. 12×19	19. 17×18
5. 15×12	10. 18×15	15. 15×14	20. 14×19

With the multiplication of larger numbers, which are both just above the same base, it is particularly important to remember that the numbers of digits in each surplus are the same as the number of noughts in the base. In the following example, a base of 100 is used which is written down above the sum.

Multiply 115 by 107

As before, the surpluses above the base of 100 are set down on the right.

$$
\begin{array}{r}
(100) \\
115 + 15 \\
\times\ 107 + 07 \\
\hline
122\ /\ 05 \\
1 \\
\hline
123\ /\ 05
\end{array}
$$

$100 + 15 + 7 = 122$
or $115 + 107 - 100 = 122$
or $115 + 7 = 122$
or $107 + 15 = 122$
$7 \times 15 = 105$, but since the right-hand portion has only two digits we must carry the 1 of 105 to the left.

The answer is 12305

Exercise 1f

1. 104×103	9. 106×105	17. 1006×1005	25. 107×107
2. 111×108	10. 144×104	18. 1044×1004	26. 145×104
3. 107×109	11. 110×113	19. 1010×1013	27. 1007×1333
4. 112×106	12. 112×107	20. 1012×1007	28. 15×16
5. 106×111	13. 113×103	21. 1013×1003	29. 142×110
6. 101×107	14. 109×127	22. 1009×1007	30. 1067×1004
7. 114×105	15. 103×155	23. 1003×1515	31. 1066×1005
8. 123×102	16. 121×104	24. 1421×1004	32. 1234×1002

How does it work?

A geometrical demonstration is useful for understanding how *All from nine and the last from ten* multiplication works. The example which follows is for multiplying 12 and 13, both of which are above the base of ten.

The method sets out this product as follows:-

$$
\begin{array}{r}
12 + 2 \\
\times\ 13 + 3 \\
\hline
15 / 6
\end{array}
$$

In this sum, the cross-addition is 13 + 2 = 15 but due to the place value it is really 130 + 20 = 150. The final product is 2 × 3 = 6.

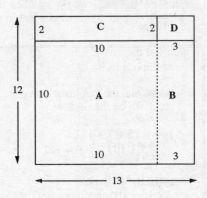

Taking the base of a rectangle as 13 units and the height as 12 units the area will be the product of 12 and 13. By partitioning the rectangle into four sections the area may be found by adding the areas of the sections.

Sections **A** and **B**, taken together, have an area of 10 × 13 = 130 square units.

Section **C** has an area of 2 × 10 = 20. The cross-addition 130 + 20 is therefore equivalent to the area of A, B and C together.

The final section, **D**, has an area of 2 × 3 = 6, and is equivalent to the right-hand part of the *All from nine* product.

Exercise 1g Mixed examples

1. 96 × 98	**11.** 109 × 109	**21.** 998 × 122
2. 94 × 88	**12.** 1234 × 9993	**22.** 198 × 102
3. 101 × 134	**13.** 1034 × 1000	**23.** 9876 × 9997
4. 14 × 18	**14.** 1876 × 1002	**24.** 1564 × 1010
5. 998 × 967	**15.** 463 × 990	**25.** 1001 × 1001
6. 124 × 105	**16.** 765 × 995	**26.** 19191 × 99998
7. 888 × 994	**17.** 1245 × 1007	**27.** 99999 × 93693
8. 16 × 17	**18.** 101 × 199	**28.** 17685 × 10009
9. 104 × 109	**19.** 989 × 991	**29.** 99990 × 45455
10. 9 × 3	**20.** 120 × 108	**30.** 10005 × 17650

Exercise 1h Use *All from nine* for each multiplication

1. Find the complements of the following:
   - a) 96
   - b) 897
   - c) 7065
   - d) 780
   - e) 5981
   - f) 34521
   - g) 99980
   - h) 10900.

2. Multiply 98 by 68.

3. Multiply 985 by 992.

4. Find the product of 97 and 65 (product is the answer to a multiplication).

5. 104 × 116.

6. Find the cost of 95 pens at 99p each.

7. A theatre auditorium has 105 rows each with 110 seats. How many seats are there altogether?

8. Find 9997 times 4680.

9. In one week a shopkeeper sold 107 bottles of lemonade at £1.15 each. How much did he receive for the lemonade?

10. Find the product of 98 and 97 and multiply your answer by 9994.

11. In one year a furniture manufacturer sold 1112 dining tables at £1007 each. How much did he receive for this sale?

12. A printer is required to produce 115 copies of a book each consisting of 106 pages. How many pages are produced?

13. A rectangular field measures 98 m by 71 m. What is its area?

14. Find the product of 106 and 103 and multiply your answer by 10003.

15. If a bricklayer can lay 850 bricks in a day, how many bricks can he lay in 992 days?

16. Find the following products:
   - (a) 9 × 9
   - (b) 99 × 99
   - (c) 999 × 999
   - (d) 9999 × 9999
   - (e) 11 × 11
   - (f) 111 × 111
   - (g) 1111 × 1111
   - (h) 11111 × 11111

Above and below

When one number is above the base and the other is below we use a vinculum to signify the minus number in the product and then 'devinculate' at the end again using *All from nine and the last from ten.*

The word 'vinculum' (*v* pronounced as *w*) comes from the Latin meaning *chain* or *bond* and is a line placed above a number to indicate a negative quantity or a deficiency. Thus $2\overline{3}$ is two tens less three units, that is 17. Vinculums are useful for calculations with numbers involving large digits.

When a number has several successive vinculum digits it may be 'devinculated' using the *All from nine and the last from ten* sutra.

Devinculate $4\overline{231}$ $4\overline{231} = 3769$

This stands for four thousand less two hundreds, less three tens, less one unit.
To devinculate, reduce the 4 by 1 and find the *All from 9* complement of the vinculum digits.

Exercise 1i 'Devinculate' the following:

1. $4\overline{2}$	11. $34\overline{2}$	21. $4\overline{2}\,\overline{1}$	31. $6\overline{3}4\overline{2}$
2. $3\overline{1}$	12. $12\overline{1}$	22. $3\overline{2}\,\overline{2}$	32. $5\overline{1}\,\overline{2}3$
3. $6\overline{4}$	13. $56\overline{4}$	23. $53\overline{1}$	33. $7\overline{1}\,\overline{1}\,\overline{1}$
4. $2\overline{1}$	14. $87\overline{3}$	24. $6\overline{1}\,\overline{1}$	34. $8\overline{2}05$
5. $7\overline{2}$	15. $654\overline{2}$	25. $43\overline{2}$	35. $5\overline{8}\,\overline{9}7$
6. $5\overline{3}$	16. $709\overline{1}$	26. $57\overline{1}\,\overline{2}$	36. $782\overline{7}\,\overline{6}$
7. $3\overline{3}$	17. $894\overline{2}$	27. $573\overline{1}\,\overline{4}$	37. $876\overline{5}4\overline{3}$
8. $1\overline{1}$	18. $20\overline{1}$	28. $202\overline{3}$	38. $9\overline{1}50\overline{3}$
9. $8\overline{2}$	19. $90\overline{3}$	29. $503\overline{4}$	39. $7\overline{4}3\overline{5}\,\overline{1}$
10. $9\overline{4}$	20. $10\overline{4}$	30. $1700\overline{1}\,\overline{4}$	40. $200\overline{2}\,\overline{4}3\overline{6}$

Here is an example where one number is above the base and the other is below.

---

108 × 94

108 is 8 more than the base and so the surplus is put down as +08. For 94, the complement is 06 and –06 is put down. The product of +8 and –6 is –48 and this is set down as $\overline{48}$.	$108 + 08$ $\times\ 92 - 06$ $\overline{102/\overline{48}}$ $101/52$

The left-hand part is found either by cross-adding, 94 + 8 = 102, or by cross-subtracting, 108 – 6 = 102.

To devinculate the $\overline{48}$ we take 1 away from the digit immediately to the left, that is 2 – 1 = 1, and use *All from nine and the last from ten* on 48 to obtain 52.

Exercise 1j   Above and below

1. 94 × 108	**9.** 92 × 112	**17.** 998 × 1004	**25.** 15 × 9
2. 95 × 103	**10.** 104 × 93	**18.** 1005 × 995	**26.** 18 × 9
3. 92 × 108	**11.** 108 × 96	**19.** 997 × 1001	**27.** 9 × 12
4. 105 × 99	**12.** 99 × 101	**20.** 986 × 1004	**28.** 11 × 9
5. 107 × 91	**13.** 98 × 148	**21.** 1112 × 997	**29.** 9 × 17
6. 90 × 104	**14.** 102 × 76	**22.** 1234 × 996	**30.** 8 × 11
7. 98 × 110	**15.** 67 × 103	**23.** 1008 × 981	**31.** 11 × 7
8. 97 × 101	**16.** 78 × 104	**24.** 1010 × 976	**32.** 8 × 15

Exercise 1k Further practice - below the base

1. 99 × 98	**7.** 81 × 98	**13.** 82 × 94
2. 96 × 99	**8.** 84 × 98	**14.** 64 × 92
3. 98 × 97	**9.** 86 × 97	**15.** 86 × 91
4. 96 × 98	**10.** 85 × 97	**16.** 90 × 99
5. 95 × 97	**11.** 41 × 98	**17.** 80 × 99
6. 85 × 98	**12.** 73 × 96	**18.** 70 × 98

19. 70 × 97   **28.** 989 × 999   **37.** 888 × 991

20. 95 × 90   **29.** 999 × 987   **38.** 857 × 993

21. 84 × 90   **30.** 999 × 889   **39.** 748× 996

22. 87 × 90   **31.** 984 × 998   **40.** 833 × 994

23. 95 × 80   **32.** 997 × 985   **41.** 948 × 995

24. 90 × 83   **33.** 996 × 987   **42.** 757 × 994

25. 70 × 92   **34.** 986 × 996   **43.** 795 × 992

26. 999 × 999   **35.** 995 × 985   **44.** 916 × 989

27. 999 × 993   **36.** 478 × 998   **45.** 406 × 997

Exercise 1l Further practice - above the base

1. 11 × 11   **11.** 101 × 101   **21.** 1121 × 1002

2. 11 × 12   **12.** 102 × 101   **22.** 1235 × 1003

3. 10 × 12   **13.** 103 × 101   **23.** 1524 × 1002

4. 13 × 10   **14.** 102 × 102   **24.** 1002 × 1463

5. 12 × 12   **15.** 102 × 103   **25.** 1213 × 1005

6. 15 × 12   **16.** 150 × 103   **26.** 10123 × 10004

7. 16 × 14   **17.** 190 × 102   **27.** 11321 × 10003

8. 18 × 12   **18.** 132 × 104   **28.** 12123 × 10005

9. 16 × 17   **19.** 105 × 121   **29.** 115322 × 100003

10. 13 × 17   **20.** 104 × 133   **30.** 1234321 × 1000006

Exercise 1m   Further practice of above and below

1. 12 × 7   **11.** 89 × 109   **21.** 1002 × 998

2. 8 × 12   **12.** 105 × 92   **22.** 1022 × 998

3. 9 × 14   **13.** 94 × 108   **23.** 1033 × 997

4. 13 × 7   **14.** 107 × 89   **24.** 986 × 1002

5. 11 × 6   **15.** 104 × 92   **25.** 990 × 1012

6. 13 × 9   **16.** 105 × 95   **26.** 1013 × 995

7. 9 × 16   **17.** 104 × 94   **27.** 997 × 1018

8. 8 × 14   **18.** 103 × 67   **28.** 995 × 1013

9. 9 × 19   **19.** 107 × 92   **29.** 1239 × 998

10. 8 × 13   **20.** 146 × 98   **30.** 953 × 1008

Chapter 2 - Multiplication by *Vertically and Crosswise*

The general case

In the previous chapter, all the multiplication sums had at least one of the numbers to be multiplied close to a particular base of·10, 100, 1000, etc. The *All from nine* method is clearly a special case formula since not all numbers to be multiplied will be close to a single base. We now proceed to deal with the general formula which is applicable to all cases of multiplication. The sutra for this is, *Vertically and Crosswise*.

There are many applications of this short rule and a simple example will show how it works in practice.

Suppose we have to multiply 42 by 13.

Starting at the left, multiply the two left-hand most digits, vertically, that is, 4 × 1 = 4, and set the answer down underneath as the left-hand most part of the answer.

$$\begin{array}{r} 4\ \ 2 \\ \times\ \underline{1\ \ 3} \\ 4 \end{array}$$

We then multiply 4 by 3 and 2 by 1, crosswise, and add these two products together, 4 × 3 = 12 and 2 × 1 = 2, and 12 + 2 = 14. Set down the 4 as the next answer digit and carry the 1 to the left.

$$\begin{array}{r} 4\ \ 2 \\ \times\ \underline{1\ \ 3} \\ 4\ \ 4 \\ 1 \end{array}$$

We multiply 2 by 3, vertically, and set down the answer, 6, as the right-hand most answer digit.

Add in the carry digit to give the answer 546.

$$\begin{array}{r} 4\ \ 2 \\ \times\ \underline{1\ \ 3} \\ 4\ 4\ 6 \\ \underline{1} \\ 5\ 4\ 6 \end{array}$$

The vertically and crosswise method may also be started from the right-hand end of the numbers. The advantage is that carry digits can be added in as the working proceeds and so the answer comes in one line instead of two. Care must be taken with setting out and it is generally easier if spaces are left between the digits.

$$\begin{array}{r} 4\ \ 2 \\ \times\ \underline{1\ \ 3} \\ 5\ 4\ 6 \\ 1 \end{array}$$

The steps are as follows:

2 × 3 = 6   (4 × 3) + (2 × 1) = 14   (4 × 1) + 1 = 5

Exercise 2a Use *Vertically and Crosswise*. Work the first half starting from the left and the second half starting from the right.

1. 21 × 23	11. 26 × 14	21. 23 × 23
2. 16 × 13	12. 34 × 14	22. 56 × 26
3. 19 × 13	13. 41 × 51	23. 38 × 32
4. 27 × 14	14. 15 × 45	24. 42 × 39
5. 16 × 32	15. 14 × 39	25. 71 × 53
6. 13 × 21	16. 49 × 15	26. 84 × 67
7. 35 × 12	17. 16 × 53	27. 91 × 75
8. 24 × 13	18. 12 × 48	28. 10 × 11
9. 76 × 11	19. 59 × 17	29. 34 × 11
10. 35 × 22	20. 42 × 15	30. 26 × 11

Exercise 2b Problems

1. Multiply 46 by 32.

2. Find the product of 23 and 48.

3. What is 53 times 84?

4. Multiply forty-two by twenty-eight.

5. Find the cost of sixteen radios at £53 each.

6. A block of stamps has 24 rows with 12 in each row. How many stamps are there in the block?

7. If a packet of biscuits costs 64p, find the cost of a whole box containing forty-eight packets.

8. Find the cost of 28 yards of dress fabric if one yard costs £34.

9. A car-park can fit 35 rows of cars with 51 in each row. Find the number of cars that can fit into the car-park.

10. Calculate the number of hours in the month of January.

The *Vertically and Crosswise* method may easily be extended to multiplying numbers containing any number of digits but for now we take up the case of multiplying two three-digit numbers.

Multiply 362 by 134

Starting from the left, the first answer digit is $3 \times 1 = 3$.

$$\begin{array}{r} 362 \\ \times\ 134 \\ \hline 3 \end{array}$$

The next answer digit is the sum of the cross-product of the four left-hand most digits, that is $(3 \times 3) + (6 \times 1) = 15$.

$$\begin{array}{r} 362 \\ \times\ 134 \\ \hline 35 \\ 1 \end{array}$$

The middle step is to add the cross-product of all six digits in the following order, $(3 \times 4) + (6 \times 3) + (2 \times 1) = 32$.

$$\begin{array}{r} 362 \\ \times\ 134 \\ \hline 352 \\ 13 \end{array}$$

The sum of the cross-product of the four right-hand most digits gives the next answer digit, that is $(6 \times 4) + (2 \times 3) = 30$.

$$\begin{array}{r} 362 \\ \times\ 134 \\ \hline 3520 \\ 133 \end{array}$$

The final step is the product of the two right-hand most digits, $2 \times 4 = 8$.

After adding up the carry digits the answer is found to be 48508.

$$\begin{array}{r} 362 \\ \times\ 134 \\ \hline 35208 \\ 133\quad \\ \hline 48508 \end{array}$$

The diagram below may help remember the vertically and crosswise pattern required for multiplying two three-digit numbers together. Each dot represents a digit in the number and the lines joining the dots stand for digits to be multiplied.

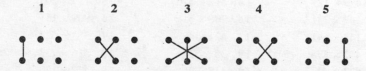

$$1 \qquad 2 \qquad 3 \qquad 4 \qquad 5$$

Again, these may also be worked starting from the right with the added advantage of adding in the carry digits and getting the answer in one line. Shown below is the previous example worked from the right-hand side starting with the final digits of each number.

The numbers to be multiplied may be set down with a space between each digit. This will help with the correct order for the answer digits.

$$\begin{array}{r} 3 \quad 6 \quad 2 \\ \times\ 1 \quad 3 \quad 4 \\ \hline 8 \end{array}$$

Starting from the right, $2 \times 4 = 8$.

The second step is the crosswise product,
$6 \times 4 + 2 \times 3 = 24 + 6 = 30$.
0 is put down and there is 3 to carry.

$$\begin{array}{r} 3 \quad 6 \quad 2 \\ \times\ 1 \quad 3 \quad 4 \\ \hline 0\ 8 \\ 3 \end{array}$$

The middle step is $3 \times 4 + 6 \times 3 + 2 \times 1 = 32$, and with the carry 3 this is 35.

The fourth step is $3 \times 3 + 6 \times 1 = 15$, and with the carry digit this is 18.

$$\begin{array}{r} 3 \quad 6 \quad 2 \\ \times\ 1 \quad 3 \quad 4 \\ \hline 8\ 5\ 0\ 8 \\ 1\ 3\ 3 \end{array}$$

The final step is $3 \times 1 + 1 = 4$

This method reduces the number of lines of working.

$$\begin{array}{r} 3 \quad 6 \quad 2 \\ \times\ 1 \quad 3 \quad 4 \\ \hline 4\ 8\ 5\ 0\ 8 \\ 1\ 3\ 3 \end{array}$$

Exercise 2c Find the following products: if the number has only two digits then you may fill the empty hundreds column with a nought. Do the first ten starting each sum at the left.

1. 123×121	11. 412×312	21. 312×212
2. 144×162	12. 423×203	22. 203×133
3. 127×354	13. 270×131	23. 364×623
4. 309×341	14. 400×413	24. 789×121
5. 477×121	15. 512×370	25. 117×203
6. 147×231	16. 208×51	26. 909×131
7. 143×641	17. 421×48	27. 353×522
8. 402×375	18. 35×374	28. 516×733
9. 523×423	19. 318×25	29. 777×120
10. 415×634	20. 78×324	30. 45×433

Exercise 2d Problems

1. Find the product of 135 and 216.

2. Multiply one hundred and two by 640.

3. There are 505 matches in a large box and a carton contains 124 such boxes. Find the number of matches in a carton.

4. A bookshop sells 563 copies of a book at £7.25 per book. How much was taken for the sale of the books?

5. Find the result of multiplying 387 by 24.

6. A fruit-picker can harvest 56 boxes of strawberries in one hour. If she works for 126 hours over a three week period, how many boxes does she fill?

7. In one evening a cinema sells 346 tickets at £3.25 each. How much is received for the sale of these tickets?

8. Find the cost of 144 eggs at 15p each.

9. A man pays £364 per month for a mortgage. Find how much he will have paid over a period of 25 years.

10. There are 16 ounces in a pound, and 112 pounds in a hundredweight. Find the number of ounces in a hundredweight.

11. Given that there are 20 hundredweight in a ton, use your answer to the previous question to find the number of ounces in a ton.

12. A printer wishes to reproduce a certain book containing 234 pages. Find the total number of pages in making 250 copies.

13. In making sponge cakes for a garden party, Amelia follows a recipe which requires 225 g of flour for each cake. How much flour will she need for 14 spongecakes?

14. A carpenter needs 24 pieces of shelving-board, each of which is 146 cm long. What is the total length of board required?

15. At a theatre there are 350 tickets at £18 and 425 tickets at £12 for each performance and there are two performances a day, seven days a week. Find the total possible box-office sales for the whole week.

For multiplying larger numbers together the pattern is extended. For example for two four-digit numbers there are seven steps to obtain the answer. To do this we may employ "Dr Pickles' knitting pattern".

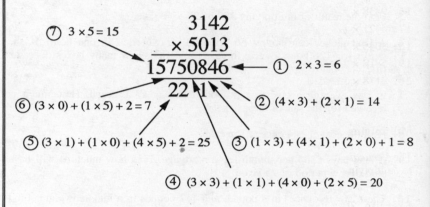

Working from the right

⑦ $3 \times 5 = 15$

$$\begin{array}{r} 3142 \\ \times\, 5013 \\ \hline 15750846 \\ 22\ 1 \end{array}$$

① $2 \times 3 = 6$

② $(4 \times 3) + (2 \times 1) = 14$

⑥ $(3 \times 0) + (1 \times 5) + 2 = 7$

⑤ $(3 \times 1) + (1 \times 0) + (4 \times 5) + 2 = 25$

③ $(1 \times 3) + (4 \times 1) + (2 \times 0) + 1 = 8$

④ $(3 \times 3) + (1 \times 1) + (4 \times 0) + (2 \times 5) = 20$

Working from the left

$$\begin{array}{r} 3142 \\ \times\, 5013 \\ \hline 15530746 \\ 22\ 1 \\ \hline 15750846 \end{array}$$

1. $(5 \times 3) = 15$

2. $(0 \times 3) + (1 \times 5) = 5$

3. $(1 \times 3) + (0 \times 1) + (5 \times 4) = 23$

4. $(3 \times 3) + (1 \times 1) + (0 \times 4) + (5 \times 2) = 20$

5. $(3 \times 1) + (1 \times 4) + (0 \times 2) = 7$

6. $(3 \times 4) + (1 \times 2) = 14$

7. $(3 \times 2) = 6$

Exercise 2e* Work either from the left or from the right.

1. 1213 × 1121	6. 1112 × 2031	11. 4000 × 3012
2. 1402 × 1032	7. 1053 × 1041	12. 4233 × 2003
3. 1200 × 3014	8. 4302 × 3075	13. 2710 × 1321
4. 1321 × 4012	9. 1123 × 2223	14. 7100 × 4313
5. 5013 × 3102	10. 3150 × 4034	15. 5712 × 8320

16. 9438 × 5741	21. 7212 × 9021	26. 617 × 1321
17. 4421 × 1234	22. 6403 × 1033	27. 53 × 5611
18. 3045 × 9874	23. 364 × 6023	28. 5216 × 33
19. 5818 × 2505	24. 7819 × 212	29. 137 × 1280
20. 8178 × 1324	25. 1176 × 512	30. 45 × 9860

Multiplying large numbers

The *Vertically and crosswise* pattern should now be familiar and may be applied to multiplying numbers of any size. All this can be done in one line.

Exercise 2f*

1. 11,213 × 11,321	11. 4,000,010 × 5,231,000
2. 14,402 × 11,232	12. 5,292 × 21
3. 53,218 × 31,121	13. 23,142 × 13
4. 413,242 × 867,541	14. 114,231 × 43
5. 43 × 543,131	15. 57 × 1,120,232
6. 231,204 × 112	16. 131 × 64,531
7. 413,211 × 52,401	17. 43 × 213,006
8. 4,352,413 × 1,234,231	18. 11× 2,435
9. 1,425,321 × 5,001,521	19. 21,324,321 × 11
10. 34,251,201 × 21,165,421	20. 534,211,121 × 11

Multiplication by 11

On looking at the answers to the last three questions it may be clear that there is a quick method for multiplying by 11. There is a sutra for this special case of multiplying but because it comes under the jurisdiction of vertically and crosswise it is called a sub-sutra.

This special sub-sutra is *Only the the last two digits*.

The following simple example illustrates this very easy method.

13,423 × 11

Write down the number, as shown on the right, with a nought placed at both ends. This is a nought sandwich.   0134230

Add the final two digits, 3 + 0 = 3, and write the answer below the 0.   0134230
    3

For the tens digit, add the final two digits to that point, that is 2 + 3 = 5.   0134230
    53

Conitnue to add adjacent digits, that is, 4 + 2 = 6, 3 + 4 = 7 and 1 + 3 = 4, 0 + 1 = 1   0134230
    47653

The answer is 147,653.   0134230
    147653

With a little practice this method can be applied without writing but some care must be taken when carry digits are involved.

Exercise 2g Multiply the following by 11:

1. 32	**6.** 78	**11.** 231	**16.** 646,453
2. 54	**7.** 98	**12.** 532	**17.** 549,241
3. 62	**8.** 65	**13.** 3,542	**18.** 63,457,271
4. 16	**9.** 46	**14.** 43,211	**19.** 90,026,452
5. 71	**10.** 77	**15.** 231,450	**20.** 53,626,409,830

20

Multiplication by 12

Another sutra may be used to obtain the product of any number with 12. The formula is *The ultimate and twice the penultimate*.

This is very similar to multiplication by 11 but we just double the digit to the left before adding.

65214 × 12

Again we start with the nought sandwich.
The ultimate digit is 0 and the penultimate digit is 4, so the ultimate plus twice the penultimate is 0 + 8 = 8.

$$\frac{0652140}{8}$$

For the tens column, the ultimate is 4 and the penultimate is 1, so 4 + 2 = 6.

$$\frac{0652140}{68}$$

Likewise, 1 + 4 = 5 and 2 + 10 = 12. With 12 we set down 2 and carry 1.

$$\frac{0652140}{2568}$$
$$1$$

5 + 12 + carry 1 = 18 and again we carry 1.

$$\frac{0652140}{782568}$$
$$1\ 1$$

The final step is 6 + 0 + carry 1 = 7.

The answer is 782568.

Exercise 2h Multiply the following by 12:

1. 23	**6.** 87	**11.** 312	**16.** 5,342
2. 14	**7.** 69	**12.** 413	**17.** 8,691
3. 32	**8.** 95	**13.** 4,201	**18.** 70,043
4. 41	**9.** 46	**14.** 4,452	**19.** 2,536,540,503
5. 52	**10.** 74	**15.** 1,543	**20.** 9,999,999,999

Multiplying numbers with final noughts

Numbers with noughts at the end are easily dealt with by placing the multiplier in a convenient place.

320,000 × 14

If we were to place the multiplier 14 in the tens and units column of 320,000, the vertically and crosswise pattern would become somewhat awkward.

$$\begin{array}{r} 320000 \\ \times\ 14 \\ \hline 4480000 \\ 1 \end{array}$$

The solution is to have the 14 directly below the 32 when setting out. In fact, the sum may be treated as 32 × 14 and then the noughts can be added at the end.

2100 × 42000

$$\begin{array}{r} 2100 \\ \times\ 42000 \\ \hline 88200000 \end{array}$$

Similarly when both numbers end with noughts add the total number of noughts in both numbers at the end.

The sutra for these type is *The total of final noughts in the numbers to be multiplied equals the final noughts in the product.*

Exercise 2i The most convenient place to set out the numbers must be chosen before writing down each sum.

1. 2100 × 13	**11.** 620 × 140	**21.** 1000 × 20,000
2. 16,000 × 14	**12.** 3500 × 230	**22.** 620 × 9800
3. 2200 × 21	**13.** 510 × 510	**23.** 74,000 × 32,000
4. 360 × 21	**14.** 150 × 450	**24.** 4,200,000 × 231
5. 450,000 × 25	**15.** 7400 × 5500	**25.** 662 × 24,200,000
6. 3300 × 63	**16.** 24,000 × 150	**26.** 12,800 × 2,270,000
7. 5100 × 98	**17.** 160 × 990,000	**27.** 910 × 7,500
8. 41 × 520000	**18.** 51,000 × 3600	**28.** 13,000 × 10,100
9. 32 × 67000	**19.** 530 × 170,000	**29.** 324,000 × 15,100
10. 72 × 12,000	**20.** 4200 × 5000	**30.** 24,600 × 1,100,000

Chapter 3 - Division

The nature of division

The number one is indivisible. To experience this a person must be at one with himself. The opposite is when the mind and attention are scattered and divided, unable to concentrate.

> *Here, O son of Kuru, there is one thought of a resolute nature.*
> *Many-branched and endless are the thoughts of the irresolute.*
>
> [Gita 2:41]

In the play of number we pretend that the one can be divided. In the same way, the Absolute or God pretends and appears to be divided in all the multifarious manifestations within the universe.

When we pretend to divide the number one, there are three ways that this division is expressed. Take the example of 1 divided by 2 or 2 into 1. The first expression is 2 into 1 = 0 remainder 1. In this case the answer is nought and the remainder is one. So the result of this attempted division is to give nothing with the original one remaining at the end. The one remaining was there at the beginning and is there at the end. Nothing has happened to the one.

Simple division

Exercise 3a Divide leaving whole-number remainders. Give answers only.

1. 3⌋5	11. 4⌋19	21. 8⌋23	31. 33⌋10
2. 5⌋7	12. 3⌋13	22. 9⌋38	32. 22⌋43
3. 2⌋3	13. 2⌋17	23. 5⌋63	33. 11⌋25
4. 3⌋1	14. 8⌋12	24. 6⌋33	34. 16⌋35
5. 5⌋1	15. 6⌋13	25. 7⌋76	35. 13⌋40
6. 4⌋1	16. 5⌋19	26. 4⌋35	36. 20⌋92
7. 5⌋2	17. 3⌋20	27. 8⌋50	37. 15⌋35
8. 3⌋0	18. 4⌋17	28. 6⌋71	38. 12⌋92
9. 5⌋4	19. 7⌋12	29. 9⌋78	39. 14⌋30
10. 2⌋5	20. 3⌋10	30. 1⌋23	40. 52⌋1

```
3 | 4 3 2 7          3 into 4 is 1 remainder 1
  |   1 1            The remainder, 1, is annexed to the 3, making 13.
    1 4 4 2 r 1      3 into 13 is 4 remainder 1.
                     This remainder is annexed to the 2, making 12.
                     3 into 12 is 4.
                     3 into 7 is 2 remainder 1.
                     The answer is 1442 remainder 1.
```

Exercise 3b Leave whole number remainders.

1. 3 | 807

2. 4 | 576

3. 6 | 376

4. 3 | 557

5. 4 | 732

6. 5 | 773

7. 2 | 987

8. 4 | 893

9. 3 | 649

10. 6 | 812

11. 2 | 543

12. 2 | 731

13. 8 | 547

14. 3 | 605

15. 4 | 497

16. 5 | 8553

17. 3 | 2401

18. 7 | 6344

19. 6 | 2330

20. 8 | 5032

Exercise 3c Set each division out as in the last exercise.

1. Divide 3501 by 3.

2. How many fours are there in 1768?

3. Divide three thousand eight hundred and fifty two by nine.

4. If £4826 is shared between two people, how much does each receive?

5. An aging farmer wishes to divide his 30000 acres of land equally amongst his four sons. How much land does each son inherit?

6. Six copies of the same book cost £64.02. How much is each book?

24

7. A junior school has two hundred and fifty two pupils and nine classes. If each class has the same number of children, how many are there in a class?

8. How many sevens are there in two thousand and nine?

9. Seven hundred and forty five cars passed a certain point on a motorway in five hours. On average, how many cars passed by per hour?

10. Calculate seven thousand three hundred and ninety nine divided by five.

The second way of expressing $1 \div 2$ is as the fraction, $\frac{1}{2}$. Here the line between the two numbers stands for the division symbol, $\div$, and so $\frac{1}{2}$ shows one divided by two without an answer. By giving this the name *half* we pretend that the one can be divided. What is staring us in the face is an incomplete division. This is the reason for this type of fraction to be called vulgar. Any fraction expressed with a top and a bottom number is called vulgar, the original meaning of which was *common*, *not refined* or *rude*. The sense of unrefined relates to the incomplete division.

Exercise 3d Express the following divisions as vulgar fractions.

1. $1 \div 3$	**6.** $3 \div 2$	**11.** 3 into 2	**16.** 7 divided by 9
2. $5 \div 9$	**7.** $4 \div 6$	**12.** 5 into 1	**17.** 4 divided by 7
3. $12 \div 13$	**8.** $5 \div 4$	**13.** 4 into 1	**18.** $3 \div 8$
4. $3 \div 4$	**9.** $8 \div 12$	**14.** 7 into 6	**19.** 7 into 3
5. $5 \div 24$	**10.** $9 \div 10$	**15.** 4 into 3	**20.** 5 into 10

Consider the divisions, $6 \div 3 = 2$ and $10 \div 5 = 2$. The numbers in the division are different but the answers are the same. We can change many division sums into more simple division sums by dividing the numbers involved. For example, $20 \div 10 = 2 \div 1$. The sutra for this is *Proportionately*.

Exercise 3e Express the following divisions in their simplest form.

1. $4 \div 2$	**6.** $16 \div 12$	**11.** $24 \div 16$	**16.** $19 \div 11$
2. $6 \div 2$	**7.** $20 \div 15$	**12.** $32 \div 20$	**17.** $28 \div 20$
3. $15 \div 3$	**8.** $30 \div 12$	**13.** $45 \div 10$	**18.** $50 \div 25$
4. $8 \div 6$	**9.** $6 \div 3$	**14.** $18 \div 14$	**19.** $100 \div 12$
5. $12 \div 8$	**10.** $18 \div 9$	**15.** $21 \div 15$	**20.** $96 \div 60$

The third method for expressing the division of one uses a decimal point. The division of 2 into 1 is made by pretending that the 1 is 10. To signify that this is not really the case a dot, or decimal point is placed between the one and the nought, making 1.0. We then say 2 into 10 is 5 and arrive at 0.5 as the answer. But the 5 has, in fact, come out of the ten, that is, the one together with the nought.

$$2\underline{\big|1.0} \atop 0.5$$

If there is no decimal point in the dividend but there is a remainder then a decimal point must be placed after the units digit with a following nought. Noughts must be added until the division is brought to completion. The sutra for this is *By completion and non-completion.*

$671 \div 4$

4 into 6 = 1 remainder 2. The 2 is written below and to the left of 7, making 27.
4 into 27·= 6 remainder 3.
4 into 31 = 7 remainder 3. Since we still have a remainder to divide a decimal point is written after the 1, a nought is added and the dividend is then 30.
4 into 30 = 7 remainder 2. Again there is a remainder and so we add a 0.
 4 into 20 = 5 and with no remainder the division is complete.

$$4\underline{\big|\,6\;7\;1\,.\;0\;0} \atop {\;\;2\;3\;\;\;\,3\;2 \atop \overline{1\;6\;7\,.\;7\;5}}$$

Exercise 3f

1. $5 \div 2$	**6.** $65670 \div 4$	**11.** $27 \div 6$	**16.** $23.143 \div 2$
2. $10 \div 4$	**7.** $1.34 \div 5$	**12.** $435 \div 8$	**17.** $4.012 \div 5$
3. $12 \div 5$	**8.** $34.56 \div 5$	**13.** $67.2 \div 5$	**18.** $567.3 \div 4$
4. $23 \div 2$	**9.** $621.1 \div 4$	**14.** $3469 \div 4$	**19.** $1023 \div 8$
5. $535 \div 4$	**10.** $5 \div 8$	**15.** $94387 \div 8$	**20.** $3.7685 \div 10$

Exercise 3g Copy and complete the following table.

DIVISION	WHOLE NUMBER REMAINDERS	VULGAR FRACTION	DECIMAL FRACTION
1 ÷ 2 or 2 into 1	0 rem 1	$\frac{1}{2}$	0.5
1 ÷ 3 or 3 into 1	0 rem 1	$\frac{1}{3}$	0.333...
2 ÷ 5 or 5 into 2			0.4
1 ÷ 10 or 10 into 1			
3 ÷ 2 or			
13 ÷ 2 or			
1 ÷ 4 or 4 into 1			0.25
5 ÷ 4 or			
9 ÷ 4 or			
3 ÷ 10 or			
5 ÷ 15 or			
1 ÷ 7			0.142857...

Division by All from 9 and the last from 10

The complement of a number may be used in division for the case in which the divisor is just a little less than a base, such as when dividing by 9, 8 or 96, etc. The *All from 9* rule is very useful for such divisions and makes the work easy and simple.

Before commencing with the method there are four names to do with division which must be learnt and understood. These are, divisor, dividend, quotient and remainder. The following rhyme will help with this:

> *The divisor is the number that divides the dividend,*
> *the answer's in the quotient, the remainder's at the end.*

For 17 ÷ 5 = 3 rem. 2, 5 is the divisor, 17 is the dividend, 3 is the quotient and 2 is the remainder.

The example on the next page illustrates the *All from 9* division method and how to set out the sums.

27

Divide 111 by 8

For a single digit divisor a space of one line is left before drawing the answer line. A remainder stroke is placed so that the number of digits in the divisor, one, is the same as the number of digits after the stroke.

8 | 1 1 / 1

The complement of the divisor, 2, is written below the 8.

8 | 1 1 / 1
2
_____
      1

The first digit of the dividend is brought straight down into the answer.

The first quotient digit, 1, is multiplied by the complement, 2, and the answer is placed below the next dividend digit.

8 | 1 1 / 1
2 | 2
_____
    1

This second column is added up, $1 + 2 = 3$, and the answer is the next quotient digit.
The new quotient digit, 3, is multiplied by the complement, 2, giving 6 which is placed in the next column. The remainder column is then added up and the answer is 13 remainder 7.

8 | 1 1 / 1
2 | 2 6
_____
  1 3 / 7

Exercise 3h Use *All from 9* division.

1. 8 | 22

2. 8 | 31

3. 8 | 101

4. 8 | 102

5. 7 | 13

6. 7 | 20

7. 9 | 21

8. 9 | 24

9. 9 | 40

10. 9 | 33

11. 8 | 23

12. 9 | 61

13. 9 | 42

14. 9 | 31

15. 9 | 100

16. 9 | 1401

17. 9 | 2401

18. 9 | 4000

19. 9 | 2330

20. 9 | 18

Division by *All from 9* may be extended for cases where the divisor has more than one digit. Following from the rule on page 5 concerning the number of noughts in the base, the number of digits in the remainder portion must be the same as the number of noughts in the base of the divisor. This will determine where the remainder stroke is to be placed in the dividend.

Divide 1374 by 878

The base of the divisor is 1000 with three noughts. This provides us with the number of digits required after the remainder stroke in the dividend, three. The stroke is placed between 1 and 3 and the remainder stroke in the answer is placed in line with the one above.

$$\begin{array}{r|l} 8\,7\,8 & 1\,/\,3\,7\,4 \\ 1\,2\,2 & \\ \hline & 1\,/ \end{array}$$

The complement of 878, found by *All from nine and the last from ten* is 122 and is written below the divisor.

$$\begin{array}{r|l} 8\,7\,8 & 1\,/\,3\,7\,4 \\ 1\,2\,2 & \quad\ 1\,2\,2 \\ \hline & 1\,/ \end{array}$$

The first quotient digit, 1, is brought straight down into the answer.

$$\begin{array}{r|l} 8\,7\,8 & 1\,/\,3\,7\,4 \\ 1\,2\,2 & \quad\ 1\,2\,2 \\ \hline & 1\,/\,4\,9\,6 \end{array}$$

$1 \times 122 = 122$, and this is placed below 374 with the digits in line.

374 + 122 gives the remainder and so the answer is 1 remainder 496

Exercise 3i *All from 9* division

1. 88⌐121

2. 76⌐111

3. 83⌐132

4. 79⌐107

5. 83⌐144

6. 73⌐129

7. 779⌐1111

8. 866⌐1234

9. 8877⌐12034

10. 8907⌐13103

11. 7999⌐12131

12. 790⌐1212

13. 887⌐1223

14. 893⌐1555

15. 828⌐1133

16. 867⌐1313

17. 93⌐121

18. 987⌐1248

In the previous exercise each dividend has one more digit than its divisor. We now take up the case where there are a larger number of digits in the dividend. The following example illustrates the method

---

$10014 \div 88$

The remainder stroke is placed so that the number of digits on its right is the same as the number of digits in the divisor, (two).

$$\begin{array}{c|c} 8\ 8 & 1\ 0\ 0\ /\ 1\ 4 \\ 1\ 2 & \\ \hline & \\ \end{array}$$

There are three digits to the left of the remainder stroke and this gives the number of spaces to be left before the answer line is drawn.

The complement of 88, that is 12, is written down below the divisor.

$$\begin{array}{c|c} 8\ 8 & 1\ 0\ 0\ /\ 1\ 4 \\ 1\ 2 & 1\ 2 \\ \hline & 1\ 1 \\ \end{array}$$

1 is brought down. $1 \times 12 = 12$ and this is placed below the next two digits of the dividend.

The second column is added up, $0 + 1 = 1$, and this gives the next answer digit.

$$\begin{array}{c|c} 8\ 8 & 1\ 0\ 0\ /\ 1\ 4 \\ 1\ 2 & 1\ 2 \\ & \quad\ 1\quad 2 \\ \hline & 1\ 1\ 3 \\ \end{array}$$

The complement is now multiplied by the second answer digit, $12 \times 1 = 12$, and the result is written in the next two columns

The third column is added up for the next answer digit, $0 + 2 + 1 = 3$.

$$\begin{array}{c|c} 8\ 8 & 1\ 0\ 0\ /\ 1\ 4 \\ 1\ 2 & 1\ 2 \\ & \quad\ 1\quad 2 \\ & \qquad\quad 3\ 6 \\ \hline & 1\ 1\ 3\ /\ 7\ 0 \\ \end{array}$$

The complement is multiplied by the third answer digit, $12 \times 3 = 36$ and this result is set below the next two digits of the dividend.

The remainder portion is added up, (giving 70) and the final answer is 113 remainder 70.

Exercise 3j

1. 89 $\lfloor$1021

2. 88 $\lfloor$1122

3. 86 $\lfloor$1111

4. 89 $\lfloor$10021

5. 89 $\lfloor$11001

6. 88 $\lfloor$10010

7. 79 $\lfloor$1001

8. 78 $\lfloor$1010

9. 889 $\lfloor$10101

10. 888 $\lfloor$10011

11. 887 $\lfloor$11243

12. 879 $\lfloor$11283

13. 798 $\lfloor$10158

14. 889 $\lfloor$101025

15. 879 $\lfloor$101003

16. 898 $\lfloor$101007

17. 8888 $\lfloor$101011

18. 8897 $\lfloor$112131

The next step is to find out what to do when the addition of digits in a column comes to more than ten. The following example illustrates this.

Divide 9 into 4261.

4 is brought down.

$4 \times 1 = 4, 2 + 4 = 6$.

$6 \times 1 = 6, 6 + 6 = 12$.

$12 \times 1 = 12, 1 + 12 = 13$

```
9 | 4  2  6 /  1
1 |    4  6  12
    4  6 12 / 13
    4  7  2 / 13
    4  7  3 /  4
```

In the third column 12 is kept as a single number until the next line when the 1 of 12 is carried to the left.

In the remainder column 13 is actually larger than the divisor, 9, and so must be redivided. 9 into 13 is 1 remainder 4 and this 1 is carried to the left.

Exercise 3k

1. $9\lfloor\overline{2413}$

2. $9\lfloor\overline{1361}$

3. $9\lfloor\overline{3463}$

4. $9\lfloor\overline{31313}$

5. $9\lfloor\overline{3573}$

6. $9\lfloor\overline{888}$

7. $9\lfloor\overline{4477}$

8. $9\lfloor\overline{12415}$

9. $8\lfloor\overline{1231}$

10. $8\lfloor\overline{1321}$

11. $8\lfloor\overline{444}$

12. $8\lfloor\overline{3030}$

13. $8\lfloor\overline{11111}$

14. $9\lfloor\overline{2727}$

15. $9\lfloor\overline{2828}$

16. $9\lfloor\overline{24680}$

17. $9\lfloor\overline{4647}$

18. $9\lfloor\overline{37111}$

19. $9\lfloor\overline{77077}$

20. $9\lfloor\overline{1977}$

The unique property of division by *All from 9 and the last from 10* is that the main working requires no division at all but only addition.

Division by Transpose and Adjust

Where the divisor is a little more than the base then we use a method very similar to *All from 9* division. The sutra is *Transpose and adjust.*

This method of division takes the divisor and *transposes* all the numbers greater than the base into vinculum numbers. In the sum itself vinculum numbers have to be added to ordinary numbers and so the next exercise has some practice for this.

$7 + \bar{3} = 4$ A vinculum is a deficiency and so when the deficiency of 3 is added to 7 the answer is 4 which is the same as $7 - 3 = 4$

Exercise 3l Oral.

1. $5 + \bar{1}$

2. $6 + \bar{3}$

3. $7 + \bar{2}$

4. $9 + \bar{5}$

5. $3 + \bar{3}$

6. $6 + \bar{1}$

7. $7 + \bar{6}$

8. $8 + \bar{5}$

9. $5 + \bar{3}$

10. $9 + \bar{2}$

11. $23 + \bar{1}\bar{1}$

12. $34 + \bar{2}\bar{1}$

13. $55 + \bar{1}\bar{2}$

14. $64 + \bar{1}\bar{2}$

15. $78 + \bar{3}\bar{1}$

16. $14 + \bar{4}$

17. $24 + \bar{2}\bar{1}$ **20.** $75 + \bar{6}\bar{2}$ **23.** $6 + \bar{2} + \bar{3}$ **26.** $7 + \bar{4} + \bar{3}$

18. $48 + \bar{3}\bar{5}$ **21.** $8 + \bar{1} + \bar{1}$ **24.** $9 + \bar{4} + \bar{1}$ **27.** $8 + \bar{2} + \bar{6}$

19. $98 + \bar{7}\bar{3}$ **22.** $9 + \bar{2} + \bar{1}$ **25.** $8 + \bar{3} + \bar{2}$ **28.** $9 + \bar{5} + \bar{1}$

The following example illustrates how to proceed with this method of division.

$256 \div 11$

$$
\begin{array}{c|cc}
11 & 2\ 5\ /\ 6 \\
\bar{1} & \bar{2}\ \ \bar{3} \\
\hline
 & 2\ 3\ /\ 3
\end{array}
$$

The base of the divisor is 10. The divisor, 11, is one more than the base and so the surplus is 1. This 1 is transposed into $\bar{1}$ and written underneath.

The rest of the process is very much as before. 2 is brought down, $2 \times \bar{1} = \bar{2}$. $\bar{2}$, which is written below the next digit 5. $5 + \bar{2} = 3$, gives the next answer digit. $3 \times \bar{1} = \bar{3}$. $6 + \bar{3} = 3$ which gives the remainder.

Exercise 3m

1. $11 \,|\, 132$	**9.** $13 \,|\, 148$	**17.** $12 \,|\, 1479$	**25.** $11 \,|\, 56227$
2. $11 \,|\, 144$	**10.** $12 \,|\, 288$	**18.** $12 \,|\, 25477$	**26.** $13 \,|\, 27469$
3. $11 \,|\, 159$	**11.** $11 \,|\, 465$	**19.** $13 \,|\, 14318$	**27.** $14 \,|\, 16954$
4. $11 \,|\, 267$	**12.** $12 \,|\, 256$	**20.** $13 \,|\, 27438$	**28.** $12 \,|\, 399888$
5. $12 \,|\, 169$	**13.** $11 \,|\, 1245$	**21.** $14 \,|\, 29694$	**29.** $11 \,|\, 477539$
6. $12 \,|\, 133$	**14.** $11 \,|\, 2468$	**22.** $13 \,|\, 39158$	**30.** $12 \,|\, 363759$
7. $12 \,|\, 269$	**15.** $11 \,|\, 15789$	**23.** $12 \,|\, 37207$	**31.** $14 \,|\, 155555$
8. $12 \,|\, 389$	**16.** $12 \,|\, 1369$	**24.** $12 \,|\, 49369$	**32.** $13 \,|\, 28886$

For larger divisors, all the digits are transposed into vinculum numbers except for the first 1 of the divisor. Particular care must be taken when setting these sums out as the number of lines required depends on the number of digits of the dividend which lie to the left of the remainder stroke.

$$23689 \div 112$$

$$
\begin{array}{r|l}
112 & 2\,3\,6\,/\,8\,9 \\
\overline{1}\,\overline{2} & \overline{2}\,\overline{4} \\
 & \quad\ \overline{1}\ \ \overline{2} \\
 & \qquad\quad \overline{1}\,\overline{2} \\
\hline
 & 2\,1\,1\,/\,5\,7
\end{array}
$$

The base of the divisor is 100 and since this has two zeros we allow two digits after the remainder stroke. The surplus of 12 is transposed to $\overline{1}\,\overline{2}$ and this is written below 112.

There are three digits to the left of the remainder stroke and this provides the number of lines needed for working. 2 is brought down as the first answer digit.

$2 \times \overline{1}\,\overline{2} = \overline{2}\,\overline{4}$ and this is set below the next two dividend digits, 3 and 6.

The second column is added, that is $3 + \overline{2} = 1$, to give the next answer digit.

$1 \times \overline{1}\,\overline{2} = \overline{1}\,\overline{2}$ which is put into the next two columns, below the 6 and 8.

The sum of the third column is $6 + \overline{4} + \overline{1} = 1$, and this is the third answer digit.

$1 \times \overline{1}\,\overline{2} = \overline{1}\,\overline{2}$ which is set down below the last two dividend digits.

The remainder is added up, $9 + \overline{2} = 7$ and $8 + \overline{2} + \overline{1} = 5$.

The answer is 211 remainder 57.

Exercise 3n Further division by *Transpose and Adjust*

1. $111\,\big|\,2458$	6. $103\,\big|\,10569$	11. $1112\,\big|\,12343$	16. $1111\,\big|\,34699$
2. $112\,\big|\,1236$	7. $102\,\big|\,16453$	12. $1203\,\big|\,25483$	17. $1212\,\big|\,26897$
3. $113\,\big|\,2384$	8. $101\,\big|\,24557$	13. $1104\,\big|\,12789$	18. $1204\,\big|\,14448$
4. $112\,\big|\,1486$	9. $110\,\big|\,15542$	14. $1211\,\big|\,27868$	19. $1363\,\big|\,13981$
5. $111\,\big|\,1278$	10. $105\,\big|\,10623$	15. $1003\,\big|\,21188$	20. $123\,\big|\,25953$

So far this chapter has dealt with three types of division: simple division, *All from 9* division and *Transpose and Adjust* division. Choices have to be made as to which method is most suitable. Simple division is generally used where the divisor has one digit, such as 4 or 7. For the choice between *All from 9* division and *Transpose and Adjust* division the base of the divisor must be found. Where the divisor is a little less than a base then use *All from 9* and where the divisor is a little more than the base then use *Transpose and Adjust*. The case for a divisor nowhere near a base is taken up in a later chapter and comes under Straight division.

Exercise 3o Inspect the divisor before deciding which method to use.

1. 9 ⌐13220	**6.** 88 ⌐12013	**11.** 106 ⌐15921	**16.** 988 ⌐211356
2. 11 ⌐24365	**7.** 7 ⌐82506	**12.** 3 ⌐86704	**17.** 104 ⌐312749
3. 4 ⌐35463	**8.** 112 ⌐25772	**13.** 97 ⌐25109	**18.** 5 ⌐445362
4. 12 ⌐15649	**9.** 6 ⌐43780	**14.** 998 ⌐12121	**19.** 96 ⌐320212
5. 8 ⌐1101	**10.** 89 ⌐11013	**15.** 1103 ⌐23284	**20.** 121 ⌐146785

Chapter 4 - Subtraction by *All from 9 and the last from 10*

Complements

In this chapter, the *All from nine* sutra is used for subtraction. We have already seen how the complement of a number is obtained by using the *All from nine and the last from ten* rule and relates any number back to unity

Subtraction using complements

In the simple case, such as 365 – 215, when the sum is set out we find that all of the top row digits are greater than or equal to the digits directly below. In this example, each digit is subtracted from the one above.

$$
\begin{array}{r}
365 \\
- 215 \\
\hline
150 \\
\end{array}
$$

Complements are used when this is not the case. The basic method is to take the difference of the two digits and, when the bottom row digit is larger, write down the complement of the difference. When complements are no longer needed we subtract an extra 1 from the next left-hand column. To see how this works in practice follow the steps in the example below.

Subtract 3876 from 5322.

Starting from the right, 6 is more than 2, so we take the difference, 4, and write down its complement from 10 (since it is the last), that is 6.

$$
\begin{array}{r}
5322 \\
- 3876 \\
\hline
6 \\
\end{array}
$$

In the next column, the difference between 7 and 2 is 5 and the complement (from 9) is 4.

$$
\begin{array}{r}
5322 \\
- 3876 \\
\hline
46 \\
\end{array}
$$

For the hundreds column, the difference between 8 and 3 is 5 and the complement of this is 4.

$$
\begin{array}{r}
5322 \\
- 3876 \\
\hline
446 \\
\end{array}
$$

In the thousands column, 5 is greater than 3 and so we can finish using complements. This is done by reducing the answer by 1 after the ordinary subtraction, that is, 5 – 3 – 1 = 1.

$$
\begin{array}{r}
5322 \\
- 3876 \\
\hline
1446 \\
\end{array}
$$

The answer is 1446.

Exercise 4a

1. 4121 – 2787	**6.** 7231 – 6452	**11.** 34121 – 15678	**16.** 42374 – 7485
2. 5432 – 1567	**7.** 8191 – 6292	**12.** 35133 – 16249	**17.** 53611 – 7899
3. 6000 – 4872	**8.** 4242 – 1353	**13.** 27000 – 18123	**18.** 48764 – 19976
4. 5132 – 1763	**9.** 5612 – 1777	**14.** 57988 – 18999	**19.** 13478 – 9589
5. 3221 – 1762	**10.** 4111 – 1444	**15.** 10000 – 6987	**20.** 62488 – 3489

Starting with complements in the middle of a sum

To start using complements at any point in the subtraction treat the particular column as if it was the first on the right.

Subtract 19670 from 56381

a) In the first two columns on the right, the digits in the top row are greater than those below. $1 - 0 = 1$, $8 - 7 = 1$.

$$\begin{array}{r} 56381 \\ -19670 \\ \hline 11 \end{array}$$

b) In the hundreds column, 6 is greater than 3 and so we start using complements here. Difference is 3, complement (from 10) is 7.

$$\begin{array}{r} 56381 \\ -19670 \\ \hline 711 \end{array}$$

c) In the next column, the difference 3, the complement (from 9) is 6.

$$\begin{array}{r} 56381 \\ -19670 \\ \hline 6711 \end{array}$$

d) For the last step, where 5 is greater than 1, we take an extra 1 off to finish using complements, $5 - 1 - 1 = 3$.

$$\begin{array}{r} 56381 \\ -19670 \\ \hline 36711 \end{array}$$

Exercise 4b

1. 4327 – 1515	6. 8241 – 4341	11. 32467 – 14533	16. 76589 – 16688
2. 3672 – 1981	7. 643 – 171	12. 76019 – 29128	17. 43723 – 19780
3. 4849 – 2954	8. 9730 – 1820	13. 32456 – 14321	18. 32346 – 18223
4. 3760 – 1910	9. 7578 – 2921	14. 66220 – 49110	19. 76542 – 17691
5. 7328 – 1631	10. 13147 – 9453	15. 43720 – 9810	20. 64321 – 15430

Finishing with complements in the middle of a sum

The procedure for finishing with complements at any particular column in a subtraction requires that the digit in the top row is greater than the digit directly below. The process is to subtract and then take 1 off.

Subtract 3459 from 6753

a) In the units column, the difference is 6, and the complement is 4.

$$\begin{array}{r} 6753 \\ -\,3459 \\ \hline 4 \end{array}$$

b) In the tens column, 5 is not greater than 5 and so we stay with the complements. Difference is 0, complement, 9.

$$\begin{array}{r} 6753 \\ -\,3459 \\ \hline 94 \end{array}$$

c) 7 is greater than 4, so $7 - 4 - 1 = 2$.

$$\begin{array}{r} 6753 \\ -\,3459 \\ \hline 294 \end{array}$$

d) In the left hand column, $6 - 3 = 3$.

e) The answer is 3294.

$$\begin{array}{r} 6753 \\ -\,3459 \\ \hline 3294 \end{array}$$

Exercise 4c

1.	5713 – 1246	**9.**	468 – 129	**17.**	32400 – 11378	**25.**	47823 – 25365
2.	2311 – 1179	**10.**	334 – 215	**18.**	46000 – 12187	**26.**	54262 – 11373
3.	6234 – 1078	**11.**	7811 – 4622	**19.**	32544 – 12359	**27.**	63974 – 22887
4.	7843 – 1237	**12.**	3817 – 1968	**20.**	67813 – 64404	**28.**	72381 – 31296
5.	6894 – 3726	**13.**	7318 – 5109	**21.**	79308 – 45219	**29.**	84623 – 53164
6.	7564 – 1299	**14.**	6453 – 1239	**22.**	53462 – 12678	**30.**	12345 – 11999
7.	3546 – 1378	**15.**	7013 – 3008	**23.**	60981 – 20895	**31.**	50256 – 20178
8.	2354 – 1068	**16.**	5453 – 1239	**24.**	46875 – 12999	**32**	76512 – 12634

The general case of subtraction

The general case is where complements are only used when necessary in a subtraction.sum There are four points to remember with *All from nine* subtraction:

1) Go into complements when the digit in the bottom row is larger than the one above.

2) The first complement is from ten and the rest are from nine.

3) Come out of complements when the digit in the top row is larger than the one below.

4) When coming out of complements drop 1 in that column.

The example on the next page shows how to start and finish using complements more than once in a single subtraction.

671245 − 380674

$$\begin{array}{r} 671245 \\ -\ 380674 \\ \hline 1 \end{array}$$

a) 5 − 4 = 1

$$\begin{array}{r} 671245 \\ -\ 380674 \\ \hline 71 \end{array}$$

b) Difference 3, complement 7.

$$\begin{array}{r} 671245 \\ -\ 380674 \\ \hline 571 \end{array}$$

c) Difference 4, complement 5.

$$\begin{array}{r} 671245 \\ -\ 380674 \\ \hline 0571 \end{array}$$

d) 1 − 0 − 1 = 0

e) Difference 1, complement 9.

$$\begin{array}{r} 671245 \\ -\ 380674 \\ \hline 90571 \end{array}$$

f) 6 − 3 − 1 = 2

g) The answer is 290571.

$$\begin{array}{r} 671245 \\ -\ 380674 \\ \hline 290571 \end{array}$$

Exercise 4d

1. 54326 − 12784	6. 765432 − 345678	11. 846123 − 728321	16. 363239 − 177190
2. 71209 − 34326	7. 326542 − 123456	12. 723068 − 91129	17. 217829 − 9183
3. 64156 − 2374	8. 36271 − 2123	13. 432157 − 81623	18. 462142 − 191806
4. 835421 − 642561	9. 100000 − 76543	14. 534087 − 80089	19. 361526 − 45619
5. 945632 − 456789	10. 932640 − 175294	15. 145629 − 8917	20. 948134 − 419918

The word *minus* means subtract or take away and comes from the Latin word meaning *less*.

Exercise 4e Problems

1. Find the difference between £763 and £489.

2. Subtract 23478 from 56712.

3. What is 6050 minus 489?

4. Subtract £23000 from £52500.

5. Find the difference between the heights of William and Jessica if William is 167 cm tall and Jessica is 129 cm tall.

6. A builder has a pile of 1200 bricks. If he uses 956 of them to build a wall, how many are left unused?

7. A furniture store has 2154 pieces of furniture for sale. If 1961 are unsold at the end of a month, how many have been sold during that month?

8. A man has £2923 in a savings account and spends £1635 on having a garage built. How much does he have left?

9. A theatre has a seating capacity of eight hundred. On one evening there were one hundred and sixty four spare seats. How many people were in the audience that night?

10. A newspaper shop had 3564 newspapers for sale in a week. How many were sold if there were 780 left at the end of the week?

11. In a town in Peru there were 1230 homes. An earthquake destroyed 851 of these homes. How many were left?

12. A man owes the bank £680. Find his remaining debt when he pays back £495 of the outstanding amount.

13. A farmer has 3025 lambs and sells 896 of them at the sheep market. How many does he have after the sale?

14. A book has 198 pages. If I have read 69 of them, how many pages do I have left to read?

15. A man bought set of screw-drivers which cost £7.42. How much change should he receive from a twenty pound note?

Turbo Subtraction

When "in" complements, whenever the digits are the same the answer is 9, when the digits differ by 1 the answer is 8 and when the digits differ by 2 the answer is 7. With practice this can be utilised to great effect and difficult subtractions can be worked out at high speed.

In the first example, at the right-hand end, the 8 and 3 give 5 as the answer digit. Thereafter, the difference is zero and the complement of zero is 9. There is nothing to calculate and once the sameness is seen the answer 9 can be put straight down.

$$\begin{array}{r} 733333333 \\ -\ 233333338 \\ \hline 499999995 \end{array}$$

Similarly, in the second example, after the right-hand end digits have been dealt with the numbers in each column are seen to be the same and so 9 is the answer digit in each case.

$$\begin{array}{r} 8544532 \\ -\ 1544536 \\ \hline 6999996 \end{array}$$

When the difference is 1 the answer digit is 8. Again, no calculation is required! We just have to recognise that the bottom digit in each column is one more than the digit above.

$$\begin{array}{r} 95463501 \\ -\ 26574619 \\ \hline 68888882 \end{array}$$

Where the difference is 2 the answer digit is 7.

$$\begin{array}{r} 6437124 \\ -\ 2659348 \\ \hline 3777776 \end{array}$$

Exercise 4f

1.	475864 − 175869	**6.**	8354243 − 3454368	**11.**	7000000 − 1212024	**16.**	5305645 − 1646746
2.	375640 − 175648	**7.**	5087432 − 2187448	**12.**	6342106 − 1342217	**17.**	7064732 − 2178868
3.	376548 − 187659	**8.**	6023132 − 144337	**13.**	7645031 − 6666138	**18.**	6121632 − 2333333
4.	734234 − 245348	**9.**	675342 − 186567	**14.**	7343023 − 3676359	**19.**	9008000 − 1231231
5.	634123 − 256349	**10.**	612006 − 12119	**15.**	8411203 − 7444637	**20.**	12453721 − 2543839

Chapter 5 - Prime and Composite Numbers

When two numbers are multiplied together the answer is called the **product**.

Thus we say, for example, the product of 2 and 7 is 14.

Numbers which are multiplied together to give a product are called **factors** of that product.

For example, 2 and 7 are factors of 14.

Any product is a **multiple** of any one of its factors.

If we take 2 as a factor then all the products formed with 2 together with other numbers are multiples of 2. For example, 4, 6, 8, 10, 12, 14, and so on, are all multiples of 2.

We ordinarily think of the world as a multiplicity. It is said that the wise man sees only one.

> *When to the man of realisation all beings become the very Self, then what delusion and what sorrow can there be for that seer of oneness?*
> [Isa Upanishad]

One is a factor of every number. This is because any number can be thought of as a product of one and itself. For example, $23 = 23 \times 1$.

Express 24 in terms of all its factors.

$$24 = 1 \times 24$$
$$= 2 \times 12$$
$$= 3 \times 8$$
$$= 4 \times 6$$

Exercise 5a Express the following numbers in terms of all their factors.

1. 12	6. 15	11. 32	16. 28
2. 6	7. 16	12. 36	17. 64
3. 8	8. 19	13. 40	18. 100
4. 14	9. 7	14. 56	19. 50
5. 20	10. 30	15. 18	20. 112

Highest common factor

The highest common factor of two or more numbers is the highest number which can divide those numbers exactly.

For example, the highest common factor of 10 and 15 is 5. The factors of 10 are 1, 2, 5 and 10; the factors of 15 are 1, 3, 5 and 15. Of factors which are common to both 10 and 15, 5 is the highest and so it is called the highest common factor.

Exercise 5b Find the HCF of the following, *By mere inspection*

1. 12, 18	**6.** 18, 30	**11.** 20, 28	**16.** 16, 24
2. 10, 20	**7.** 20, 25	**12.** 35, 49	**17.** 32, 40
3. 12, 15	**8.** 15, 25	**13.** 64, 8	**18.** 22, 44
4. 6, 8	**9.** 9, 16	**14.** 80, 30	**19.** 30, 45
5. 12, 24	**10.** 8, 18	**15.** 15, 35	**20.** 36, 60

Exercise 5c Find the HCF of the following, *By mere inspection*

1. 4, 6, 12	**6.** 3, 6, 12	**11.** 10, 20, 25	**16.** 10, 15, 30
2. 3, 6, 9	**7.** 8, 12, 16	**12.** 24, 36, 48	**17.** 16, 15, 30
3. 2, 4, 8	**8.** 3, 9, 15	**13.** 12, 15, 18	**18.** 16, 48, 64
4. 4, 8, 12	**9.** 6, 9, 18	**14.** 12, 18, 30	**19.** 14, 21, 35
5. 4, 12, 16	**10.** 5, 15, 20	**15.** 20, 30, 40	**20.** 18, 27, 36

Prime numbers

Prime numbers are only divisible by one and themselves.

A prime number is like the man that remains steadfast in himself. He cannot be divided by anything that is not himself. He stands alone unmoved when everything around him is in turmoil.

For some reason, many mathematicians do not include 1 as a prime number. 1 is really the prime of primes. As described before, 1 is really indivisible.

3, 11 and 17 are examples of prime numbers. Can you think of others?
If you take any number, multiply it by 4 and either add or subtract 1, can you always arrive at a prime number? For example, $7 \times 4 + 1 = 29$.

Exercise 5d

1. Write down the following numbers in a row and draw a circle round those which are prime:

    10 11 12 13 14 15 16 17 18 19 20

2. What is the next prime number after 31?

3. Write down all the prime numbers between 40 and 60.

4. Write down all the numbers between 20 and 40 which are not prime.

5. What is the product of the first three prime numbers, the first four prime numbers and the first five prime numbers?

6. Copy and complete the following table:

Number, n	n × n	Add n	Add 17	Is it prime?
1	1	2	19	Yes
2	4	6	23	Yes
3	9	12		
4				
5				
6				
7				
8				
9				
20				

Composite numbers

Numbers which are not prime are called **composite**. This means that composite numbers may be thought of as products of other numbers. For example, 12 is composite because it may be split up into factors, 3 × 4 or 2 × 6.

All composite numbers are multiples of their factors.

Every composite number may be expressed as the product of factors which are primes. To find these prime factors we divide the number by the smallest prime starting with 2. We continue to divide each answer by 2 until this is no longer possible. The answer is then divided by 3, 5, 7, and higher primes until the answer itself is a prime number. The number can then be expressed as the product of prime factors. The sutra is *By mere observation*.

Express 24 as the product of prime factors.

$24 = 2 \times 12$
$\quad = 2 \times 2 \times 6$
$\quad = 2 \times 2 \times 2 \times 3$

2 into 24 = 12, therefore $24 = 2 \times 12$
We now take the 12 and decompose it into its factors, $12 = 2 \times 6$ and likewise, $6 = 2 \times 3$.
The chart is as shown on the left. The result is that 24 is expressed as a product of four numbers all of which are primes.

Exercise 5e Express each number as the product of its prime factors.

1. 8	6. 18	11. 30	16. 40
2. 10	7. 15	12. 21	17. 36
3. 16	8. 22	13. 27	18. 42
4. 20	9. 24	14. 14	19. 64
5. 6	10. 9	15. 35	20. 81

Lowest common multiple

The lowest common multiple of two or more numbers is the lowest number into which those numbers can divide.

For example the lowest common multiple of 6 and 8 is 24. This is because of multiples of 6, that is, 6, 12, 18, 24, 30, 36, etc and of multiples of 8, that is 8, 16, 24, 32, 40, 48, etc, some multiples are common to both. These common multiples are 24, 48, 72, 96, etc. Of these common multiples 24 is the lowest and is therefore called the LCM.

Exercise 5f Find, *By mere inspection*, the LCM of the following:

1. 4, 6	6. 8, 12	11. 5, 12	16. 2, 3, 4
2. 2, 3	7. 4, 5	12. 10, 15	17. 4, 5, 3
3. 4, 8	8. 10, 6	13. 25, 10	18. 4, 6, 8,
4. 8, 10	9. 5, 15	14. 15, 20	19. 2, 5, 4
5. 5, 7	10. 3, 5	15. 4, 16	20. 4, 5, 6

There is a simple method for finding the lowest common multiple of two numbers when the answer is not obvious. The sutra for this is *Proportionately*.

Find the lowest common multiple of 24 and 30.

The numbers are set down with a small space between. Underneath these numbers, and slightly to the left, write down the highest common factor, in this case 6. Divide both numbers by 6 and write the answers below, 4 and 5.
The LCM is the product of these three numbers, that is $6 \times 4 \times 5 = 6 \times 20 = 120$.

24 30
6   4   5

24 30
$6 \times 4 \times 5 = 120$

Exercise 5g Use the method above to find the LCM of the following:

1. 6, 8	**6.** 10, 4	**11.** 12, 8	**16.** 9, 15
2. 4, 6	**7.** 15, 10	**12.** 6, 20	**17.** 15, 25
3. 10, 12	**8.** 15, 20	**13.** 6, 9	**18.** 6, 27
4. 6, 10	**9.** 12, 14	**14.** 25, 30	**19.** 8, 18
5. 8, 14	**10.** 14, 4	**15.** 40, 60	**20.** 24, 28

Note that when, of two numbers, the first is a factor of the second, such as 7 and 14, then the first is the highest common factor of both and the second is the lowest common multiple of both.

To find the LCM of three numbers the simplest way is to find the LCM of two of them and then find the LCM of the answer to this and the third number.

Find the LCM of 16, 20 and 24.

For 16 and 20, the LCM is 80. The problem is then to find the LCM of 80 and 24. Again, using *Proportionately*, the answer is found to be 240.

16 20
$4 \times 4 \times 5 = 80$

80 24
$8 \times 10 \times 3 = 240$

47

Exercise 5h Use the method above to find the LCM of the following:

1. 3, 6, 12	**6.** 4, 8, 16	**11.** 6, 9, 8	**16.** 10, 15, 36
2. 6, 8, 10	**7.** 2, 5, 10	**12.** 8, 9, 12	**17.** 8, 10, 12
3. 4, 5, 6	**8.** 3, 5, 10	**13.** 6, 10, 15	**18.** 5, 6, 7
4. 4, 6, 14	**9.** 3, 8, 12	**14.** 12, 20, 36	**19.** 8, 14, 20
5. 3, 7, 8	**10.** 10, 15, 30	**15.** 8, 12, 18	**20.** 6, 15, 25

Coprime numbers

Two numbers are **coprime** when their highest common factor is one.

For example, 4 is not a prime number because it can be divided by 2, 9 is likewise not a prime number because 3 is a factor. 4 and 9 are called coprime because their highest common factor is 1. When two numbers are coprime their lowest common multiple is the product. For example, with 4 and 9, the LCM is 4 × 9 = 36.

Since 1 is a factor of all numbers, every number is related to every other number through 1.

> *This is the truth: the sparks, though of one nature with the fire, leap from it; uncounted beings leap from the Everlasting, but these, O friend, merge into It again.*

> [Mundaka Upanishad: 2,1,1]

Exercise 5i Copy and complete this table showing coprimeness between numbers. If two numbers are coprime put a cross and if they are not, put a dot. The first few have been done for you.

	2	3	4	5	6	7	8	9	10
2	·	X	·	X	·	X	·	X	·
3	X	·	X	X	·	X	X	·	X
4	·	X	·						
5									
6									
7									
8									
9									
10									

Summary of definitions for primes and composite numbers

EXAMPLES

1. When two numbers are multiplied together the answer is called the product.

   The product of 4 and 6 is 24.

2. Numbers which are multiplied together to give a product are called factors of that product.

   3 and 5 are factors of 15.

3. One is a factor of every number.

   $1 \times 17 = 17$

4. Any product is a multiple of any one of its factors.

   20 is a multiple of 5 since $5 \times 4 = 20$.

5. The highest common factor of two or more numbers is the highest number which can divide those numbers exactly.

   Of 12 and 16, 4 is the HCF.

6. Prime numbers are only divisible by one and themselves.

   17 is prime because its only factors are 1 and 17.

7. Numbers which are not prime are called composite.

   22 is composite because 2 and 11 are factors as well as 1 and 22.

8. Every composite number may be expressed as the product of factors which are primes.

   $36 = 2 \times 2 \times 3 \times 3$

9. The lowest common multiple of two or more numbers is the lowest number into which those numbers can divide.

   The LCM of 8 and 12 is 24.

10. Two numbers are coprime when their highest common factor is one.

    6 and 35 are coprime.

11. Since 1 is a factor of all numbers, every number is related to every other number through 1.

Exercise 5j Problems

1. Write down all the factors of 48.

2. List the multiples of 3 which lie between 60 and 80.

3. List all the numbers less than 30 which are both multiples of 2 and multiples of 3.

4. List all the factors of 36 which are also factors of 30.

5. Write down the multiples of 9 up to 90. Sum the digits. What do you find?

6. What is the HCF of 56 and 72?

7. Express 48 as the product of prime factors.

8. Find the LCM of 12 and 18.

9. What is the LCM of 3, 7 and 15?

10. Write down two numbers which are coprime, one of which is a multiple of 2 and the other a multiple of 3.

11. Write down a composite number which has the first five whole numbers as factors.

12. Find the LCM of the first nine numbers.

13. Helena climbs three stairs with each pace and Jonathan climbs four. If they both start together at the bottom, after how many stairs will they step onto the same stair?

14. Alpa and Suki meet at the library on a Saturday. After this, Alpa returns every three days and Suki returns every five days. after how many days will they meet again at the library? Which day of the week is this?

15. Two brothers have paces measuring 24 in and 30 in, respectively. If they both start together, after what distance will their steps coincide?

16. What is the lowest price which must be paid for a whole number of crayons at 45 p each which could also buy a whole number of pencils at 25 p each?

17. Martha is 48 years old and her husband, Hugh, is 56. Their daughter, Andrea, is twice the highest common factor of her parent's ages. How old is Andrea?

Chapter 6 - Fractions

Common or vulgar fractions arise from pretending to divide the one which is unity. The line in between the two numbers in the fraction stands for the division sign. Thus, for example, $\frac{3}{5}$ represents the division $3 \div 5$.

If we have 12 m of rope and divide it into two equal parts, each part will be 6 m long. Each of these equal parts is called one-half of the whole rope, and its relation to the 12 m is expressed as $\frac{1}{2}$. Thus 6 m is $\frac{1}{2}$ of 12 m. Consequently, $\frac{1}{2}$ of a quantity is that which is obtained when the quantity is divided by 2, or into 2 equal parts.

Exercise 6a What is $\frac{1}{2}$ of each of the following quantities?

1. £6	**6.** 150 feet	**11.** 38 g	**16.** 98 minutes
2. 48 p	**7.** 16 pints	**12.** 56 litres	**17.** 264 acres
3. 32 m	**8.** 112 hours	**13.** 11 tons	**18.** 6432 years
4. 50 cm	**9.** 62 days	**14.** 3 seconds	**19.** 1500 sq.ft
5. 120 miles	**10.** 86 km	**15.** 5 mm	**20.** $135

If we divide 12 m of rope into three equal parts there will be 4 m of rope in each part. Each part is called one third, or $\frac{1}{3}$, of the whole 12 m of rope. Consequently $\frac{1}{3}$ of a quantity is obtained when we divide that quantity by 3, or into 3 equal parts. If we then take two of these equal parts we have two thirds, or $\frac{2}{3}$, of the whole.

So the number on the bottom of the fraction shows into how many parts a quantity has been divided. The number on the top shows how many of these parts have been taken. For this reason the number on the bottom is called the **denominator** and the number on the top is called the **numerator**.

In relation to a quantity there are two ways in which to understand a fraction. For example, with $\frac{2}{3}$, we may consider it to be $\frac{1}{3}$ of 2 units or as 2 lots of $\frac{1}{3}$.

To find a fraction of any quantity, multiply the quantity by the numerator and divide by the denominator, or conversely, divide by the denominator and multiply by the numerator.

Find $\frac{5}{6}$ of £3.24

$$£3.24 \div 6 = £0.54$$
$$£0.54 \times 5 = \underline{£2.70}$$

or $£3.24 \times 5 = £16.20$
$$£16.20 \div 6 = \underline{£2.70}$$

Exercise 6b Find:

1. $\frac{1}{3}$ of £2.40   6. $\frac{2}{3}$ of £4.50   11. $\frac{3}{10}$ of 40 min   16. $\frac{2}{3}$ of 63 cm

2. $\frac{1}{4}$ of 12 kg   7. $\frac{2}{5}$ of 15 sec   12. $\frac{4}{5}$ of £25   17. $\frac{3}{5}$ of 45 in

3. $\frac{1}{5}$ of 20 m   8. $\frac{3}{4}$ of 20 mm   13. $\frac{3}{8}$ of 24 kg   18. $\frac{2}{9}$ of 81 hours

4. $\frac{1}{8}$ of 32 ft   9. $\frac{2}{9}$ of $18   14. $\frac{5}{6}$ of 30 m   19. $\frac{4}{10}$ of £3.50

5. $\frac{1}{6}$ of 36 g   10. $\frac{3}{5}$ of 55 litres   15. $\frac{5}{12}$ of 48 days   20. $\frac{7}{12}$ of 240 miles

Equivalent fractions

Two fractions are equivalent when their value is the same. For example, $\frac{3}{6}$ has the same value as $\frac{1}{2}$. When the numerator and denominator of a fraction are coprime, that is their highest common factor is 1, then the fraction is in lowest terms.

To bring a fraction to lowest terms, divide both the numerator and denominator by their highest common factor.

Bring $\frac{16}{24}$ to lowest terms.

$$\frac{16}{24} = \frac{2}{3}$$

The HCF of 16 and 24 is 8.
8 into 16 = 2 and 8 into 24 = 3.

Exercise 6c Bring to lowest terms:

1. $\frac{2}{6}$ 6. $\frac{6}{8}$ 11. $\frac{16}{24}$ 16. $\frac{20}{30}$ 21. $\frac{16}{30}$

2. $\frac{5}{10}$ 7. $\frac{9}{12}$ 12. $\frac{21}{28}$ 17. $\frac{15}{30}$ 22. $\frac{24}{28}$

3. $\frac{7}{14}$ 8. $\frac{10}{15}$ 13. $\frac{18}{24}$ 18. $\frac{6}{15}$ 23. $\frac{27}{45}$

4. $\frac{8}{16}$ 9. $\frac{12}{16}$ 14. $\frac{8}{24}$ 19. $\frac{12}{18}$ 24. $\frac{32}{96}$

5. $\frac{2}{10}$ 10. $\frac{15}{20}$ 15. $\frac{10}{25}$ 20. $\frac{20}{32}$ 25. $\frac{28}{84}$

Exercise 6d Write down the missing number, sutra - *Proportionately.*

1. $\frac{1}{3} = \frac{}{9}$ 9. $\frac{1}{5} = \frac{3}{}$ 17. $\frac{4}{5} = \frac{16}{}$ 25. $\frac{20}{} = \frac{5}{11}$

2. $\frac{3}{10} = \frac{6}{}$ 10. $\frac{7}{12} = \frac{}{36}$ 18. $\frac{11}{12} = \frac{33}{}$ 26. $\frac{2}{} = \frac{10}{25}$

3. $\frac{2}{5} = \frac{}{35}$ 11. $\frac{2}{3} = \frac{10}{}$ 19. $\frac{2}{3} = \frac{}{12}$ 27. $\frac{}{6} = \frac{50}{60}$

4. $\frac{1}{5} = \frac{5}{}$ 12. $\frac{1}{5} = \frac{}{10}$ 20. $\frac{3}{7} = \frac{9}{}$ 28. $\frac{}{7} = \frac{6}{14}$

5. $\frac{3}{4} = \frac{12}{}$ 13. $\frac{1}{6} = \frac{3}{}$ 21. $\frac{21}{} = \frac{3}{10}$ 29. $\frac{28}{35} = \frac{4}{}$

6. $\frac{2}{3} = \frac{}{9}$ 14. $\frac{2}{3} = \frac{}{18}$ 22. $\frac{}{20} = \frac{4}{5}$ 30. $\frac{15}{40} = \frac{3}{}$

7. $\frac{3}{4} = \frac{6}{}$ 15. $\frac{5}{9} = \frac{}{27}$ 23. $\frac{}{40} = \frac{1}{8}$ 31. $\frac{2}{15} = \frac{16}{}$

8. $\frac{4}{5} = \frac{}{10}$ 16. $\frac{1}{4} = \frac{}{12}$ 24. $\frac{2}{} = \frac{4}{6}$ 32. $\frac{7}{50} = \frac{35}{}$

Improper fractions and mixed numbers

An **Improper Fraction** has its numerator greater than its denominator. For example, $\frac{5}{3}$ is an improper fraction because 5 is greater than 3.

All improper fractions are greater than 1.

A **Mixed Number** has a whole number part and a fractional part. For example, $3\frac{2}{5}$ is a mixed number because it has a whole number, 3, mixed with the fraction, $\frac{2}{5}$.

When changing an improper fraction into a mixed number, divide the denominator into the numerator. The remainder gives the numerator of the remaining fraction.

$\frac{17}{5} = 3\frac{2}{5}$

5 into 17 goes 3 remainder 2.
3 is the whole number and 2 is the numerator of the remaining fraction.

Explanation: $\frac{17}{5} = \frac{15 + 2}{5} = \frac{15}{5} + \frac{2}{5} = 3 + \frac{2}{5} = 3\frac{2}{5}$

Exercise 6e Change to mixed numbers or whole numbers.

1. $\frac{6}{2}$ 6. $\frac{13}{5}$ 11. $\frac{36}{6}$ 16. $\frac{53}{6}$ 21. $\frac{82}{11}$

2. $\frac{3}{2}$ 7. $\frac{18}{6}$ 12. $\frac{40}{7}$ 17. $\frac{32}{8}$ 22. $\frac{59}{12}$

3. $\frac{8}{4}$ 8. $\frac{19}{2}$ 13. $\frac{48}{8}$ 18. $\frac{60}{7}$ 23. $\frac{93}{12}$

4. $\frac{9}{4}$ 9. $\frac{15}{3}$ 14. $\frac{39}{5}$ 19. $\frac{38}{9}$ 24. $\frac{77}{9}$

5. $\frac{11}{2}$ 10. $\frac{29}{6}$ 15. $\frac{60}{11}$ 20. $\frac{33}{10}$ 25. $\frac{64}{5}$

When changing mixed numbers into improper fractions multiply the whole number by the denominator and add the numerator. This will give the numerator of the improper fraction. The denominator remains the same.

$9\frac{2}{3} = \frac{29}{3}$

The whole number, 9, is multiplied by the denominator, 3, to give 27. The 2 of $\frac{2}{3}$ is then added to 27 to give the new numerator, 29.

Exercise 6f Convert to improper fractions:

1. $1\frac{1}{4}$ 3. $3\frac{3}{5}$ 5. $5\frac{1}{4}$ 7. $3\frac{3}{8}$ 9. $3\frac{4}{9}$

2. $4\frac{1}{5}$ 4. $4\frac{3}{4}$ 6. $6\frac{1}{8}$ 8. $2\frac{1}{10}$ 10. $5\frac{7}{10}$

11. $11\frac{2}{3}$ **14.** $8\frac{2}{9}$ **17.** $8\frac{6}{7}$ **20.** $6\frac{3}{5}$ **23.** $5\frac{9}{10}$

12. $12\frac{5}{6}$ **15.** $10\frac{5}{8}$ **18.** $12\frac{7}{10}$ **21.** $7\frac{1}{9}$ **24.** $9\frac{1}{12}$

13. $9\frac{7}{8}$ **16.** $5\frac{5}{9}$ **19.** $11\frac{4}{11}$ **22.** $4\frac{6}{7}$ **25.** $8\frac{3}{5}$

Multiplying fractions

Fractions are multiplied by multiplying the two numerators together and multiplying the two denominators together.

Before this takes place always bring the product to lowest terms. If there is any factor, greater than 1, common to any one of the numerators and any one of the denominators then those numbers should both be divided by that common factor. This simplifies the multiplication and saves having to bring the answer to lowest terms afterwards.

$$\frac{2}{9} \times \frac{15}{23}$$

$$= \frac{2}{3} \times \frac{5}{23} = \frac{10}{69}$$

The HCF of 9 and 15 is 3.
3 into 9 = 3 and 3 into 15 = 5, therefore replace 9 and 15 by 3 and 5.
$2 \times 5 = 10$ and $3 \times 23 = 69$
The answer is $\frac{10}{69}$

Exercise 6g Leave answers as mixed numbers where necessary.

1. $\frac{3}{4} \times \frac{1}{2}$ **6.** $\frac{4}{9} \times \frac{1}{7}$ **11.** $\frac{5}{6} \times \frac{1}{4}$ **16.** $\frac{3}{4} \times \frac{16}{21}$

2. $\frac{2}{3} \times \frac{5}{7}$ **7.** $\frac{3}{7} \times \frac{2}{5}$ **12.** $\frac{2}{3} \times \frac{7}{9}$ **17.** $\frac{21}{22} \times \frac{11}{27}$

3. $\frac{1}{3} \times \frac{2}{5}$ **8.** $\frac{2}{5} \times \frac{3}{5}$ **13.** $\frac{3}{4} \times \frac{1}{5}$ **18.** $\frac{8}{9} \times \frac{33}{44}$

4. $\frac{1}{2} \times \frac{7}{8}$ **9.** $\frac{4}{5} \times \frac{15}{16}$ **14.** $\frac{10}{11} \times \frac{33}{35}$ **19.** $\frac{4}{15} \times \frac{25}{64}$

5. $\frac{3}{4} \times \frac{4}{7}$ **10.** $\frac{1}{7} \times \frac{3}{5}$ **15.** $\frac{7}{8} \times \frac{4}{21}$ **20.** $\frac{2}{3} \times \frac{33}{44}$

21. $\frac{7}{9} \times \frac{3}{21}$ **24.** $\frac{8}{9} \times \frac{27}{40}$ **27.** $\frac{11}{16} \times \frac{8}{9} \times \frac{4}{5}$ **30.** $\frac{5}{7} \times \frac{3}{8} \times \frac{21}{30}$

22. $\frac{3}{4} \times \frac{5}{7}$ **25.** $\frac{3}{7} \times \frac{5}{9} \times \frac{14}{15}$ **28.** $\frac{5}{6} \times \frac{8}{25} \times \frac{3}{4}$ **31.** $\frac{1}{2} \times \frac{7}{12} \times \frac{18}{35}$

23. $\frac{5}{11} \times \frac{4}{25}$ **26.** $\frac{11}{21} \times \frac{30}{31} \times \frac{7}{55}$ **29.** $\frac{3}{10} \times \frac{5}{9} \times \frac{6}{7}$ **32.** $\frac{7}{11} \times \frac{8}{9} \times \frac{33}{56}$

Multiplication of mixed numbers

Before mixed numbers can be multiplied they should be converted into improper fractions.

$$2\frac{1}{3} \times 1\frac{1}{5} = \frac{7}{3} \times \frac{6}{5} = \frac{14}{5} = 2\frac{4}{5}$$

$2\frac{1}{3}$ is converted to $\frac{7}{3}$ and $1\frac{1}{5}$ becomes $\frac{6}{5}$.

The fractions are then cancelled down, multiplied and simplified in the usual way.

The order of steps for multiplying fractions together is as follows:

1. Convert any mixed or whole numbers into improper fractions,
2. cancel down any numerator with any denominator,
3. multiply,
4. check to see that the fraction is in lowest terms,
5. convert to a mixed number if the answer is an improper fraction.

$$4 \times 1\frac{3}{5} = \frac{4}{1} \times \frac{8}{5} = \frac{32}{5} = 6\frac{2}{5}$$

In this example the whole number is converted into a fraction, $4 = \frac{4}{1}$, as well as the mixed number, before multiplying.

Exercise 6h

1. $\frac{2}{5} \times 1\frac{1}{2}$

2. $2\frac{1}{2} \times \frac{4}{5}$

3. $3\frac{1}{4} \times \frac{3}{13}$

4. $4\frac{2}{3} \times 2\frac{2}{5}$

5. $2\frac{1}{5} \times \frac{5}{22}$

6. $1\frac{1}{4} \times \frac{2}{5}$

7. $2\frac{1}{3} \times \frac{3}{8}$

8. $2\frac{1}{5} \times \frac{10}{11}$

9. $3\frac{1}{2} \times 4\frac{2}{3}$

10. $4\frac{1}{4} \times \frac{4}{21}$

11. $2\frac{2}{3} \times 5\frac{1}{4}$

12. $3\frac{5}{7} \times 1\frac{1}{13}$

13. $8\frac{1}{3} \times 3\frac{3}{5}$

14. $2\frac{1}{10} \times \frac{6}{7}$

15. $6\frac{3}{10} \times 1\frac{4}{21}$

16. $4\frac{2}{7} \times 2\frac{1}{10}$

17. $6\frac{1}{4} \times 1\frac{3}{5}$

18. $5 \times \frac{3}{5}$

19. $2\frac{1}{7} \times 14$

20. $3\frac{1}{8} \times 4$

21. $\frac{1}{6} \times 9$

22. $18 \times \frac{1}{9}$

23. $4 \times 3\frac{3}{8}$

24. $3\frac{1}{5} \times 2\frac{1}{2} \times 1\frac{3}{4}$

25. $6\frac{2}{5} \times 1\frac{7}{8} \times \frac{7}{12}$

26. $2\frac{4}{7} \times 4\frac{2}{3} \times 1\frac{1}{4}$

27. $3\frac{2}{3} \times 1\frac{1}{5} \times \frac{3}{22}$

28. $1\frac{1}{18} \times 1\frac{4}{5} \times 3\frac{1}{3}$

29. $4\frac{4}{5} \times 1\frac{5}{18} \times 3\frac{3}{4}$

30. $7\frac{1}{2} \times 1\frac{1}{3} \times \frac{9}{10}$

Division of fractions

The division of one fraction by another is an application of the *Transpose and adjust* sutra, which was met in another context in chapter three. This rule has a large number of uses in algebra as well as other topics but here it tells us what to do when dividing fractions. *Transpose* means turn the second fraction up-side-down and *adjust* tells us to change the sign from ÷ to ×.

$\frac{7}{16} \div \frac{5}{8}$ The second fraction, $\frac{5}{8}$, is Transposed to $\frac{8}{5}$ and the sign is Adjusted to ×. The two fractions are then cancelled down and multiplied in the usual

$\frac{7}{16} \times \frac{8}{5} = \frac{7}{10}$ way to give the answer of $\frac{7}{10}$.

Exercise 6i

1. $8 \div \frac{4}{5}$

2. $18 \div \frac{6}{7}$

3. $40 \div \frac{8}{9}$

4. $72 \div \frac{8}{11}$

5. $28 \div \frac{14}{15}$

6. $15 \div \frac{5}{6}$

7. $14 \div \frac{7}{8}$

8. $\frac{21}{32} \div \frac{7}{8}$

9. $\frac{9}{25} \div \frac{3}{10}$

10. $44 \div 1\frac{4}{7}$

11. $\frac{3}{56} \div 1\frac{9}{14}$

12. $\frac{21}{22} \div \frac{7}{11}$

13. $\frac{8}{75} \div \frac{4}{15}$

14. $\frac{35}{42} \div \frac{5}{6}$

15. $27 \div \frac{9}{13}$

16. $\frac{28}{27} \div \frac{4}{9}$

17. $35 \div \frac{5}{7}$

18. $\frac{22}{45} \div \frac{11}{15}$

19. How many halves are there in 7?

20. How many quarters are there in 5?

21. How many times does $\frac{1}{7}$ go into 3?

22. Divide 9 by $\frac{3}{5}$.

Division of mixed numbers

As with multiplication all mixed numbers must first be converted into improper fractions.

$2\frac{1}{2} \div 3\frac{1}{3}$ $2\frac{1}{2}$ is converted to $\frac{5}{2}$ and $3\frac{1}{3}$ becomes $\frac{10}{3}$.

$\frac{5}{2} \div \frac{10}{3}$ The two fractions are then divided by *Transpose and Adjust*.

$\frac{5}{2} \times \frac{3}{10} = \frac{3}{4}$

Exercise 6j Leave answers in lowest terms and as mixed numbers if necessary.

1. $5\frac{4}{9} \div \frac{14}{27}$

2. $3\frac{1}{8} \div 3\frac{3}{4}$

3. $7\frac{1}{5} \div 1\frac{7}{20}$

4. $8\frac{1}{4} \div 1\frac{3}{8}$

5. $6\frac{2}{3} \div 2\frac{4}{9}$

6. $4\frac{2}{7} \div \frac{9}{14}$

7. $5\frac{5}{8} \div 6\frac{1}{4}$

8. $6\frac{4}{9} \div 1\frac{1}{3}$

9. $5\frac{1}{4} \div 2\frac{11}{12}$

10. $7\frac{1}{7} \div 1\frac{11}{14}$

11. $10\frac{2}{3} \div 1\frac{7}{9}$

12. $8\frac{4}{5} \div 3\frac{3}{10}$

13. $11\frac{1}{4} \div \frac{15}{16}$

14. $9\frac{1}{7} \div 1\frac{11}{21}$

15. $31\frac{1}{2} \div 5\frac{5}{8}$

16. $9\frac{3}{4} \div 1\frac{5}{8}$

17. $12\frac{1}{2} \div 8\frac{3}{4}$

18. $10\frac{5}{6} \div 3\frac{1}{4}$

19. $22\frac{2}{3} \div 1\frac{8}{9}$

20. $\frac{2}{5} \div 1\frac{11}{15}$

21. $8\frac{3}{4} \div 3\frac{1}{2}$

22. Divide $7\frac{1}{2}$ by $\frac{5}{8}$

23. Divide $\frac{5}{8}$ by $1\frac{1}{4}$

24. Divide $1\frac{1}{5}$ into 12

25. Divide $1\frac{1}{6}$ into $9\frac{1}{3}$

Exercise 6k Problems

1. A girl had a book of 104 pages and she read $\frac{1}{8}$ of it. How many pages had she read?

2. What fraction of 8 pints is 3 half-pints?

3. A boy had £24.00 and spent £6.00 of it. What fraction of his money did he spend?

4. Find $\frac{3}{8}$ of £1000.

5. A boy spent $\frac{1}{2}$ of his money in one shop and $\frac{1}{4}$ of it in another. He then had 40 p left. How much did he begin with?

6. One third of a lamp-post is painted black and the remaining 6m yellow. What is the length of the part which is black?

7. What is the value of $\frac{1}{12}$ of 192?

8. $\frac{9}{10}$ of a length of timber, $1\frac{1}{4}$ m long, is removed. How much is left?

9. Find the product of $6\frac{7}{8}$ and $2\frac{2}{11}$.

10. What is the value of $\frac{3}{5}$ of $3\frac{3}{4}$?

11. Find how many times $2\frac{1}{6}$ will divide into $5\frac{5}{12}$.

12. When fully loaded a lorry can carry $3\frac{1}{4}$ tons of sand. Find how much it can deliver in carrying $9\frac{1}{2}$ loads.

13. What is 55 m as a fraction of 100 m?

14. Multiply $\frac{1}{4}$ by $\frac{1}{4}$ and divide the result by $\frac{1}{32}$.

15. My father is 180 cm tall. I am 4 cm taller than $\frac{2}{3}$ of his height. How tall am I?

16. If $\frac{3}{4}$ of a quantity of liquid is 30 l, what is $\frac{7}{8}$ of the same amount?

17. A man wishes to build an extension to his house and council planning regulations allow an increase of $\frac{1}{5}$ of the original floor space. If the floor space in his house is 1600 sq.ft., what is the largest floor space allowed for the extension?

18. If a car can travel 240 miles on a full tank of petrol, how far can it go when it has used up $\frac{5}{6}$ of the tank?

19. What fraction of 6 min 40 sec is 1 min 20 sec?

20. A train carries 576 passengers. Of these $\frac{7}{8}$ travelled first class. In another train there were $\frac{7}{8}$ as many passengers, and $\frac{7}{8}$ of these travelled first class. How many more first class passengers were there in the first train than in the second?

Chapter 7 - Algebra

First Principles

Algebra is used to express the universal laws of mathematics. The effect of these laws may also be expressed in arithmetic and geometry. For example, there is one law by which $3 \times 6 = 6 \times 3$. In algebra, this may be expressed as $a \times b = b \times a$ where a and b are any numbers.

To aid the study of algebra letters are used to represent numbers. We usually use those of the English alphabet. One of the Vedic sutras is *Individuality and Totality* and provides that a letter can stand for a particular number or for any number in general. If a letter is given a particular value then in the same piece of work it keeps the same value. For, if we say "let $x = 1$", we do not mean that x must always have the value 1, but only in the particular example we are considering.

An **algebraic expression** is a collection of numbers some or all of which are represented as letters, such as $ab + 3c - ad$. It may consist of one or more **terms**, which are separated from each other by the signs $+$ and $-$. Thus, $ab + c - ad$ is an expression consisting of three terms.

Note: When no sign is placed before a term the sign $+$ is understood.

Expressions are either **simple** or **compound**. A simple expression has only one term, such as $5ab$ or $-2x^2y$. A compound term consists of two or more terms. A simple expression is sometimes called a **monomial**. An expression consisting of two terms, such as $3a - 4bc$, is called a **binomial** and an expression consisting of three terms is called a **trinomial**. An expression with any number of terms is called a **polynomial**, which means 'many named'.

Exercise 7a Write down the number of terms in each of the following expressions:

1. $ab + cd$

2. $2a + 4b - c$

3. $3x + 4y - 2z + 1$

4. $a + ab + abc - c$

5. $x^2 + 2x - 54$

6. $3ab - 4x^2$

7. $7x^3 - 2x^2y + 3xyz + 2$

8. $x + xy - 2y + 4 - z$

When two or more quantities are multiplied together the result is called the **product**. Thus in $3 \times 5 = 15$, the product is 15. In algebra the product of two quantities a and b is usually written as ab. So $a \times b = ab$.

Each of the quantities multiplied together to form a product is called a **factor**. For example, in $5ab$, which is the same as $5 \times a \times b$ the factors are 5, a, and b. When a product has more than one letter as its factors then these letters are customarily written in alphabetical order and so we write ab and not ba.

When one of the factors in a term is a number then it is called a **coefficient**. For example, in $5ab$, 5 is the coefficient. The coefficient of any term is always written on the left and so we write $5ab$ and not $ab5$ or any other combination.

Note: When the coefficient is unity it is usually omitted. So we do not write $1a$, but simply a.

Exercise 7b Find the values of the following:

1. $y + 6$ if $y = 5$	6. $n - 4$ if $n = 14$	11. $4a + 2$ if $a = 8$
2. $y - 4$ if $y = 8$	7. $6 + s$ if $s = 12$	12. $6f + 3$ if $f = 4$
3. $5 + h$ if $h = 0$	8. $9 - p$ if $p = 6$	13. $5c - 9$ if $c = 3$
4. $7t$ if $t = 8$	9. $2 - p$ if $p = 2$	14. $7 - 4y$ if $y = 4$
5. $7w - 4$ if $w = 2$	10. $3q$ if $q = 11$	15. $6 - 2k$ if $k = 2$

E.g. If $a = 2$, $b = 3$ and $c = 5$, find the value of $3ab + 4c$.

$3ab + 4c = 3 \times 2 \times 3 + 4 \times 5 = 18 + 20 = 38$

Exercise 7c Given that $a = 3$, $b = 5$, $x = 2$, $y = 1$ and $z = 0$, find the values of the following:

1. $2x + 3$	9. $b - 1$	17. $4x + 8z$
2. $3a - 2$	10. $3a$	18. $5z + 1$
3. $11 - b$	11. $2b - xy$	19. $y \times y \times y$
4. $3 + x + 5a$	12. $3b - 7$	20. $2y + 3x - z$
5. $b + 7$	13. $x - 2$	21. $4abx$
6. $9y$	14. $5 + 2x$	22. $2xyz$
7. $a \times a$	15. $7 + z$	23. $ab + xy$
8. $3 + z$	16. $7y$	24. $5ax - 3by$

Exercise 7d Find the values of the following expressions:

1. $3a + 2b$ when $a = 4$ and $b = 7$
2. $5x - 3y$ when $x = 5$ and $y = 4$
3. $3p + 4q$ when $p = 2$ and $q = 5$
4. $5m - 2n$ when $m = 3$ and $n = 5$
5. $7g + 2h$ when $g = 3$ and $h = 4$
6. $8p - 8q$ when $p = 3$ and $q = 3$
7. $3h + 7k$ when $h = 5$ and $k = 1$
8. ab when $a = 3$ and $b = 4$

9. pqr when $p = 2$, $q = 3$ and $r = 4$
10. $p + q + r$ when $p = 2$, $q = 3$ and $r = 4$
11. $4h - h \times h$ when $h = 3$
12. $ab - b$ when $a = 6$ and $b = 7$
13. $pq - 2p$ when $p = 0$ and $q = 13$
14. $x + xy$ when $x = 9$ and $y = 3$
15. $2xy - 6y$ when $x = 10$ and $y = 15$

Simplifying

Terms which do not differ, or when they differ only in their numerical coefficients are called **like terms**, otherwise they are called **unlike terms**. For example, $3a$, $7a$; and $5a^2b$, $-2a^2b$ are pairs of like terms because they are the same except for their numerical coefficients.

Algebraic expressions can be **simplified** by collecting up like terms.

Simplify $4x + 3x - 5x$
$4x + 3x - 5x = 2x$

Simplify $4a + 2b - a + 6b - c$
$4a + 2b - a + 6b - c = 3a + 8b - c$

Exercise 7e Simplify by collecting like terms:

1. $3p + 9p$
2. $6q + 7q$
3. $4y + 7y$
4. $8d + 5d$
5. $2a + 2a + 2a$

6. $11q - q$
7. $11w - 8w$
8. $14m - 5m$
9. $14h - 9h$
10. $7x - 7$

11. $3x + 4y + 4x + 2y$
12. $9c - 8c + 7b - 7b$
13. $7g + 8m - 3g - 5m$
14. $5y + 3w + 8y - 3w$
15. $8h - 7n + 3h - 8n$

16. $9h + 8m - 7h$ **21.** $5y + 8q + 7y + 6y$ **26.** $3m + 8m - 3y + 5m$

17. $9y + 5z + 5z - 8w$ **22.** $7k - 5k + 7 + 8$ **27.** $7h + 6k - 4h + 8k$

18. $7 + 13h - 8h + 5$ **23.** $4g + 6h + 3g + 8g$ **28.** $7m + 5a - m - 2a$

19. $9m + 9n - 7m + 7n$ **24.** $6n + 4w + 6w - 4n$ **29.** $9k + 7w - 8k + 8w$

20. $8x + y - 7x + 4y$ **25.** $4k + 3q + 5k - 2q$ **30.** $11w + 4q - 5w - 4q$

Exercise 7f Simplify by collecting like terms:

1. $3x + 4y + 4x + 2y$

2. $6m + 5k + 4m + 9k$

3. $4a + 2a + 5k + 7k$

4. $8 + 3y + 7 + 8y$

5. $3p + 2m + 3m + 2m$

11. $3a + 6b + 4a$

12. $4g + 8h + 5g - 6h$

13. $7w + 6y + 7y + 3w$

14. $9m + 9n - 7m + 7n$

15. $8x + y - 7x + 4y$

16. $9c - 8c + 7b - 7b$

17. $7k - 5k + 7 + 8$

18. $4g + 6h + 3g + 8g$

19. $5w + w + 2q + 3w - q$

20. $6h + 7k + 3h + 4h - 7k + 2h$

6. $8x + 6c + 8x$

7. $5y + 8q + 7y + 6y$

8. $3x + 2x + 7x + 5x + m$

9. $3a + 2b + 4c + 2c + 3a$

10. $2a + 8g + 4a + 5g + 6a$

21. $7g + 8m - 3g - 5m$

22. $6n + 4w + 6w - 5n$

23. $4k + 3q + 5k - 2q$

24. $7x + 8m - 5x + 7m$

25. $3m + 8m - 3y + 5m$

26. $7a + 6b - 4a + 8b$

27. $5y + 3w + 8y - 3w$

28. $7m + 5a - m - 2a$

29. $2q + 2q - 3 + q$

30. $7 + 13h - 8h + 5$

Simple Equations

An **equation** is a statement that two algebraic expressions are equal.

For example, $4x + 2 = 14$, is an equation which states that the expression $4x + 2$ is equal to 14.

The parts of an equation, which are separated by an equals sign, are called the **sides** of the equation. Every equation has a *right-hand* side and a *left-hand* side. In the equation above, the left-hand side is $4x + 2$, and the right-hand side is 14.

The equation, $4x + 2 = 14$, is only found to be true when $x = 3$. The value 3 is said to **satisfy** the equation.

The letter whose value is to be found is called the **unknown quantity**. Before the value is known it is unknown, like the unmanifest or something in a dark room which you cannot see. You know that it is there but not what it is. The process of finding its value is called **solving the equation**. This process brings the unknown into the known or the unmanifest into the manifest, like switching on a light in the dark room. The value found by solving the equation is called the **solution**.

Thus in $4x + 2 = 14$, x is the unknown quantity and once solved, as $x = 3$, the value of x becomes known. $x = 3$ is called the solution.

For the simplest of equations the method of finding the solution is given by the sutra, *By mere observation*.

Solve $3x = 6$ $\therefore \underline{x = 2}$	3 times a certain number is equal to 6, and by mere observation the answer must be 2.

Exercise 7g Solve, *By mere observation*

1. $x + 2 = 5$

2. $M + 1 = 4$

3. $q + 3 = 6$

4. $a + 2 = 7$

5. $a + 3 = 5$

6. $w + 4 = 7$

7. $b + 5 = 9$

8. $m + 3 = 4$

9. $y + 6 = 9$

10. $m + 7 = 7$

11. $x + 6 = 13$

12. $8 + y = 14$

13. $3 + z = 11$

14. $15 = x + 7$

15. $6 + y = 14$

16. $m - 2 = 3$

17. $k - 4 = 1$

18. $x - 3 = 5$

19. $3 = h - 5$

20. $g - 9 = 1$

21. $3 = x - 3$

22. $y - 4 = 5$

23. $b - 2 = 6$

24. $0 = f - 3$

25. $x - 5 = 5$

26. $2 = y - 1$

27. $m - 3 = 8$

28. $n + 7 = 9$

29. $8 = 7 + y$

30. $6 = 8 - x$

Exercise 7h Solve, *By mere observation*

1. $3m = 12$	**11.** $2x = 32$	**21.** $32 = 5x$
2. $5k = 15$	**12.** $30 = 6h$	**22.** $72 = 8y$
3. $7w = 14$	**13.** $4g = 4$	**23.** $636 = 6p$
4. $3q = 6$	**14.** $6 = 6m$	**24.** $180 = 3b$
5. $3a = 9$	**15.** $96 = 12v$	**25.** $84 = 12x$
6. $60 = 3y$	**16.** $0 = 3y$	**26.** $4z = 32$
7. $20 = 4c$	**17.** $7 = 7m$	**27.** $7y = 28$
8. $7k = 63$	**18.** $9 = 3k$	**28.** $1 = 3z$
9. $6m = 48$	**19.** $1 = 2x$	**29.** $0 = 7n$
10. $45 = 9k$	**20.** $0 = 5y$	**30.** $88 = 11a$

Solving equations by Transpose and Adjust

The sutra for solving most equations is *Transpose and Adjust*. *Transpose* here means to take one term or number from one side of the equation over to the other side. *Adjust* tells us to change the sign to the opposite, thus × becomes ÷ and vice versa, and + becomes − and vice versa. The transposing and adjusting is carried out until the unknown term stands by itself and thereby becomes known.

We will begin with easy examples for although the solution may be obvious immediately, a system is required so that harder examples may be tackled at a later stage. The aim of solving an equation is to obtain x by itself on the left and the number that x is equal to on the right. In order to bring this about with an example, such as $x + 13 = 18$, we *transpose* the 13 from the left side of the equation over to the right side and *adjust* its sign from + to − which is the opposite.

Solve $x + 13 = 18$

$$x + 13 = 18$$
$$x = 18 - 13$$
$$\therefore x = 5$$

13 is transposed to the right-hand side of the equal sign and the sign of it, which was +, is changed to a −. The right-hand side is then $18 - 13 = 5$.

Note: When setting out always keep the = signs vertically in line.

Solve $4 = 2 + x$

$4 = 2 + x$
$4 - 2 = x$
$\therefore x = 2$

On looking at the equation we can see that on the right, 2 is added to x. In order to obtain x by itself this 2 must be transposed to the other side of the equation with the inevitable change of sign from + to −. The answer would then be $2 = x$, but is customarily expressed as $x = 2$ since this is grammatically correct.

Solve $x - 12 = 56$

$x - 12 = 56$
$x = 56 + 12$
$\therefore x = 68$

In this example, x stands together with −12. For x to stand by itself the 12 must be transposed to the other side. The sign for 12 changes to a + and the answer is then $x = 68$.

Exercise 7i   Solve, by *Transpose and Adjust*, setting them out as shown above:

1. $m + 7 = 12$
2. $h + 6 = 14$
3. $10 = x + 4$
4. $a + 18 = 140$
5. $100 = n + 13$
6. $94 = y + 7$
7. $25 + x = 120$
8. $90 = 3 + x$
9. $y - 5 = 256$
10. $4 = b - 82$

11. $24 = x + 20$
12. $x - 5 = 29$
13. $40 = z + 34$
14. $41 = a - 23$
15. $b + 28 = 42$
16. $c - 17 = 21$
17. $38 = d - 12$
18. $9 = t - 14$
19. $300 = 10 + x$
20. $a + 44 = 82$

21. $x - 15 = 57$
22. $48 = 12 + y$
23. $c + 19 = 31$
24. $b - 120 = 101$
25. $42 = y - 7$
26. $96 = z - 24$
27. $9 + c = 23$
28. $24 = z + 19$
29. $s - 29 = 71$
30. $x + 51 = 235$

The next type of equation uses multiplication and division. Where a number is multiplying x the transposed form will be a division, and vice versa. The following examples show this type.

Solve $6x = 42$ Since $6x$ means $6 \times x$, when the 6 is transposed to the other side the $\times$ is adjusted to a $\div$. This is

$$x = \frac{42}{6}$$ then $42 \div 6$ which is written as a fraction. On dividing 42 by 6 the answer is found to be 7.

$$\therefore x = 7$$

Here are two further examples, the second of which requires two transpositions.

Solve $\dfrac{x}{3} = 7$ Solve $\dfrac{30}{y} = 6$ $30 = 6 \times y$

$$x = 7 \times 3$$ $$\frac{30}{6} = y$$

$$\therefore x = 21$$ $$\therefore y = 5$$

Exercise 7j Solve, by *Transpose and Adjust*, setting them out as shown above.

1. $4c = 36$ 6. $6y = 48$ 11. $147 = 7x$

2. $11a = 77$ 7. $44 = 4m$ 12. $4 = 4c$

3. $3h = 27$ 8. $2n = 2$ 13. $5g = 5$

4. $48 = 8a$ 9. $6w = 54$ 14. $7x = 343$

5. $6 = 2m$ 10. $42 = 7q$ 15. $9y = 9$

16. $\dfrac{x}{3} = 5$ 21. $\dfrac{x}{2} = 5$ 26. $9 = \dfrac{y}{3}$

17. $\dfrac{k}{2} = 3$ 22. $\dfrac{y}{3} = 4$ 27. $\dfrac{m}{2} = 16$

18. $\dfrac{w}{5} = 2$ 23. $2 = \dfrac{h}{5}$ 28. $3 = \dfrac{y}{8}$

19. $3 = \dfrac{y}{4}$ 24. $\dfrac{p}{3} = 7$ 29. $\dfrac{y}{4} = 8$

20. $7 = \dfrac{n}{3}$ 25. $\dfrac{a}{2} = 2$ 30. $1 = \dfrac{n}{3}$

31. $\frac{100}{x} = 50$ **36.** $\frac{15}{g} = 3$ **41.** $1 = \frac{5}{p}$

32. $\frac{39}{y} = 3$ **37.** $6 = \frac{30}{a}$ **42.** $\frac{14}{x} = 2$

33. $\frac{32}{z} = 4$ **38.** $\frac{10}{b} = 2$ **43.** $\frac{35}{c} = 7$

34. $3 = \frac{9}{m}$ **39.** $\frac{8}{k} = 4$ **44.** $5 = \frac{60}{y}$

35. $\frac{6}{x} = 3$ **40.** $8 = \frac{8}{d}$ **45.** $\frac{50}{w} = 2$

Multiplication

If a and b are two numbers then the product, 'a times b' is equal to 'b times a'. Algebraically this is written as $ab = ba$, or $a \times b = b \times a$. For example, $5 \times 3 = 3 \times 5$.

To multiply terms together, multiply the coefficients together and write that product first and then write down the product of the letters.

Simplify $3 \times b \times 2 \times a$

$$3 \times b \times 2 \times a = 3 \times 2 \times b \times a$$
$$= 6 \times b \times a$$
$$= 6ab$$

Multiplying the numbers together first gives 6. The product of the letters is ab and so the answer is $6ab$.

Exercise 7k Simplify, remembering to give the letters in alphabetical order:

1. $3 \times a \times 4 \times c$

2. $2 \times a \times b \times 3 \times 4 \times c$

3. $4 \times t \times 5 \times r \times s$

4. $a \times 4 \times 6 \times b$

5. $b \times a \times 2 \times c \times 6$

6. $x \times 4 \times y \times 6$

7. $3 \times x \times 2 \times y \times 1 \times z$

8. $a \times 6 \times b \times 2 \times c \times 4$

9. $7 \times d \times c \times b \times 3$

10. $b \times 2 \times a \times 4 \times c \times 4$

11. $5x \times 7$

12. $3 \times 2b$

13. $m \times n \times q \times p \times 3$

14. $3a \times 4b$

15. $7a \times 4c \times 2b$

16. $5x \times 4y \times 2z$

17. $3a \times 4b \times 6x$

18. $2p \times 6q$

19. $3a \times 5b \times c$

20. $3m \times 2n \times 9p \times q$

69

Brackets

When an expression is placed within brackets then it is to be treated as a single entity. A number appearing outside a bracket means that the quantity inside the bracket should be multiplied by that number.

For example, $a(b + c)$ means: first add b and c and then multiply the result by a. An example with numbers is $4(5 + 3) = 4 \times (5 + 3) = 4 \times 8 = 32$.

Exercise 71 $7(2 + 4) = 7 \times 6 = 42$. Calculate the following in this way, showing the same steps:

1. $5(3 + 1)$	**4.** $4(2 + 8)$	**7.** $5(8 - 6)$	**10.** $7(8 - 3)$
2. $6(4 + 3)$	**5.** $\frac{1}{2}(5 + 3)$	**8.** $4(7 - 2)$	**11.** $\frac{3}{4}(2 + 6)$
3. $10(3 + 5)$	**6.** $\frac{1}{3}(7 + 5)$	**9.** $5(8 + 3)$	**12.** $\frac{2}{5}(18 - 3)$

$7(2 + 4) = 7 \times 2 + 7 \times 4 = 14 + 28 = 42$. Calculate the following in this way, showing the same steps:

13. $5(3 + 1)$	**15.** $3(2 + 12)$	**17.** $7(8 - 3)$	**19.** $3(5 - 2)$
14. $4(2 + 8)$	**16.** $6(7 + 2)$	**18.** $5(8 - 6)$	**20.** $4(7 - 5)$

This last method has to be used for multiplying out brackets with algebraic expressions. This is because in the example $a(b + c)$, the $b + c$ in the brackets cannot be simplified. Remembering that $a(b + c) = a \times (b + c)$ we can see that

$$a(b + c) = a \times b + b \times c$$
$$= ab + ab$$

To multiply out the brackets we multiply everything inside the bracket by the term immediately outside the bracket.

Here are some examples:

$3(a + b) = 3a + 3b$	$5(x - y) = 5x - 5y$
$a(3 + b) = 3a + ab$	$y(x - 7) = xy - 7y$

Exercise 7m Multiply out the brackets:

1. $3(c + d)$
2. $7(e + f)$
3. $9(g + h)$
4. $4(k + m)$
5. $6(n - p)$
6. $2(q - r)$
7. $\frac{1}{2}(t - v)$
8. $\frac{2}{3}(x - y)$
9. $a(b + c)$
10. $d(e - f)$

11. $g(h - k)$
12. $m(n + p)$
13. $a(b + 4)$
14. $c(d - 6)$
15. $e(2 + f)$
16. $g(5 - h)$
17. $2(a + 4)$
18. $4(b - 2)$
19. $5(c - 3)$
20. $7(d + 3)$

21. $8(2 + e)$
22. $3(3 - f)$
23. $2(6 - g)$
24. $6(d - 3)$
25. $5(1 - h)$
26. $3(2a + 5)$
27. $2(3b - 2)$
28. $4(2c - 3)$
29. $5(3d + 1)$
30. $6(3 + 2h)$

31. $2a(b + 4)$
32. $3k(4 - m)$
33. $3c(d - 5)$
34. $2n(5 - p)$
35. $4e(f + 1)$
36. $6q(q + 2)$
37. $5g(h - 1)$
38. $3t(t - 3)$
39. $3h(7k + 5n)$
40. $5g(3h - 1)$

To simplify an expression containing brackets we first multiply out the brackets and then collect like terms. When a bracket does not have a multiplyng number immediately to the left then 1 is understood to be that multiplier For example, $(9x - 3) = 1(9x - 3) = 9x - 3$ and again, $-(9x - 3) = -1(9x - 3) = -9x + 3$.

$$6x + 3(x - 2) = 6x + 3x - 6$$
$$= 9x - 6$$
$$2 + (3x - 7) = 2 + 3x - 7$$
$$= 3x - 5$$

Expanding the bracket gives $3x - 6$.
In the second example, there is a + sign immediately to the left of the bracket.
In this case we take the bracket as $1(3x - 7)$ which is equal to $3x - 7$.

Exercise 7n Simplify the following expressions:

1. $2x + 4(x + 1)$
2. $3 + 5(2x + 3)$
3. $3(x + 1) + 4$
4. $6(2x - 3) + 2x$
5. $7 + 2(2x + 5)$
6. $3x + 3(x - 5)$

7. $2(x + 4) + 3(x + 5)$
8. $6(2x - 3) + 5(x - 1)$
9. $3x + (2x + 5)$
10. $4 + (3x - 1)$
11. $3x - 2(3x + 4)$
12. $5 - 4(5 + x)$

13. $7c - (c + 2)$
14. $5x - 4(2 + x)$
15. $9 - 2(4x + 1)$
16. $7a - (a + 6)$
17. $10 - 4(3x + 2)$
18. $40 - 2(1 + 5w)$

71

19. $6y - 3(3y + 4)$ **23.** $2m + 4(3m - 5)$ **27.** $4 - (6 - x)$

20. $8 - 3(2 + 5z)$ **24.** $7 - 2(3x + 2)$ **28.** $10f + 3(4 - 2f)$

21. $5x + 4(5x + 3)$ **25.** $x + (5x - 4)$ **29.** $7 - 2(5 - 2s)$

22. $42 - 3(2c + 5)$ **26.** $9 - 2(4g - 2)$ **30.** $7x + 8x - 2(5x + 1)$

Simplifying with Indices

When a product has all its factors the same then it may be written as one factor to the power of the number of factors. For example, the product $2 \times 2 \times 2 \times 2$, has four factors and can therefore be written as 2^4, which is read as, *two to the power of 4.*

Again, the product $a \times a \times a$, has three factors and can therefore be written as a^3. The number 3, in this case, is called the **power** or **index** of a.

Note: when the index is 2, such as 5^2, it is usually read as five *squared*. Similarly when the index is 3, such as 7^3, it is frequently read as seven *cubed*. The origin of this is ancient Greece. The ancient Greek mathematicians often used to think of numbers as magnitudes so that a line of length 1 could be doubled in length to make 2, and so on. On multiplying two lengths together the result is the area of a rectangle and if the two lengths are the same the result is the area of a square. Similarly on multiplying three lengths together we can arrive at the volume of a cube. For the same reason square centimetres are written as cm^2 and cubic centimatres are written as cm^3.

Simplify $2 \times 2 \times 2 \times 2 \times 2 \times 2$ Simplify $a \times a \times a \times b \times b$

$2 \times 2 \times 2 \times 2 \times 2 \times 2 = 2^6$ $a \times a \times a \times b \times b = a^3 \times b^2$
$= a^3 b^2$

Exercise 7p Simplify:

1. $2 \times 2 \times 2$ **5.** $6 \times 6 \times 6 \times 6 \times 6$ **9.** $7 \times 7 \times 7 \times 7$

2. $1 \times 1 \times 1 \times 1 \times 1$ **6.** 7×7 **10.** $4 \times 4 \times 4 \times 4 \times 4$

3. $5 \times 5 \times 5$ **7.** $3 \times 3 \times 3 \times 3 \times 3$ **11.** $a \times a \times a \times b \times b$

4. $3 \times 3 \times 3 \times 3$ **8.** $8 \times 8 \times 8$ **12.** $a \times b \times b \times c \times c$

13. $d \times d \times d \times d \times a$ 19. $t \times u \times u \times v \times v$ 25. $x \times y \times y \times y \times x \times x$

14. $x \times x \times x \times x \times x \times x$ 20. $g \times g \times g \times h \times h$ 26. $a \times b \times a \times c \times c$

15. $x \times y \times y \times z$ 21. $x \times y \times x \times y \times y$ 27. $m \times m \times n \times n \times n \times m$

16. $c \times c \times d \times d \times c$ 22. $a \times b \times b \times c \times c \times c$ 28. $p \times q \times p$

17. $e \times f \times f \times f \times f$ 23. $p \times p \times p \times p \times p \times q$ 29. $a \times b \times a \times b \times a$

18. $b \times b \times b \times a$ 24. $a \times b \times c \times c \times c \times c$ 30. $r \times s \times t \times r \times s \times t$

When multiplying two numbers which are the same and which both have indices then add the indices to find the index of the product.

Since $a^3 = aaa$, and $a^2 = aa$,

$$\text{then } a^3 \times a^2 = aaa \times aa = aaaaa = a^5 = a^{3+2}.$$

The rule governing this is expressed as *The index of a letter in a product is the sum (of the indices) in the factors*. This is sometimes called the index law for multiplication.

Exercise 7q Simplify: (Remember that $x^1 = x$:)

1. $y^2 \times y^3$ 11. $h^2 \times h^2$ 21. $a^2 \times a^3$

2. $m^3 \times m^2$ 12. $n^3 \times n^2$ 22. $m^4 \times m^8$

3. $k^4 \times k^2$ 13. $p^4 \times p^4$ 23. $k^2 \times k^6$

4. $c^3 \times c^3$ 14. $y^3 \times y$ 24. $n^5 \times n^3$

5. $b^4 \times b^5$ 15. $w \times w^2$ 25. $b^5 \times b^7$

6. $m^4 \times m^3$ 16. $3^2 \times 3^3$ 26. $h^{11} \times h^7$

7. $b^2 \times b^7$ 17. $2^4 \times 2^5$ 27. $x^{20} \times x^{30}$

8. $n^2 \times n^2$ 18. $k \times k^5$ 28. $y^{40} \times y^{50}$

9. $h^5 \times h^5$ 19. $x \times x$ 29. $d^{200} \times d^{100}$

10. $r^3 \times r^6$ 20. $x \times x^2$ 30. $a^{12} \times a^{21}$

To multiply two simple expressions together we write the product of the coefficients first and then the products of the various other factors.

$3k^4 \times 5k^3 = 15k^7$ The product of the coefficients is $3 \times 5 = 15$.
The product of the other terms, by adding the indices, is k^7.

Exercise 7r Simplify:

1. $2m^2 \times 2m^5$

2. $5w^3 \times 3w^2$

3. $2c^4 \times 2c^3$

4. $3k^3 \times 2c^2$

5. $4p^5 \times 5p^4$

6. $6y^5 \times 3$

7. $4m^3 \times m^2$

8. $n^4 \times 3n^3$

9. $3g^3 \times 5g^5$

10. $a^3 \times 3$

11. $3x^2 \times 5x$

12. $2q \times 3q^3$

13. $4c \times 2c$

14. $8h^2 \times 7h^5$

15. $9n^9 \times 6n^6$

16. $8m^7 \times 9m^8$

17. $6q^5 \times 8$

18. $5b \times b^5$

19. $v \times 4v$

20. $7d^4 \times 6d^8$

21. $5v \times 5v^2$

22. $5y^2 \times 6y^5$

23. $7w^5 \times 5w$

24. $2p^7 \times 4p^8$

25. $9q^4 \times q^5$

26. $s^3 \times s^2$

27. $8m^4 \times m$

28. $4r \times r^3$

29. $6n^5 \times n^4$

30. $12a^{12} \times 5a^7$

Chapter 8 - Practice and Revision 1

Read each question carefully and set out each sum correctly so as to show working. The page numbers given in brackets show where to find each topic.

Exercise 8a Addition

1. $\begin{array}{r} 34 \\ + 52 \\ \hline \end{array}$	4. $\begin{array}{r} 133 \\ + 483 \\ \hline \end{array}$	7. $\begin{array}{r} 786 \\ + 189 \\ \hline \end{array}$	10. $\begin{array}{r} 2067 \\ + 7856 \\ \hline \end{array}$
2. $\begin{array}{r} 27 \\ + 49 \\ \hline \end{array}$	5. $\begin{array}{r} 437 \\ + 786 \\ \hline \end{array}$	8. $\begin{array}{r} 94875 \\ + 5638 \\ \hline \end{array}$	11. $\begin{array}{r} 9978 \\ + 7584 \\ \hline \end{array}$
3. $\begin{array}{r} 23 \\ 45 \\ + 14 \\ \hline \end{array}$	6. $\begin{array}{r} 221 \\ 324 \\ + 102 \\ \hline \end{array}$	9. $\begin{array}{r} 2214 \\ 403 \\ + 2133 \\ \hline \end{array}$	12. $\begin{array}{r} 99 \\ 476 \\ + 6758 \\ \hline \end{array}$

13. Add together 2435, 456 and 98768

14. Find the sum of £2.34, £82.55 and £12.95

Exercise 8b Subtraction

1 $\begin{array}{r} 76 \\ - 34 \\ \hline \end{array}$	3. $\begin{array}{r} 123 \\ - 67 \\ \hline \end{array}$	5. $\begin{array}{r} 6574 \\ - 2398 \\ \hline \end{array}$	7. $\begin{array}{r} 345627 \\ - 145672 \\ \hline \end{array}$
2. $\begin{array}{r} 83 \\ - 58 \\ \hline \end{array}$	4. $\begin{array}{r} 6324 \\ - 1878 \\ \hline \end{array}$	6. $\begin{array}{r} 7234 \\ - 2919 \\ \hline \end{array}$	8. $\begin{array}{r} 5463721 \\ - 1918293 \\ \hline \end{array}$

9. Subtract 456 from 923

10. Subtract £34.65 from £78.11

11. What is the value of 700 take away 344?

12. Take 654 m from 1145 m

13. Find the difference between 3767 and 1298

14. Find 3543 minus 987

Exercise 8c Single-digit multiplication

1 $\begin{array}{r} 113 \\ \times\ \ 3 \\ \hline \end{array}$	3. $\begin{array}{r} 246 \\ \times\ \ 3 \\ \hline \end{array}$	5. $\begin{array}{r} 2531 \\ \times\ \ 7 \\ \hline \end{array}$	7. $\begin{array}{r} 5043 \\ \times\ \ 9 \\ \hline \end{array}$
2. $\begin{array}{r} 216 \\ \times\ \ 2 \\ \hline \end{array}$	4. $\begin{array}{r} 461 \\ \times\ \ 4 \\ \hline \end{array}$	6. $\begin{array}{r} 1285 \\ \times\ \ 8 \\ \hline \end{array}$	8. $\begin{array}{r} 894371 \\ \times\ \ \ \ \ 6 \\ \hline \end{array}$

Exercise 8d Use Nikhilam multiplication to find,

1. $\begin{array}{r} 8 \\ \times 9 \end{array}$	5. $\begin{array}{r} 64 \\ \times 97 \end{array}$	9. $\begin{array}{r} 12 \\ \times 14 \end{array}$	13. $\begin{array}{r} 1112 \\ \times 1007 \end{array}$	17. $\begin{array}{r} 104 \\ \times 98 \end{array}$
2. $\begin{array}{r} 95 \\ \times 93 \end{array}$	6. $\begin{array}{r} 998 \\ \times 992 \end{array}$	10. $\begin{array}{r} 103 \\ \times 106 \end{array}$	14. $\begin{array}{r} 10001 \\ \times 10078 \end{array}$	18. $\begin{array}{r} 1053 \\ \times 997 \end{array}$
3. $\begin{array}{r} 98 \\ \times 97 \end{array}$	7. $\begin{array}{r} 877 \\ \times 995 \end{array}$	11. $\begin{array}{r} 172 \\ \times 103 \end{array}$	15. $\begin{array}{r} 8 \\ \times 11 \end{array}$	19. $\begin{array}{r} 134 \\ \times 92 \end{array}$
4. $\begin{array}{r} 86 \\ \times 98 \end{array}$	8. $\begin{array}{r} 9947 \\ \times 9998 \end{array}$	12. $\begin{array}{r} 1002 \\ \times 1013 \end{array}$	16. $\begin{array}{r} 112 \\ \times 97 \end{array}$	20. $\begin{array}{r} 10005 \\ \times 9997 \end{array}$

Exercise 8e Use Vertically and Crosswise

1 $\begin{array}{r} 21 \\ \times 23 \end{array}$	3. $\begin{array}{r} 66 \\ \times 66 \end{array}$	5. $\begin{array}{r} 87 \\ \times 65 \end{array}$	7. $\begin{array}{r} 325 \\ \times 643 \end{array}$
2. $\begin{array}{r} 46 \\ \times 72 \end{array}$	4. $\begin{array}{r} 70 \\ \times 54 \end{array}$	6. $\begin{array}{r} 121 \\ \times 223 \end{array}$	8. $\begin{array}{r} 1004 \\ \times 7031 \end{array}$

9. Find the product of 65 and 24

10. Multiply 364 by 24

11. Find the cost of 72 bricks at 65p each.

12. Given that there are 24 hours in a day and 365 days in a year, find the number of hours in a year.

13. If a pilgrim can walk 28 miles in a day, how many miles will he travel in 32 days?

14. A rectangular floor requires 35 tiles across the width and 52 tiles along its length. How many tiles are needed to cover the whole floor?

Exercise 8f Simple Division

1 $3\overline{)3609}$	3. $3\overline{)73242}$	5. $5\overline{)78230}$	7. $9\overline{)867584}$
2. $2\overline{)2146}$	4. $4\overline{)236}$	6. $6\overline{)137}$	8. $7\overline{)21434}$

9. Divide 315 by 7

10. How many thirds are there in 2?

11. Share £108 into four equal groups.

12. If six bags of cement cost £21, how much does one bag cost?

13. How many fours are there in 200?

14. Find the remainder when 23457 is divided by 9.

15. A pack of 52 cards is dealt out to four players. How many cards will each receive?

16. A merchant wishes to divide his profits of £400,000 equally amongst his four sons. If he first has to pay half in tax, how much will each son receive?

Exercise 8g Use division by *All from nine and the last from ten* to find,

1. 9|123   **4.** 9|2131   **7.** 8|111   **10.** 979|2453 **13.** 96|2400

2. 9|113   **5.** 9|2301   **8.** 889|1322 **11.** 827|2100 **14.** 89|12102

3. 9|1210   **6.** 88|213   **9.** 88|1023 **12.** 97|1423 **15.** 935|21234

Exercise 8h Division by *Transpose and Adjust*

1. 11|158   **3.** 11|277   **5.** 13|13279   **7.** 14|16954   **9.** 112|1456

2. 11|259   **4.** 12|269   **6.** 13|27699   **8.** 12|241579 **10.** 113|2395

Exercise 8i Write down the missing words:

1. When two numbers are multiplied together the answer is called the

_____ .

2. Numbers which are multiplied together to give a product are called _____ of that product.

3. One is a factor of _____ number.

4. Any product is a _____ of any one of its factors.

5. The highest common factor of two or more numbers is the highest number which can _____ those numbers exactly.

6. Prime numbers are only _____ by one and themselves.

7. Numbers which are not prime are called _____.

8. Every composite number may be expressed as the product of factors which are _____.

9. The lowest common multiple of two or more numbers is the _____ number into which those numbers can _____.

10. Two numbers are coprime when their _____ _____ _____ is one.

11. Since _____ is a factor of all numbers, every number is related to every other number through _____.

Exercise 8j Primes and composite numbers

1. Find the HCF of 36 and 45.

2. Find the LCM of 16 and 12.

3. What is the next prime after 29?

4. Is 39 composite or prime?

5. Give the four pairs of factors of 24.

6. Express 24 as the product of prime factors.

7. What is the HCF of 28, 24 and 48?

8. What is the LCM of 24 and 32?

9. What is the HCF of 24 and 9?

10. Are 24 and 9 coprime?

11. What is the HCF of 9 and 16?

12. Are 9 and 16 coprime?

Exercise 8k Fractions

1. Express $\frac{8}{10}$ in its simplest form.

6. How many halves are there in $3\frac{1}{2}$?

2. Bring $\frac{12}{16}$ to lowest terms.

7. Find half of £47.

3. Express $4\frac{5}{6}$ as an improper fraction.

8. What is $\frac{2}{3}$ of 12?

4. Write $\frac{22}{5}$ as a mixed number.

9. Find the missing number in
$$\frac{9}{10} = \frac{45}{}$$

5. How many quarters are there in 3?

10. What is the next number in the sequence, $1\frac{1}{3}$, $2\frac{2}{5}$, $3\frac{3}{7}$, ?

Exercise 8l Multiplication and division of fractions

1. $\frac{2}{5} \times \frac{3}{7}$ **5.** $\frac{2}{9} \times \frac{3}{8}$ **9.** $3\frac{3}{4} \times 6\frac{2}{5}$ **13.** $\frac{4}{11} \div \frac{3}{22}$ **17.** $4\frac{1}{8} \div 2\frac{1}{4}$

2. $\frac{1}{3} \times \frac{1}{2}$ **6.** $\frac{5}{12} \times \frac{4}{5}$ **10.** $7\frac{1}{2} \times 3\frac{1}{5}$ **14.** $\frac{2}{3} \div 1\frac{1}{9}$ **18.** $\frac{11}{16} \div 22$

3. $\frac{2}{3} \times \frac{3}{4}$ **7.** $\frac{15}{44} \times \frac{11}{25}$ **11.** $7\frac{1}{7} \times 9\frac{1}{10}$ **15.** $\frac{5}{6} \div 10$ **19.** $5\frac{3}{5} \div 2\frac{4}{5}$

4. $\frac{2}{3} \times \frac{9}{10}$ **8.** $\frac{8}{15} \times \frac{5}{12}$ **12.** $\frac{1}{4} \div \frac{2}{5}$ **16.** $1\frac{1}{5} \div \frac{3}{10}$ **20.** $\frac{17}{18} \div 3\frac{2}{5}$

Exercise 8m

Find the value of,

1. $y + 6$ if $y = 7$ **3.** $5 + r$ if $r = 16$ **5.** $5p - 4$ if $p = 3$

2. $y - 4$ if $y = 12$ **4.** $7s$ if $s = 9$ **6.** $6x - 3$ if $x = 12$

Given that $a = 2$, $b = 4$, $c = 5$, find the values of the following:

7. $2a + 3$ **12.** $b - a + c$ **17.** $a + b - c$

8. $3b - 2$ **13.** $5a - 2c$ **18.** abc

9. $14 - c$ **14.** $4b - ac$ **19.** $ab + bc - ac$

10. $2 + a + 3b$ **15.** $ab - 7$ **20.** $bc \div a$

11. $4b - 5$ **16.** $bc - 20$ **21.** $10ab \div c$

Simplify by collecting like terms:

22. $a + a + a$	**27.** $12p - p$	**32.** $3a + 4b + 4a + 2b$
23. $b + b + b + b$	**28.** $5w + w$	**33.** $7c - 7c + 7d - 7d$
24. $c + c + c - c - c$	**29.** $11n - 3n$	**34.** $6g + 8h - 3g - 5h$
25. $2a + a + a$	**30.** $8h - 9h + 8h$	**35.** $5x + 2y + 8x - y$
26. $2x - 2x + 3x$	**31.** $5y - 7$	**36.** $4y - 8z + 7y - 9z$

Exercise 8n Solve

1. $x + 4 = 7$	**7.** $40 = 2b$	**13.** $q + 3 = 28$	**19.** $88 = 8c$
2. $x + 5 = 9$	**8.** $50 = 5c$	**14.** $40 = x + 3$	**20.** $16 = 8m$
3. $b - 2 = 13$	**9.** $0 = 3a$	**15.** $t - 5 = 39$	**21.** $36w = 72$
4. $z - 5 = 0$	**10.** $14 = 7p$	**16.** $64 = h + 34$	**22.** $21 = 7k$
5. $3 = x - 1$	**11.** $4d = 12$	**17.** $23 = 12 + y$	**23.** $3x = 393$
6. $n - 6 = 9$	**12.** $7r = 56$	**18.** $p + 19 = 41$	**24.** $100y = 100$

Exercise 8o Expand the brackets and simplify where possible:

1. $2(c + d)$	**4.** $4(a - b)$	**7.** $9(2 + x)$	**10.** $4a(b + 4)$
2. $5(e + f)$	**5.** $a(b + c)$	**8.** $4(3 - y)$	**11.** $2k(4 - m)$
3. $8(g + h)$	**6.** $a(b - 4)$	**9.** $5(6 - g)$	**12.** $5c(d - 4)$

13. $3x + 5(x + 2)$	**15.** $2(x + 3) + 4(x + 2)$	**17.** $8c - (c + 5)$
14. $2 + 6(2x + 9)$	**16.** $5(2x - 1) + 4(x - 2)$	**18.** $6x - 3(5 + x)$

Exercise 8p Simplify:

1. $f \times f \times f \times f$	**5.** $a \times b \times a \times b \times b$	**9.** $d^2 \times d^2$	**13.** $2y^2 \times y^5$
2. $b \times b \times b$	**6.** $r \times s \times r \times r \times s$	**10.** $b^3 \times b$	**14.** $5w^3 \times 2w^2$
3. $p \times p \times p \times p$	**7.** $a^2 \times a^3$	**11.** $x^3 \times x^3$	**15.** $4x^2 \times 3x$
4. $a \times b \times b \times c \times c$	**8.** $n^3 \times n^2$	**12.** $m^4 \times m^8$	**16.** $3q \times 6q^3$

Exercise 8q Mixed Problems

1. How many socks will be required to fill 8 packs when each pack contains three pairs?

2. What is the product of 5 and 23?

3. If 7 is one factor of 84 what is the other?

4. How many 25p stamps can be bought for £5.75?

5. Find the cost of six bottles of ink at £3.95 each.

6. Find the number of 55 cm strips of floor vinyl which can be cut from a piece 330 cm long.

7. Subtract the sum of 747 and 836 from 2312.

8. Divide 12004 by 89 by*All from 9 and the last from 10.*

9. Multiply 988 by 997.

10. Find the difference between 5245 and 6342.

11. Multiply 345 by 7.

12. A boy calculates that he can spend £1.34 a week for seven weeks and have 73p left at the end. How much does he start with?

13. Add together 4634, 103, 36854, 1534 and subtract the answer from 50000.

14. Divide £13.30 by 5.

15. 32 coaches, each with 49 passengers, are to take a group of people to a football match. How many people are there in the group?

16. Express £72 as a fraction of £120.

17. A woman buys some wool for £28.95, a knitting pattern for £5.65 and some knitting needles for £2.30. How much change does she receive from a £50 note?

18. What is the cost of x pencils at *34* pence each?

19. In a box of 60 vegetables, $\frac{2}{5}$ are potatoes, $\frac{1}{3}$ are carrots and the rest are parsnips. How many parsnips are there?

81

20. If five books cost £45 and the same number of pens cost £32, find the difference between the cost of a book and a pen.

21. Multiply 234 by 825 and write your answer in words.

22. Find the product of 1112 and 1004 and subtract one million, one hundred and eleven thousand, one hundred and eleven from your answer.

23. Use *Transpose and Adjust* to divide 2475 by 112.

24. Find the product of $\frac{3}{4}$ and $\frac{8}{15}$.

25. What fraction of a whole day is 4 hours?

26. How many seconds are there in a day?

27. A train is due to leave Victoria station at 5 48 pm. At what time does it leave if it is 35 minutes late?

28. Multiply the HCF of 24 and 36 by the LCM of 24 and 36.

29. Find the remainder when 998 is divided into 23410.

30. In the division, 5 into 17 = 3 remainder 2, which number is the dividend?

31. If $a = 5$, what is the difference between $3a$ and $a + 3$?

32. What is £457.87 taken from £1000?

33. Simplify, $3(x + 2) + 4(x + 2) + 5(x + 2) - 11(x + 2)$

34. Find the total cost of four adult theatre tickets at £6.60 each and three child tickets which are half price.

35. Eight pieces of fence cost £101.60. Find the cost of one such piece.

36. Find the lowest number which is a multiple of 4, a multiple of 9 and a multiple of 5.

37. A man sold his house for £215,250 and bought a another for £183,750. How much did he save?

38. To place an advertisement in a certain newspaper costs £7.00 plus 36p per word. How much does it cost for advertisement consisting of 28 words?

39. Divide 1321011 by 9878

Chapter 9 - Geometry 1

Geometry is concerned with space within form and shape. Just as number begins with one so geometry begins with a point which is an expression of unity. A point is a position in time and space where the forces of the Creator are concentrated ready for creation. Just as plants and trees come from seeds so all forms and shapes come from points.

A point does not have any size and, like one, it is indivisible. When we draw a point it is, in fact, a dot. It has size. We use a small dot to represent a point.

In order to divide the point we first have to expand it. The expansion is spherical and equal in all directions. This equal spherical expansion can then be divided in any way we choose. There are, however, only five ways of dividing a sphere from the centre so that all the parts are equal. These five divisions are called the Platonic forms. Their names are: tetrahedron, cube, octahedron, dodecahedron and icosahedron, and they divide the sphere into four, six, eight, twelve and twenty parts, respectively. We begin with these because they are the most perfect, being equal in all respects. These five forms or shapes are called the regular polyhedra.

Dodecahedron

The dodecahedron is the twelve-fold division of a sphere. We will begin with the internal model made up of twelve cone-like segments. These segments may be made using stiff paper or card. Each segment is pentagonal in shape and made up of five equal angles. These internal angles, for the dodecahedron are based on the measures of one, two and three. The diagram below shows the net for each of the twelve segments and this can be copied for use.

SEGMENT FOR THE DODECAHEDRON

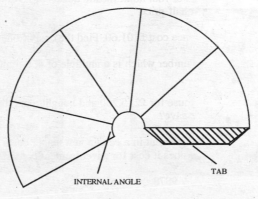

INTERNAL ANGLE

TAB

By making twelve copies of this diagram the segments for the model can be made. Accurate cutting is necessary. Each straight line should be scored and the segment folded and glued with the tab on the outside. When the segments are put together the tabs will be covered by adjacent segments.

To obtain the internal angle for the segments of the dodecahedron the following diagram may be used. It is drawn using measures of one, two and three. This diagram is the basis for all of the five Platonic polyhedra but the lines drawn show the internal angle for the dodecahedron.

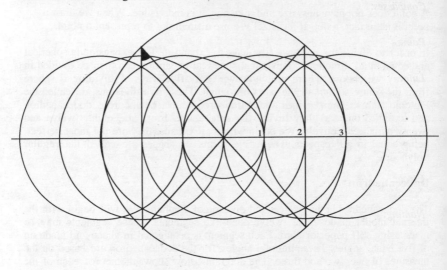

INTERNAL ANGLE FOR DODECAHEDRON

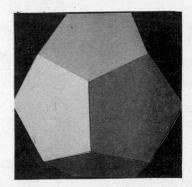

Notes on drawing

Before progressing with constructions there are several tips for drawing which you will find useful.

Equipment: A sharpened pencil with a hard lead should always be used. You will also need a straight edge or ruler, preferably made of perspex which is transparent.

Compasses: Giant bow-compasses are the best. These have a shouldered point, replaceable leads, and when set to a particular radius, do not slip.

Point: When drawing a point make it as fine as possible by touching the pencil onto the paper once.

Line: When drawing a line through two points,
a) place the pencil on one point,
b) slide the ruler up to the pencil and turn it so that it lies next to the other point,
c) place the pencil on the other point to check that the line, once drawn, will run through it,
d) draw the line once with pencil pressed gently against the ruler.

Circle: Having chosen the centre and radius draw the circle by holding the compasses at the top and leaning them over slightly.

Naming: Points are named and labelled using capital letters. Sometimes a number is used to indicate a measure. Lines are named using two or more labelled points which lie on it. For example, AB would be used to label the straight line which connects or passes through the points A and B. Circles are named by giving the point at the centre and either its radius or a point on its circumference. Angles are usually named using the three-letter notation. The point at which the two lines forming the angle meet is used as the middle letter. For example, the diagram below shows the angle formed by the two lines AB and AC which meet at A. The angle contained by these lines is therefore angle BAC.

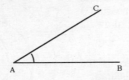

All drawing should be done on plane paper and be accurate, neat and beautiful. When drawing, only use gentle pressure so that lines, etc., are thin and light. Constructions in geometry are simple because they only involve the drawing of points, lines and circles or parts of circles.

To construct the internal angle for the dodecahedron.

For this construction, we need only a part of the diagram on the previous page.

Draw a straight line and mark a point on it. Label this point 0. Set the compasses to about an inch and with centre 0 draw a circle. This circle cuts the straight line at measure 1.

By placing the compass point where the circle cuts the straight line, increase the size to a measure of 2. With centre 0, draw a circle with measure 2 and label the straight line as shown.

With centre 1 draw another circle with measure 2 and label the point where this cuts the straight line as 3. Draw two more circles with the same measure, one with centre 2 and the other with centre 3.

With centre 0, open the compasses to a measure of 3 and draw a circle.

Draw a straight line which passes through the point 2 and the points where the two circles centred at 1 and 3 cut one another. This line should be extended so that it passes through the largest circle. From the point where this line cuts the circle with measure 3 to the original centre, 0, draw a straight line.

The angle marked with a dot is the internal angle for the dodecahedron. This angle may be copied five times around a point to form each segment for the internal model. Otherwise the segment on page 83 may be copied.

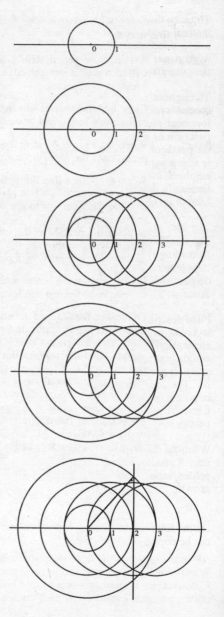

Exterior model

To make the exterior model of the dodecahedron we could cover each face of the internal model with a pentagon and we would need twelve of them. A pentagon is a five-sided shape. The *penta* of pentagon comes originally from the Sanskrit word *panca* which is the number five. We have our word *punch* (the drink) from the same root and this is a drink traditionally consisting of five ingredients.

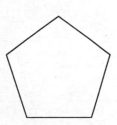

Throughout history the pentagon has been held to be of special symbolic importance. Pythagoras, one of the foremost philosophers of ancient Greece, regarded the pentagon as sacred. In the Vedic tradition, one name for the pentagon in Sanskrit is *Pancabhuja - five-armed*. This is also a name of the Vedic god *Ganesa*, who is lord of numbers, multitudes, obstacles and the five elements. Ganesa is described as having the body of a man, the head of an elephant and he rides around on a mouse.

The five-fold nature of the pentagon is an important aspect of the dodecahedron. According to Plato each polyhedron stands for an element. The cube represents the element Earth, the icosahedron - Water, the tetrahedron - Fire and the octahedron is Air. The Dodecahedron represents the great element Ether or Space.

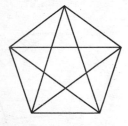

Plato describes Space as the *receptacle*. This means that it holds or contains all things made of the other elements. He describes it as invisible, formless, all-embracing, possessed of intelligibility, yet very hard to grasp. It provides position for everything that comes to be. The four elements, Air, Fire, Water and Earth, come out of the Ether and thus Ether is five-fold. This five-fold nature of Ether is represented by the pentagon.

When the diagonals of a pentagon are drawn we have a pentagram or five-pointed star. A smaller pentagon lies at the centre. Each of the diagonals is also cut in the golden ratio which is frequently found in plants and other forms of natural growth.

On the following page is the net for the exterior model of the dodecahedron. This can be copied onto stiff paper or card, cut out and glued together.

NET FOR EXTERIOR MODEL OF DODECAHEDRON

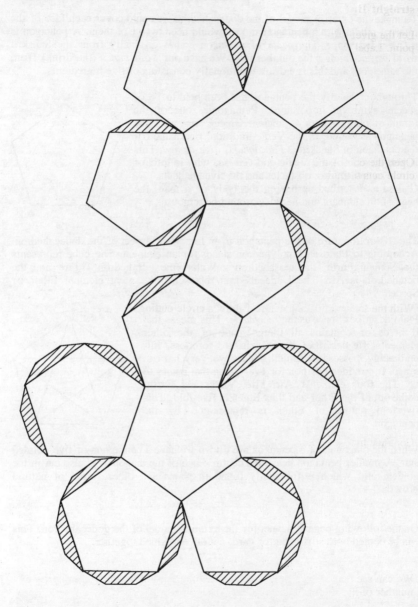

To draw a straight line any number of times as long as a given straight line.

Let the given straight line be AB. Draw a long straight line and at one end mark a point. Label this point 0.

Open the compasses to a radius AB and draw a circle at the point 0. Where this circle cuts the straight line is labelled point 1.

With the same radius and centre 1 draw a circle cutting the straight line at 2.

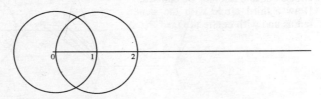

Continue in this fashion, moving in steps along the straight line.

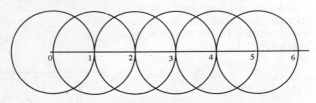

We can see that at each numbered point along the line we have made a line that number of times longer than the line AB.

To draw a perpendicular near the end of a straight line

A perpendicular is a line at right-angles to another line. For example, walls are usually perpendicular to the floor.

We start with a straight line. Near the right-hand end of this line mark a point and label it B so that the line is AB.

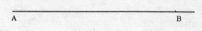

With any convenient radius draw a circle with centre B. Label the point where it cuts the line AB as C.

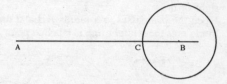

With the same radius and centre C draw a circle. Let the point above the straight line where these two circles cut one another be called D. Draw a third circle with the same radius and with centre at D.

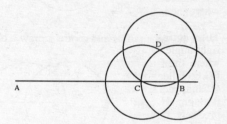

Draw a straight line through C and D and continue it so that it passes through the edge of the circle whose centre is D. Let this point be labelled E.

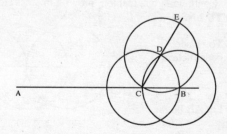

Through B and E draw the straight line, FG.

FG is perpendicular to AB.

There are many ways of drawing a perpendicular. This construction is particularly useful when we wish to have a perpendicular near the end of a straight line. You may have noticed that very little space is used to the right of the point B.

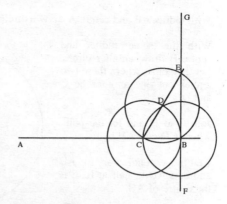

How can we test to see whether it is at right angles to AB? First of all by looking. Does it look perpendicular? If not, can you see where the inaccuracy is?

There is a simple way of testing the right-angle. Let the two points where the first circle cuts the line FG be called M and N. With centre C and radius CM draw an arc through N. If the arc passes precisely through N as well as M then these two points are exactly the same distance from C and the line FG is perpendicular to AB.

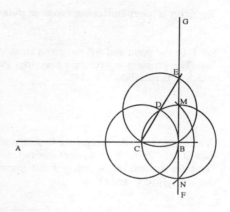

To bisect a straight line perpendicularly

To bisect means to cut something into two equal parts. The following construction divides any given line into two equal parts with a perpendicular line.

Let AB be the given line.

A ——————— B

With radius AB and centre A draw a circle.

With the same radius and centre B draw another circle. Let the points where these two circles cut one another be C and D.

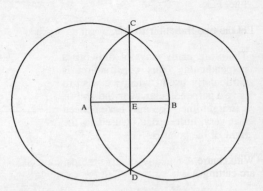

Join C to D and let the point where CD cuts AB be E.

CD is perpendicular to AB and cuts AB in half at E. E is the centre of AB.

To drop a perpendicular from a point to a given straight line.

Let P be the point and AB the given straight line. The problem is to draw a line from P which is perpendicular to AB.

With centre P set the compasses to such a size as will pass through the straight line twice. Draw the arc and let the points where it cuts the line AB be C and D.

With any radius and centre C draw an arc and with the same radius but with centre D draw another arc so that the two arcs cut each other. Let the points where they cut be Q and R.

From P draw a straight line passing through Q and R. The line PQR is perpendicular to AB.

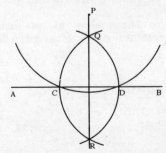

To bisect a given angle

Let the two lines AB and AC form an angle.

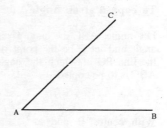

With centre A and any suitable radius draw an arc cutting AB in D and AC in E.

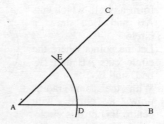

With centre D and any radius draw an arc lying between AB and AC. With the same radius but with centre E draw another arc. Let these two arcs cut at P.

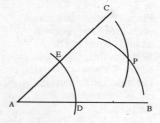

Join A to P. AP bisects the angle BAC

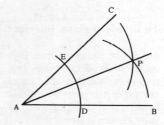

To copy a given angle

Let angle ABC be any given
angle and let P be the point on
the line PQ at which the angle
ABC is to be copied.

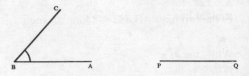

With centre B and at
such a radius which will
form a circle which cuts
AB and BC, draw a
circle.
Let the points where the
circle cuts AB and BC
be D and E.
With the same radius
draw a circle with
centre P. Let this circle
cut the straight line PQ
in S.
Place your compass
point on D and measure
a radius equal to DE.
With radius DE and
centre S draw a circle.
Let this circle cut the
circle centred at P at
the point R.

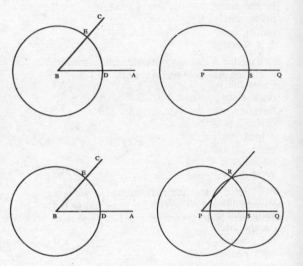

Join P to R with a straight line. The angle QPR is equal to the angle ABC.

To divide a given line into any number of equal parts.

Let AB be the given line. It is
required to divide this line
into any number of equal
parts. For the purposes of this
construction the number of
parts chosen is five.

From A draw a straight line at
an angle to AB of about half a
right angle.
Choosing any radius (such as
will allow five measures of it

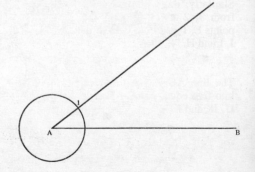

to be made on the straight line) draw a circle centred at **A**. Let this circle cut the straight line at point 1.

With the same radius and centre 1, draw a circle giving a measure of 2.
In the same way continue to draw circles, of the same radius, centred at measures of 2, 3, 4 and 5.

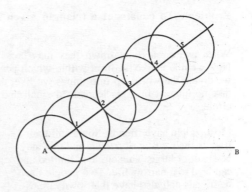

From the point of measure 5 draw a straight line to B. Let this line cut the circle with centre 5 at the point C.
Adjust the compasses to a radius from the point of measure 4 to the point C. With this radius and centre 3, draw an arc to cut the circle with centre 4 at the point D. With centre 2, draw an arc to cut the circle with centre 3 at the point E. In like manner, with centres 1 and A draw arcs to cut the circles at F and G.

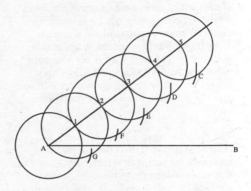

Draw a straight line from 4 through D to cut AB in K. Similarly, draw straight lines from 3, 2 and 1 through the points E, F and G to cut AB in J, I and H.

The line AB is now divided into five equal parts, AH, HI, IJ, JK and KB.

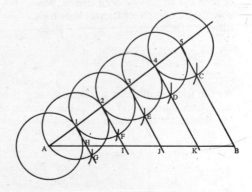

Problem: To construct a triangle given the lengths of the three sides.

When two circles are drawn they may cross over one another. They intersect. Now a circle is like the limit within which people live their lives. This is because we divide the world up into things we like, things we do not like and things we take no interest in. This leads to a small and narrow existence, like living in a circle.

Most people have friends. Some call their friends their *circle of friends* and this may be small or large. This circle is limited and can lead to a narrow life. Two people may be friends and also have their own circles of friends. Some may be within both circles whilst others are in only one circle whilst yet others may not be in either circle. Whenever you exclude someone from friendship that person is not inside your circle. The best way is not to create any circle leading to a small life. This means that other people are not cut off and you are then free to include everybody.

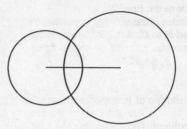

The diagram represents two friends, centred at A and B, and the circles represent the world in which they live. The distance between these two friends, the strength of their friendship, is represented by the line joining A to B. At C is a friend of both and so falls on both circles. We now have a triangle of friends shown as triangle ABC.

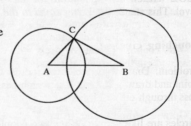

We can use this diagram to construct any sized triangle, given the lengths of the three sides. One side is used as the distance between the two centres. The other two lengths are used as the measures for the two circles.

Problem: Draw a triangle ABC with side lengths AB = 8 cm, BC = 6 cm and AC = 7 cm.

Draw a long horizontal line and on it mark two points, A and B, which are 8 cm apart. With centre A and radius 7 cm draw a circle. With centre B and radius 6 cm draw a circle. The point above the line AB where the two circles intersect is then C. Join A to C and B to C. ABC is the required triangle.

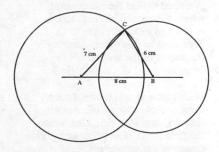

This type of triangle is called *scalene* because all the sides are of different lengths.

Problem: Draw the triangle ABC with AB = 12 cm, BC = 8 cm and AC = 8 cm.

We can see that two sides of the triangle are equal in length. Their *legs* are both the same. Such a triangle is called *isosceles*. The word *isosceles* comes from the Greek word ΙΣΟΣ (Isos) which means *equal to*. The elevators in buildings in Greece have the word ΙΣΟΣ written on the button for the ground floor level. This stands for being *equal to the ground*.

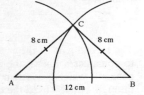

Touching circles

Problem: Draw two circles of radius 1" and 2" which touch each other at one point and draw a straight line which passes through that point but which does not pass through either circle.

Circles are like people. When two people meet there is a line joining the centre of one person to the centre of the other. It is the line of consciousness or attention. In the same way, when two circles meet, you need to establish the line joining the centres. This is the clue for the problem: to draw a line which is going to be the line joining the centres of the two circles.

We begin with one of the circles and then draw the straight line from the centre of that circle. Let the first circle have radius 2 inches and centre at A. From the centre,

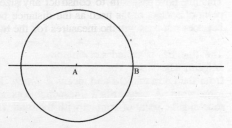

A, draw a long straight line which cuts the circle at B. B is the point at which the two circles will touch.

We need to find the exact point where the second circle is to be centred in relation to the first. This may be done by measuring the radius of the second circle from the point of contact, B.

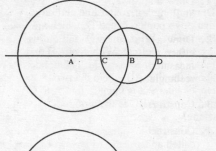

With centre B and radius 1 inch draw a circle cutting the straight line at C and D, where C is inside the first circle. The point D is the centre of the second circle.

Draw the second circle with radius 1 inch and centre D. The two circles now touch each other at the point B.

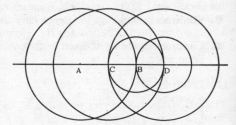

The second part of the problem is to construct a line at the point of contact which does not pass through either circle. How many such lines are there? The answer is one and this one line will be perpendicular to the line ACBD.

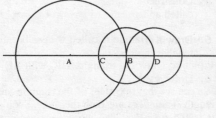

With radius 2 inches, and centre C, draw a circle. With the same radius, but with centre D, draw another circle. Let these two circles cut at E and F.

Join E to F through the point B. This line now passes through the point of contact of the two circles but does not pass within either.

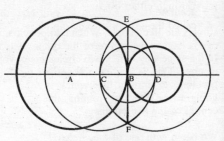

The line EF is called a *common tangent*. The word *tangent* comes from the Latin *tangere* and means *to touch*. The *tango* dance also comes from the same word. A tangent is a line which touches a circle at one point like a wheel touching the point of contact with the road. It does not pass within the circle.

Exercise 9a Drawing problems

1. Draw a straight line and on it mark a point, P. Construct a perpendicular at P.

2. Draw a straight horizontal line and on it mark two points, A and B, near either end. Construct perpendiculars at A and B. Mark off two equal measures on the perpendiculars and, connecting with a straight line, make a rectangle.

3. Construct an equilateral triangle with sides 5 cm in length.

4. Construct a triangle with base 4 cm and two equal sides of 6 cm. This is called an isosceles triangle because it has two equal sides.

5. Draw a circle of radius 2 inches. Construct a circle of radius 1 inch which touches the first circle.

6. Draw a straight line and divide it into three equal parts.

7. Construct a triangle ABC with sides AB = 8 cm, AC = 6 cm and BC = 5 cm.

8. Construct triangle PQR with sides PQ = 4 in, QR = 3 in and PR = 2 in.

9. Construct triangle UVW with UV = 7 cm, UW = 5 cm and VW = 6 cm. Drop a perpendicular from W to the line UV.

10. Construct triangle ABC with AB = 9 cm, BC = 7 cm and AC = 6 cm. Drop a perpendicular from C to AB. Similarly, drop perpendiculars from A to BC and from B to AC. The three perpendiculars meet at a point. Label this point O. With centre O and radius OA draw a circle. If your drawing is accurate the circle will pass through the points A, B and C. This circle is called the circumscribing circle.

Chapter 10 - Digital Roots

Summing digits

You may have noticed that with the nine times table all the answers have digits adding up to nine.

$$1 \times 9 = 9$$
$$2 \times 9 = 18, \quad 1 + 8 = 9$$
$$3 \times 9 = 27, \quad 2 + 7 = 9$$
$$4 \times 9 = 36, \quad 3 + 6 = 9, \text{ etc}$$

This brings us to the important idea of digital root. The **digital root** of any number is the sum of all the digits, continued until there is only one digit left. Here are some examples:-

Number	Summing digits		Digital root
71	$7 + 1 = 8$		8
231	$2 + 3 + 1 = 6$		6
85	$8 + 5 = 13$	$1 + 3 = 4$	4
7562	$7 + 5 + 6 + 2 = 20$	$2 + 0 = 2$	2

It is also a fact that the digital root of a number is the same as the remainder when that number is divided by 9. For example, $71 \div 9 = 7$ remainder 8 and $231 \div 9 = 25$ remainder 6.

The digital root of a number in fact tells us something of the quality of that number and can also help us check answers to many calculations.

Exercise 10a Find the digital roots of the following:

1. 23
2. 47
3. 89
4. 91
5. 995

6. 234
7. 173
8. 647
9. 983
10. 189

11. 3201
12. 5463
13. 5338
14. 8696
15. 46521

16. 546384
17. 748702
18. 7401275
19. 65420652
20. 463729193

Casting out nines

An easy method for finding the digital root of any number is to cast out nines and groups of digits which add up to 9. This is done by crossing out any nines in the number or any digits adding up to nine. The numbers which are left at the end are added up for the digital root. The sutra used here is *By Elimination and Retention..*

Example: Find the digital root of 19462785.

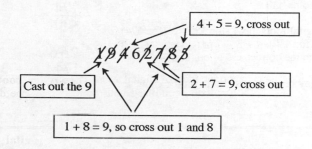

The only number which is left is 6 and this is the digital root.

If there is nothing left after having cast out nines then the digital root is 9. This is because in the process of casting out nought and nine are interchangeable. This also follows from the fact that when dividing any number by 9 and the remainder is 0 it may also be said to be 9, for example, 18 ÷ 9 = 2 remainder 0, or 1 remainder 9.

Exercise 10b Find the digital root by casting out nines:

1. 813	**11.** 6322	**21.** 897364	**31.** 367425
2. 366	**12.** 43701	**22.** 230098	**32.** 538987
3. 574	**13.** 96534	**23.** 876221	**33.** 182799
4. 722	**14.** 35096	**24.** 994652	**34.** 678321
5. 75002	**15.** 12789	**25.** 65743	**35.** 354621
6. 34625	**16.** 32811	**26.** 94804	**36.** 768511
7. 16307	**17.** 4432	**27.** 125789	**37.** 473821
8. 4565	**18.** 9798	**28.** 657483	**38.** 98076
9. 8612	**19.** 4985	**29.** 832762	**39.** 812763
10. 32366	**20.** 9876	**30.** 999987	**40.** 978132

Using digital roots to check answers

By casting out nines from all the numbers in any sum the same sum also **holds true** for the digital roots.

To take a simple example, consider the sum, 256 + 174.

On adding the two numbers the answer is found to be 430.

$$\begin{array}{r} 256 \\ + 174 \\ \hline 430 \end{array}$$

The digital roots are 4 (for 256), 3 (for 174) and 7 (for 430). 4 + 3 = 7 provides us with a check to the correctness of our sum.

This may be set out as shown on the right:

$$\begin{array}{rr} 256 & 4 \\ + 174 & + 3 \\ \hline 430 \quad 7 & 7 \end{array}$$

Exercise 10c Answer these additions and check your answers using digital roots.

1. $\begin{array}{r}326\\+784\end{array}$	6. $\begin{array}{r}75432\\+\;\;678\end{array}$	11. $\begin{array}{r}846123\\+728321\end{array}$	16. $\begin{array}{r}363239\\+177190\end{array}$
2. $\begin{array}{r}209\\+326\end{array}$	7. $\begin{array}{r}6542\\+23456\end{array}$	12. $\begin{array}{r}723068\\+\;91129\end{array}$	17. $\begin{array}{r}217829\\+\;\;\;183\end{array}$
3. $\begin{array}{r}4156\\+2374\end{array}$	8. $\begin{array}{r}36271\\+\;2123\end{array}$	13. $\begin{array}{r}432157\\+\;81623\end{array}$	18. $\begin{array}{r}462142\\+\;\;\;806\end{array}$
4. $\begin{array}{r}5421\\+2561\end{array}$	9. $\begin{array}{r}110000\\+\;76543\end{array}$	14. $\begin{array}{r}534087\\+\;80089\end{array}$	19. $\begin{array}{r}26\\+45619\end{array}$
5. $\begin{array}{r}463\\4767\\+\;\;45\end{array}$	10. $\begin{array}{r}640\\854\\+294\end{array}$	15. $\begin{array}{r}29\\65\\65\\+\;917\end{array}$	20. $\begin{array}{r}134\\7651\\8007\\+19918\end{array}$

The same should hold true for subtractions and it does, provided that we take account of the times when, in the subtraction of the digital roots, we allow for the complement to be taken. The example taken is 8245 – 1817.

$$
\begin{array}{cc}
8245 & 1 \\
-\ 1817 & -\ 8 \\
\hline
6428 \quad 2 & \overline{7} = 2 \ \text{(since } 9-7=2\text{)}
\end{array}
$$

Exercise 10d Answer the sum and check each one using digital roots

1. 54326 – 12784	**6.** 765432 – 345678	**11.** 846123 – 728321	**16.** 363239 – 177190
2. 71209 – 34326	**7.** 326542 – 123456	**12.** 723068 – 91129	**17.** 217829 – 9183
3. 64156 – 2374	**8.** 36271 – 2123	**13.** 432157 – 81623	**18.** 462142 – 191806
4. 835421 – 642561	**9.** 100000 – 76543	**14.** 534087 – 80089	**19.** 361526 – 45619
5. 945632 – 456789	**10.** 932640 – 175294	**15.** 145629 – 8917	**20.** 948134 – 419918

Usually, with additions and subtractions, it is quicker to check the sum by repeating it. There are times, however, when the digital root check is very useful for multiplications and divisions. This is an application of the rule -
The product of the sum of the digits in the factors is equal to the sum of the digits in the product.

The two numbers to be multiplied are the factors and the answer is called the product.

$$
\begin{array}{r} 322 \\ \times\ 263 \\ \hline 84686 \end{array}
\qquad
\begin{array}{r} 7 \\ \times\ 2 \\ \hline 5\quad 14 \end{array}
$$

The digital roots of 322 and 263 are 7 and 2 respectively. The product of 2 and 7 is 14 which has a digital root of 5. The digital root of the product, 84686 is also 5.

This check is not absolutely safe but does provide a useful safety net. A typical case where the check does not work is where two of the digits in the answer are interchanged by mistake. The digital root of this answer would be the same as that of the real answer.

Exercise 10e Answer the following and use digital roots to check your answers.

1. 23 × 23	**6.** 84 × 67	**11.** 789 × 121	**16.** 777 × 120
2. 56 × 26	**7.** 91 × 75	**12.** 117 × 203	**17.** 45 × 433
3. 38 × 32	**8.** 312 × 212	**13.** 909 × 131	**18.** 2312 × 2163
4. 42 × 39	**9.** 203 × 133	**14.** 353 × 522	**19.** 3254 × 1107
5. 71 × 53	**10.** 364 × 623	**15.** 516 × 733	**20.** 4233 × 2003

With division, the same rule applies but the wording is different: *The digital root of the product of the divisor and quotient, together with that of the remainder, is equal to the digital root of the dividend.* An actual example will clarify this.

$$
7\,\big|\,3\ 7\ 6\ 3\ 7
$$
$$
\underline{\ \ \ \ \ 2\ \ 5\ 4\ \ \ }
$$
$$
5\ 3\ 7\ 6\ /\ 5
$$

DR of 5376 = 3.
7 × 3 + 5 = 26, DR = 8
DR of 37637 = 8

The quotient is 5376 and has a digital root of 3. The digital root of the divisor, 7, is 7, and 7 × 3 = 21. To this we add the remainder ,5 and obtain the digital root of the answer making 8. This number should equal the digital root of the dividend, 37637,which is also 8.

Exercise 10f Answer the following and check the answers with digital roots.

1. 3⟌871

6. 5⟌763

11. 2⟌534

16. 5⟌8173

2. 4⟌536

7. 2⟌927

12. 8⟌773

17. 3⟌2991

3. 6⟌356

8. 4⟌813

13. 8⟌544

18. 7⟌63114

4. 3⟌567

9. 3⟌649

14. 3⟌688

19. 6⟌23923

5. 4⟌702

10. 6⟌822

15. 4⟌927

20. 8⟌76854

Chapter 11 - Divisibility

First Principles

One is indivisible

Any number which is not a prime is divisible.

Prime numbers are said to be divisible by one and themselves but for the purposes of divisibility we will treat them as being indivisible.

Two, five and ten

An even number is one which may be divided into two equal parts. Even numbers end in 2, 4, 6, 8 or 0.

An odd number is a number which, when divided into two, will not give two equal parts. Odd numbers end in 1, 3, 5, 7 and 9. For example, if we try to divide 43 into two equal parts the closest possibility is 21 and 22 and these are not equal.

A number is divisible by two if it ends with an even number.

A number is divisible by ten when it ends with a nought.

A number is divisible by five when it ends with nought or five.

These three numbers, two, five and ten are all closely related. Ten divided by two is five and ten divided by five is two. Two and five mirror each other. There are quick methods for multiplying and dividing numbers by 5 using this mirror-like quality. For example, $73 \div 5 = 14.6$. This is found by multiplying 73 by 2 to give 146 and then dividing by 10 to give 14.6.

To find out whether a number is divisible by either two, five or ten we just need to look at the final digit. The sutra for this is *By mere inspection*.

Exercise 11a Copy and complete the following table:

	Number	Divisible by 10?	Divisible by 2?	Divisible by 5?
1	4225	×	×	√
2.	340			
3.	67			
4.	34509			

5.	65475			
6.	34532			
7.	56090			
8.	656500			
9.	212345			
10.	600040			

Four and eight

The test for divisibility by four depends upon the final two digits. For example, how do we know whether or not 45796532 is divisible by four without actually dividing the number. The answer is that if the final two digits are divisible by four then the whole number is also. So with 45796532 we can look at the last two digits, 32, and say, 'Yes! It is divisible by four'. The sutra for this is *Only the last two digits*.

There is another sutra which helps to establish whether or not the final two digits of any number are divisible by four and this is *The ultimate and twice the penultimate*. This tells us to take the final digit and add to it twice the penultimate (the one before the final). For example with 876392, the ultimate is 2 and the penultimate is 9. So we take $2 + 2 \times 9 = 2 + 18 = 20$. Since 20 is divisible by 4 then 92 is divisible by 4 and so 876392 is also divisible by 4. The alternative to using this sutra is to learn all the multiples of 4 up to 100.

It is often possible to just look at the final two digits and realise that the number is divisible by 4. When this happens the sutra is *By mere inspection*.

Exercise 11b Copy and complete the following table, to find the *ultimate and twice the penultimate* for each multiple of four. In column A are the multiples of four, in column B are the results of adding the ultimate and twice the penultimate. If the result in column B is a two-digit number then repeat the process to form column C.

A	B	C	A	B	C	A	B	C	A	B	C
04	4		28			52			76		
08	8		32			56			80		
12	4		36	12	4	60			84		
16			40			64			88		
20			44			68	20	4	92		
24			48			72			96		

Is 450768 divisible by 4?

450768   20   Yes

$8 + 2 \times 6 = 20$ and 20 is divisible by 4, therefore, Yes.

Exercise 11c Which of the following are divisible by 4?

1. 82	**6.** 129	**11.** 12086	**16.** 100092
2. 45	**7.** 336	**12.** 47600	**17.** 3587672
3. 216	**8.** 596	**13.** 3120	**18.** 989769968
4. 735	**9.** 7158	**14.** 5050	**19.** 7576476
5. 842	**10.** 4344	**15.** 32894	**20.** 98700186

To find out if a number is divisible by eight we extend the sutra for four and instead of considering the final two digits we look at the final three digits. The rule is to find the ultimate plus twice the penultimate plus four times the pen-penultimate (*pen-penultimate* means *the one before the one before the final digit*). If this result is in the eight times table then the number is divisible by 8.

Is 7095643736 divisible by 8?

The ultimate is 6. The penultimate is 3 and two times this is 6.
The pen-penultimate is 7 and four times this is 28.
$6 + 6 + 28 = 40$, which is a multiple of 8 and so 7095643736 is divisible by 8.

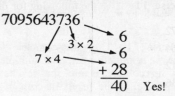

$$7095643736$$
$$3 \times 2 \longrightarrow 6$$
$$\longrightarrow 6$$
$$7 \times 4 \quad\quad + 28$$
$$\overline{\quad 40 \quad} \text{ Yes!}$$

Exercise 11d Which of the following is divisible by 8?

1. 256	**5.** 3246	**9.** 5368	**13.** 2111034	**17.** 6574602
2. 128	**6.** 9786	**10.** 2222	**14.** 600	**18.** 328886
3. 647	**7.** 3576	**11.** 87231	**15.** 57400	**19.** 9350936
4. 1286	**8.** 2178	**12.** 243558	**16.** 3217000	**20.** 5768574632

Nine and three

Three and nine are closely related because $3 \times 3 = 9$. The divisibility rules for 3 and 9 are also similar to one another.

A number is divisible by 9 if the sum of the digits is divisible by 9. In relation to digital roots a number is divisible by 9 if its digital root is 9. The digital root of any number can be found by casting out nines and this has been described in the previous chapter.

Is 6594138243 divisible by 9?

First cast out any nines and then cast out groups of digits adding up to nine.
So we cross out 9, and 6 and 3.
Cross out 5 and 4, and 1 and 8.
Cross out 2, 4 and 3.
Since all numbers have been cast out, the digital root is 9 and so the number is divisible by 9.

6594138243

6594138243

6594138243

DR = 9, Yes!

Exercise 11e Test the following for divisibility by 9

1. 72	6. 108	11. 17453	16. 8460153
2. 64	7. 145	12. 635247	17. 7685709
3. 12	8. 954	13. 6258153	18. 5433412
4. 36	9. 216	14. 556723414	19. 923456781
5. 54	10. 7299	15. 9272635443	20. 10000123

A number is divisible by 3 when the sum of the digits is divisible by 3. Again, it follows that a number is divisible by 3 when its digital root is 3, 6 or 9.

To find out whether or not a number is divisible by three we can cast out three's, sixes, and nine's and groups of numbers adding up to either three, six or nine. The sutra for casting out is *By elimination and retention*.

Is 3647224912 divisible by 3?

Writing this number down we can
immediately cross out 3, 6 and 9.
We can also cross out 7 and 2, 2 and 4 and
1 and 2. We are then left with 4. Therefore
this number is not divisible by 3.

3̸6̸4̸7̸2̸2̸4̸9̸1̸2̸

4 No!

Exercise 11f Test the following for divisibility by 3

1. 21	**6.** 31	**11.** 4321	**16.** 1438675
2. 45	**7.** 93	**12.** 111	**17.** 12540876
3. 91	**8.** 43	**13.** 222	**18.** 2345876
4. 102	**9.** 78	**14.** 444	**19.** 509739
5. 25	**10.** 84	**15.** 6578	**20.** 1324176994

Divisibility rules

Here is a summary of the divisibility rules for 2, 3, 4, 5, 8, 9 and 10:

A number is divisible by **two** if it ends with an even number.

A number is divisible by **three** when the digital root is divisible by three.

A number is divisible by **four** when the ultimate and twice the penultimate are
divisible by four, or when the number comprising the final two digits are
divisible by four.

A number is divisible by **five** when it ends with nought or five.

A number is divisible by **eight** when the ultimate, twice the penultimate and four
times the pen-penultimate is divisible by eight, or when the number comprising
the final three digits is divisible by eight.

A number is divisible by **nine** when the digital root is nine.

A number is divisible by **ten** when it ends with a nought.

Exercise 11g Which of the following numbers are divisible by the first number:-

1. 2; 43521, 6753, 546378, 768574, 35709, 214636
2. 3; 12943, 10886, 365748, 99716, 1212369, 3245463
3. 4; 812, 922, 13780, 46376, 725834, 25308
4. 5; 6987, 53425, 86709, 30004, 576800, 32530
5. 8; 4524, 1278, 19344, 789020, 85752, 25167128
6. 9; 432, 873, 606, 7857, 8427, 30708, 546299
7. 10; 3241, 63450, 5400, 65745, 9586000

Divisibility rules for composite numbers

To obtain a divisibility rule for any composite number, such as 6, 12, 15 and 18, we use combinations of the rules for their factors. For example, $6 = 2 \times 3$ and so a number which can be divided exactly by 6 must be divisible by 3 and also 2. The various rules for some of the composite numbers are given below.

A number is divisible by 6 when it is divisible by both 2 and 3.
A number is divisible by 12 when it is divisible by both 3 and 4.
A number is divisible by 15 when it is divisible by both 3 and 5.
A number is divisible by 18 when it is divisible by both 2 and 9.
A number is divisible by 20 when it ends in nought and the penultimate digit is even.
A number is divisible by 24 when it is divisible by both 3 and 8.
A number is divisible by 30 when it is divisible by both 3 and 10.
So when testing a number for its divisibility for say, 24, it must pass the test for 3 and the test for 8.

Exercise 11f Which of the following numbers are divisible by the first number:-

1. 6; 543, 256, 189, 498, 5634, 3788, 98789, 342222
2. 12; 5463, 5768, 288, 7992, 122876, 78654
3. 15; 145, 7860, 4325, 9870, 12300, 4638765
4. 18; 879, 4284, 187632, 7869043, 32054526
5. 20; 560, 790, 2400, 785400, 45210, 879880
6. 24; 126, 786, 4624, 8768, 9243, 657452
7. 30; 780, 6700, 4650, 92700, 435850

The divisibility rules for 7, 11, 13, 17, 19 and other awkward looking numbers will be left to a later stage.

Chapter 12 - Addition and Subtraction of Fractions

Adding with the same denominator

The first type of addition of fractions is where the denominators are the same. We just add the numerators and then simplify the answer.

$$\frac{7}{12} + \frac{11}{12}$$ The denominators are the same, so add the numerators.

$$\frac{7}{12} + \frac{11}{12} = \frac{18}{12}$$ The next step is to simplify the answer as far as possible by bringing to lowest terms. In this case, both the numerator and denominator are divisible by 6, their HCF.

$$\frac{18}{12} = \frac{3}{2}$$

Having been left with an improper fraction this has to be converted into a mixed number. (It is customary not to leave answers as improper fractions).

$$\frac{3}{2} = 1\frac{1}{2}$$ 2 is divided into 3 giving $1\frac{1}{2}$ as the final answer.

The whole sum may be set out in one line as follows:

$$\frac{7}{12} + \frac{11}{12} = \frac{18}{12} = \frac{3}{2} = 1\frac{1}{2}$$

Exercise 12a Set them out as shown above or write answers only.

1. $\frac{1}{4} + \frac{1}{4}$　　　4. $\frac{1}{5} + \frac{1}{5}$　　　7. $\frac{1}{7} + \frac{3}{7}$　　　10. $\frac{1}{9} + \frac{1}{9}$

2. $\frac{1}{3} + \frac{1}{3}$　　　5. $\frac{1}{7} + \frac{1}{7}$　　　8. $\frac{2}{7} + \frac{4}{7}$　　　11. $\frac{2}{9} + \frac{4}{9}$

3. $\frac{1}{9} + \frac{7}{9}$　　　6. $\frac{5}{12} + \frac{7}{12}$　　　9. $\frac{3}{10} + \frac{1}{10}$　　　12. $\frac{1}{5} + \frac{3}{5}$

13. $\frac{3}{4} + \frac{2}{4}$　　　15. $\frac{3}{8} + \frac{3}{8}$　　　17. $\frac{1}{6} + \frac{1}{6}$　　　19. $\frac{1}{7} + \frac{5}{7}$

14. $\frac{2}{3} + \frac{2}{3}$　　　16. $\frac{2}{9} + \frac{5}{9}$　　　18. $\frac{2}{5} + \frac{1}{5}$　　　20. $\frac{1}{8} + \frac{1}{8}$

Adding when one denominator is a factor of the other

When the denominators are not the same then it is possible to make them the same so that the addition or subtraction may take place. The first case is where one denominator is a factor of the other. This means that the denominator which is a factor can be multiplied by some number to make it equal to the other denominator. The following example shows how this is done.

$\frac{1}{4} + \frac{5}{12}$

$= \frac{3}{12} + \frac{5}{12}$

$= \frac{8}{12}$

$= \frac{2}{3}$

In this example, 4 is a factor of 12, so we must convert $\frac{1}{4}$ into $\frac{3}{12}$ and then add the two fractions as before.

The procedure is to find how many times one denominator goes into the other; in this case, 4 into 12 = 3.

The next step is to multiply top and bottom of $\frac{1}{4}$ by 3. Both fractions will then have the same denominator.which is called the *Lowest Common Denominator*.

This may be written out as,

$$\frac{1}{4} + \frac{5}{12} = \frac{3 + 5}{12} = \frac{8}{12} = \frac{2}{3}$$

Exercise 12b

1. $\frac{1}{2} + \frac{1}{4}$

2. $\frac{1}{3} + \frac{1}{6}$

3. $\frac{1}{4} + \frac{3}{8}$

4. $\frac{2}{5} + \frac{3}{10}$

5. $\frac{1}{3} + \frac{1}{9}$

6. $\frac{3}{4} + \frac{1}{12}$

7. $\frac{3}{16} + \frac{1}{4}$

8. $\frac{2}{5} + \frac{9}{20}$

9. $\frac{5}{6} + \frac{1}{18}$

10. $\frac{7}{20} + \frac{1}{4}$

11. $\frac{1}{12} + \frac{5}{6}$

12. $\frac{3}{4} + \frac{5}{24}$

13. $\frac{11}{15} + \frac{7}{30}$

14. $\frac{11}{12} + \frac{1}{36}$

15. $\frac{3}{8} + \frac{5}{32}$

16. $\frac{3}{7} + \frac{19}{42}$

17. $\frac{7}{18} + \frac{7}{36}$

18. $\frac{4}{5} + \frac{9}{40}$

19. $\frac{11}{15} + \frac{12}{45}$

20. $\frac{5}{12} + \frac{17}{60}$

Addition using *Vertically and Crosswise* with coprime denominators

If the denominators in the two fractions to be added are coprime, that is, their highest common factor is 1, then the *Vertically and Crosswise* sutra is brought into play. The denominator of the answer is simply obtained by multiplying the two denominators together. The numerator is obtained by calculating the sum of the cross-product of all four numbers. The following example illustrates this quick method for adding such fractions.

$\frac{2}{5} + \frac{3}{7}$	Are the denominators coprime? Yes! The denominator is $5 \times 7 = 35$
$= \frac{29}{35}$	The numerator is the sum of the cross-product, $2 \times 7 + 3 \times 5 = 14 + 15 = 29$
	Answer, $\frac{29}{35}$.

Exercise 12c All working may be done mentally so write answers only.

1. $\frac{1}{4} + \frac{2}{3}$ 7. $\frac{1}{4} + \frac{1}{5}$ 13. $\frac{1}{2} + \frac{1}{5}$ 19. $\frac{2}{9} + \frac{1}{2}$

2. $\frac{1}{2} + \frac{1}{3}$ 8. $\frac{2}{5} + \frac{1}{4}$ 14. $\frac{1}{3} + \frac{1}{5}$ 20. $\frac{3}{5} + \frac{1}{4}$

3. $\frac{1}{3} + \frac{1}{4}$ 9. $\frac{1}{2} + \frac{3}{7}$ 15. $\frac{1}{3} + \frac{3}{7}$ 21. $\frac{2}{3} + \frac{1}{8}$

4. $\frac{1}{6} + \frac{3}{5}$ 10. $\frac{1}{2} + \frac{2}{3}$ 16. $\frac{3}{4} + \frac{4}{5}$ 22. $\frac{2}{3} + \frac{5}{11}$

5. $\frac{3}{4} + \frac{1}{7}$ 11. $\frac{3}{4} + \frac{2}{3}$ 17. $\frac{7}{8} + \frac{1}{3}$ 23. $\frac{4}{7} + \frac{1}{9}$

6. $\frac{5}{9} + \frac{1}{4}$ 12. $\frac{1}{2} + \frac{3}{5}$ 18. $\frac{1}{11} + \frac{1}{12}$ 24. $\frac{2}{9} + \frac{1}{11}$

Vertically and Crosswise for non-coprime denominators

When the denominators are not coprime then we can reduce those denominators so that they are coprime. This is done by finding the HCF of the denominators and dividing each denominator by that HCF. This is an extension to the previous method but careful setting out is required so that the answer may be found easily.

$\frac{3}{4} + \frac{5}{8}$

Are the denominators coprime? No!
Write down the HCF of the denominators, 4, on the left and below the two fractions.
Divide the HCF, 4, into each of the denominators and write down the answers below. 4 into 4 = 1 and 4 into 8 = 2.

$\frac{3}{4} + \frac{5}{8} = \frac{11}{8}$

4   1   2

$= 1\frac{3}{8}$

The 1 and 2 become the new denominators and these are used in the sum of the cross-product, $(3 \times 2) + (5 \times 1) = 11$ which gives the numerator of the answer.
The denominator is the product of the HCF and the two new denominators, $4 \times 1 \times 2 = 8$.
The answer is then simplified to give $1\frac{3}{8}$.

Exercise 12d

1. $\frac{1}{4} + \frac{1}{6}$ 7. $\frac{3}{8} + \frac{5}{18}$ 13. $\frac{3}{8} + \frac{1}{12}$ 19. $\frac{5}{12} + \frac{2}{15}$

2. $\frac{3}{4} + \frac{1}{6}$ 8. $\frac{1}{15} + \frac{1}{20}$ 14. $\frac{5}{12} + \frac{1}{9}$ 20. $\frac{3}{16} + \frac{7}{20}$

3. $\frac{1}{6} + \frac{5}{9}$ 9. $\frac{5}{12} + \frac{5}{10}$ 15. $\frac{3}{4} + \frac{5}{6}$ 21. $\frac{1}{12} + \frac{1}{18}$

4. $\frac{5}{6} + \frac{1}{10}$ 10. $\frac{3}{8} + \frac{3}{10}$ 16. $\frac{7}{12} + \frac{5}{8}$ 22. $\frac{3}{20} + \frac{1}{24}$

5. $\frac{1}{14} + \frac{5}{6}$ 11. $\frac{1}{6} + \frac{1}{8}$ 17. $\frac{5}{6} + \frac{2}{9}$ 23. $\frac{7}{10} + \frac{2}{15}$

6. $\frac{1}{12} + \frac{2}{9}$ 12. $\frac{3}{10} + \frac{1}{4}$ 18. $\frac{3}{8} + \frac{5}{12}$ 24. $\frac{1}{12} + \frac{1}{14}$

Subtraction with the same denominators

$\frac{7}{15} - \frac{4}{15} = \frac{3}{15} = \frac{1}{5}$

As with addition, when the denominators are the same we can just subtract the numerators and simplify the answer as necessary.

115

Exercise 12e Write answers only or set them out as shown above.

1. $\frac{3}{8} - \frac{1}{8}$ 6. $\frac{3}{4} - \frac{1}{4}$ 11. $\frac{6}{11} - \frac{5}{11}$ 16. $\frac{15}{16} - \frac{3}{16}$

2. $\frac{4}{5} - \frac{2}{5}$ 7. $\frac{7}{8} - \frac{3}{8}$ 12. $\frac{13}{35} - \frac{6}{35}$ 17. $\frac{19}{24} - \frac{10}{24}$

3. $\frac{7}{9} - \frac{4}{9}$ 8. $\frac{9}{10} - \frac{4}{10}$ 13. $\frac{9}{40} - \frac{1}{40}$ 18. $\frac{17}{20} - \frac{5}{20}$

4. $\frac{5}{6} - \frac{1}{6}$ 9. $\frac{11}{12} - \frac{9}{12}$ 14. $\frac{11}{15} - \frac{1}{15}$ 19. $\frac{31}{52} - \frac{5}{32}$

5. $\frac{9}{25} - \frac{4}{25}$ 10. $\frac{11}{28} - \frac{3}{28}$ 15. $\frac{28}{30} - \frac{7}{30}$ 20. $\frac{19}{45} - \frac{7}{45}$

Subtraction when one denominator is a factor of the other

When one denominator is a factor of the other then the larger one is the lowest common denominator. In such a case, the fraction with the smaller denominator is converted.

$$\frac{7}{16} - \frac{3}{8} = \frac{7 - 6}{16} = \frac{1}{16}$$

8 is a factor of 16 and it goes into 16 twice. So we multiply top and bottom of $\frac{3}{8}$ by 2 to give $\frac{6}{16}$ and then subtract as usual.
The answer is then $\frac{1}{16}$.

Exercise 12f Set them out as shown in the example.

1. $\frac{1}{2} - \frac{1}{4}$ 6. $\frac{5}{6} - \frac{5}{18}$ 11. $\frac{11}{16} - \frac{5}{32}$ 16. $\frac{11}{20} - \frac{11}{80}$

2. $\frac{1}{3} - \frac{1}{6}$ 7. $\frac{8}{9} - \frac{5}{18}$ 12. $\frac{17}{30} - \frac{3}{10}$ 17. $\frac{1}{2} - \frac{5}{24}$

3. $\frac{5}{8} - \frac{1}{4}$ 8. $\frac{19}{24} - \frac{5}{12}$ 13. $\frac{5}{6} - \frac{5}{24}$ 18. $\frac{1}{5} - \frac{1}{25}$

4. $\frac{7}{9} - \frac{2}{3}$ 9. $\frac{12}{25} - \frac{3}{50}$ 14. $\frac{28}{33} - \frac{2}{3}$ 19. $\frac{29}{36} - \frac{1}{6}$

5. $\frac{4}{5} - \frac{1}{15}$ 10. $\frac{3}{5} - \frac{7}{35}$ 15. $\frac{35}{42} - \frac{8}{21}$ 20. $\frac{59}{64} - \frac{3}{8}$

116

Subtraction using *Vertically and Crosswise* with coprime denominators.

For subtraction of fractions whose denominators are coprime the process is almost the same as for addition except that instead of finding the sum of the cross-product we use the difference of the cross-product.

$$\frac{3}{7} - \frac{2}{5}$$

$$= \frac{1}{35}$$

Are the denominators coprime? Yes!
Denominator is $5 \times 7 = 35$
Numerator is the difference of the cross-product,
$3 \times 5 - 2 \times 7 = 15 - 14 = 1$

Exercise 12g Write answers only

1. $\frac{2}{3} - \frac{1}{4}$ 4. $\frac{2}{3} - \frac{1}{2}$ 7. $\frac{7}{9} - \frac{1}{2}$ 10. $\frac{4}{5} - \frac{2}{3}$

2. $\frac{1}{2} - \frac{2}{5}$ 5. $\frac{1}{2} - \frac{3}{7}$ 8. $\frac{2}{3} - \frac{1}{8}$ 11. $\frac{3}{4} - \frac{1}{3}$

3. $\frac{3}{4} - \frac{2}{3}$ 6. $\frac{1}{3} - \frac{1}{5}$ 9. $\frac{4}{5} - \frac{1}{2}$ 12. $\frac{3}{5} - \frac{1}{2}$

13. $\frac{2}{3} - \frac{3}{8}$ 16. $\frac{6}{7} - \frac{2}{5}$ 19. $\frac{2}{9} - \frac{1}{8}$ 22. $\frac{3}{4} - \frac{2}{5}$

14. $\frac{1}{2} - \frac{1}{3}$ 17. $\frac{5}{9} - \frac{1}{2}$ 20. $\frac{6}{7} - \frac{1}{2}$ 23. $\frac{4}{5} - \frac{1}{3}$

15. $\frac{5}{6} - \frac{1}{5}$ 18. $\frac{6}{11} - \frac{3}{7}$ 21. $\frac{1}{5} - \frac{1}{7}$ 24. $\frac{3}{8} - \frac{2}{9}$

***Vertically and Crosswise* with non-coprime denominators**

When the denominators are not coprime we reduce the denominators as for addition. The next example shows how this works.

$$\frac{5}{12} - \frac{3}{8}$$

$$\frac{5}{12} - \frac{3}{8} = \frac{1}{24}$$
$$4 \quad 3 \quad 2$$

Are the denominators coprime? No!
The HCF of the denominators is 4 which is put down below and to the left
4 into 12 is 3 and 4 into 8 is 2. The 12 and 8 are crossed out and the 3 and 2 are placed below them. The denominator of the answer is $4 \times 3 \times 2 = 24$. The difference of the cross-product gives the numerator, that is, $(5 \times 2) - (3 \times 3) = 1$

117

Exercise 12h

1. $\frac{5}{6} - \frac{3}{4}$ 4. $\frac{1}{6} - \frac{1}{8}$ 7. $\frac{8}{9} - \frac{5}{6}$ 10. $\frac{9}{10} - \frac{3}{4}$

2. $\frac{1}{4} - \frac{1}{6}$ 5. $\frac{7}{10} - \frac{1}{4}$ 8. $\frac{4}{9} - \frac{1}{6}$ 11. $\frac{13}{15} - \frac{3}{10}$

3. $\frac{3}{4} - \frac{1}{6}$ 6. $\frac{5}{8} - \frac{1}{12}$ 9. $\frac{5}{6} - \frac{3}{10}$ 12. $\frac{7}{8} - \frac{5}{12}$

13. $\frac{3}{10} - \frac{1}{4}$ 16. $\frac{5}{9} - \frac{1}{6}$ 19. $\frac{5}{8} - \frac{7}{12}$ 22. $\frac{5}{8} - \frac{1}{14}$

14. $\frac{3}{8} - \frac{1}{12}$ 17. $\frac{5}{6} - \frac{1}{10}$ 20. $\frac{5}{6} - \frac{2}{9}$ 23. $\frac{2}{9} - \frac{1}{12}$

15. $\frac{5}{12} - \frac{1}{9}$ 18. $\frac{5}{6} - \frac{3}{4}$ 21. $\frac{5}{12} - \frac{3}{8}$ 24. $\frac{5}{12} - \frac{2}{15}$

Summary

There are four types of additions (or subtractions) in fractions which differ according to the denominators. These are shown in the examples below.

1 $\frac{2}{5} + \frac{1}{5} = \frac{3}{5}$ The denominators are the same.

2 $\frac{2}{3} + \frac{4}{9} = \frac{6 + 4}{9}$ One denominator is a factor of the other.

$= 1\frac{1}{9}$

3 $\frac{2}{5} + \frac{3}{7} = \frac{29}{35}$ The denominators are coprime - *Vertically and Crosswise*

4 $\frac{3}{4} + \frac{5}{22} = \frac{43}{44}$ The denominators are not coprime - *Vertically*
   $\quad 2 \quad 2 \quad 11$ *and Crosswise* and reduction of denominators

Exercise 12i Before answering each question inspect the denominators to see which method to use.

1. $\frac{5}{16} + \frac{9}{16}$ 5. $\frac{2}{7} + \frac{3}{14}$ 9. $\frac{7}{10} - \frac{13}{40}$ 13. $\frac{5}{8} - \frac{1}{12}$

2. $\frac{3}{5} - \frac{3}{10}$ 6. $\frac{15}{16} - \frac{3}{4}$ 10. $\frac{5}{18} + \frac{3}{10}$ 14. $\frac{7}{10} - \frac{4}{15}$

3. $\frac{3}{4} + \frac{3}{4}$ 7. $\frac{2}{5} + \frac{5}{6}$ 11. $\frac{5}{6} + \frac{3}{8}$ 15. $\frac{1}{8} + \frac{1}{11}$

4. $\frac{19}{20} - \frac{7}{20}$ 8. $\frac{1}{12} + \frac{3}{32}$ 12. $\frac{7}{8} - \frac{2}{9}$ 16. $\frac{3}{4} + \frac{3}{10}$

Practice with mixed numbers

When a sum has mixed numbers always work out the whole number part first and then proceed with the fractional part.

$$4\frac{5}{6} - 1\frac{1}{8}$$

$4 - 1 = 3$
Are the denominators coprime? No! HCF = 2.
2 into 6 = 3, 2 into 8 = 4.
Denominator, $2 \times 3 \times 4 = 24$
Numerator, $(5 \times 4) - (1 \times 3) = 17$

$$= 3\frac{5}{6} - \frac{1}{8}$$
$$\quad 2 \quad 3 \quad 4$$

$$= 3\frac{17}{24}$$

Exercise 12j Remember to inspect the denominators first.

1. $1\frac{1}{2} + 1\frac{1}{2}$ 6. $6\frac{1}{3} + 2\frac{7}{12}$ 11. $1\frac{11}{16} + 2\frac{3}{8}$ 16. $3\frac{3}{4} + 2\frac{5}{16}$

2. $1\frac{1}{5} + 1\frac{3}{5}$ 7. $3\frac{1}{2} + 7\frac{5}{6}$ 12. $9\frac{5}{8} - 2\frac{1}{3}$ 17. $5\frac{9}{16} - 4\frac{1}{2}$

3. $1\frac{1}{2} + 4\frac{3}{4}$ 8. $4\frac{1}{8} + 9\frac{3}{16}$ 13. $2\frac{5}{8} + 4\frac{3}{8}$ 18. $4\frac{3}{4} - 3\frac{1}{6}$

4. $2\frac{3}{4} - 1\frac{3}{4}$ 9. $5\frac{3}{16} - 2\frac{1}{4}$ 14. $3\frac{7}{8} + 2\frac{5}{16}$ 19. $6\frac{9}{10} - 5\frac{4}{5}$

5. $1\frac{5}{12} + 2\frac{5}{12}$ 10. $6\frac{5}{6} + 7\frac{2}{3}$ 15. $4\frac{1}{2} - 1\frac{1}{12}$ 20. $3\frac{2}{3} + 4\frac{1}{4}$

119

Exercise 12k Problems

1. Subtract $2\frac{2}{5}$ from $7\frac{3}{4}$

2. Find the sum of $5\frac{2}{7}$ and $6\frac{3}{14}$

3. Add together $5\frac{7}{10}$ metres and $2\frac{1}{2}$ metres.

4. John walks to a village which is $12\frac{3}{4}$ miles away. How far has he left to travel after walking $7\frac{2}{5}$ miles?

5. A builder has $2\frac{1}{4}$ tons of concrete delivered on Monday, $3\frac{3}{5}$ tons delivered on Tuesday and $4\frac{3}{10}$ tons on Wednesday. How much concrete does he receive altogether?

6. A carpenter has to glue two pieces of wood together. One piece is $2\frac{5}{12}$ inches wide and the other has a width of $3\frac{3}{8}$ inches. What is the width of the two pieces when stuck together?

7. Anna lives $4\frac{1}{3}$ km from school and Lucy lives $5\frac{4}{5}$ km from school. How much further from the school does Lucy live than Anna?

8. A rectangular room at the library is $4\frac{1}{5}$ m wide and $5\frac{1}{4}$ m long. Find the total length of all four walls.

9. Three-eighths of a local park is laid out in flower beds and lawns whilst $\frac{2}{5}$ is set aside for games. What fraction of the park is set aside for other purposes?

10. Christopher was given $\frac{1}{6}$ of a fruit cake whilst Sophie and George each received one-third. What fraction of the cake was given to these children?

11. In making a cake, $1\frac{2}{5}$ kg of flour is added to $\frac{7}{8}$ kg of dried fruit. What is the total mass of the mixture?

12. One can holds $1\frac{3}{4}$ litres of petrol and another holds $7\frac{9}{10}$ litres. How much more does the larger can hold than the smaller one?

Chapter 13 - Decimal Fractions

Place Value

There are four distinct features about our number system:

1 There are only nine numbers, all others are just repetitions of these nine.
2 A nought is used to mean that there is nothing there.
3 We use a decimal point to distinguish between whole numbers and parts of a whole.
4 We use a place value system in which places to the left are ten times as big as those to the right.

In our number system the positioning of numbers is used to indicate their value. This is called place value. For instance, if 2 is written to the left of another number, such as 25, it means two tens and not two units. Without place value calculations would be extremely difficult. The principle of place value is that the place immediately to the left of any given place is ten times as large. Conversely, a position to the right is ten times as small, or one tenth of the value to the left.

There is an instrument called an abacus which was used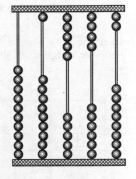
by the ancient Romans for performing calculations.
The Romans did not have our number system and so
mental calculations were very difficult. An abacus
consists of series of rods with ten beads on each rod.
Beads are moved up the rods to represent numbers.
The right-hand most rod is used for units and the next
rod to the left is used for tens. The number shown on
the abacus on the right is 1542.

In counting from one to nine the beads in the units rod
are moved up one by one. The step from nine to ten is
important. All the nine beads on the units rod are set to
nought and one bead appears on the tens rod. In this
move from nine to ten all the nine beads move into the
unmanifest; they disappear. This disappearance is represented by 0, the unmanifest, together with the one at ten. This is the stage of Self realisation.

> *The ultimate or the Absolute is one and with the start of creation it*
> *unfolds itself in nine states and there it ends. In this nine-stage*
> *creation, we see all the manifestation. When all the stages of the*
> *creation have seen their fulfilment, it once again unites in the same*
> *Absolute.*
>
> [Sri Sankaracarya Santananda Sarasvati]

Instead of having the units column as the right-hand most column we may have it somewhere in the middle. Fractions may then be included. The column to the right of the units column is for tenths, the column to the right of this is for hundredths, and so on.

Thousands	Hundreds	Tens	Units	.	tenths	hundredths	thousandths
TH	H	T	U	.	t	h	th

Decimal Point

The decimal point is used to distinguish between whole numbers and parts of a whole. For example, 0.1 is one-tenth part of one, 0.01 is a one-hundredth part of one and 0.001 is one-thousandth part of one. Again, 32.4 is three tens, two units and four tenths.

All calculations with decimal fractions are done in the same way as with whole numbers.

When reading decimal numbers never use words that are used for tens, hundreds, etc, but only the words for the individual numbers. For example, 3.78 is read as *Three point seven eight* and not as *Three point seventy-eight*.

Exercise 13a Make a copy of the table below and complete it by writing the numbers with the digits in the correct columns. The first one has been done for you.

		TH	H	T	U	.	t	h	th	t.th
	134.062		1	3	4	.	0	6	2	
1.	2.6									
2.	32.1									
3.	4556.03									
4.	0.09									
5.	7101.3									
6.	4.0017									
7.	8732.046									
8.	129.0013									
9.	670.005									
10.	0.0092									

Addition and subtraction of decimals

When adding or subtracting decimal numbers keep the decimal points in a vertical line.

Add together 2.34, 673.37 and 34.8.	$\begin{array}{r} 2\ .34 \\ 673\ .37 \\ +\ 34\ .8 \\ \hline 710\ .51 \end{array}$

Exercise 13b Adding and subtracting

1. 3.86 + 2.31
2. 5.7 + 4.91
3. 62.4 + 2.8
4. 75.8 + 32.1
5. 4.78 + 6.8
6. 3.75 + 7.2
7. 87.1 + 5.67
8. 98.2 + 0.75
9. 23.48 + 7.33
10. 34.234 + 7.89

11. 7.64 – 4.31
12. 65.5 – 32.5
13. 76.88 – 23.7
14. 8.98 – 4.73
15. 18.43 – 9.69
16. 23.42 – 8.7
17. 14.6 – 9.87
18. 28.00 – 3.95
19. 27.7 – 1.48
20. 28.4 – 4.635

21. 19.1 + 3.725
22. 0.47+ 4.9
23. 43.65 – 1.9
24. 65 – 6.5
25. 6.5 – 0.65
26. 3.4651 + 34.77
27. 1.0 – 0.87634
28. 56 – 8.97
29. 82.115 + 9.98
30. 104.7 – 67.48

Exercise 13c Problems with money

1. £0.78 + £0.65
2. £1.83 +£6.96
3. £354.75 + £42.68
4. £1.92 – £0.67
5. £100.00 – £56.45
6. £865.40 – £139.53
7. £85.74 + £28.99
8. £56.21 – £28.35
9. £43.65 – £1.90

10. Add together £3.67, £7.45 and £1.55

11. Subtract £4.98 from £12.50

12. Find the sum of £2.36, £5.55, £9.31 and £5.67

13. What is £16.80 minus £7.93?

123

14. Decrease £20.00 by £13.78

15. A man paid £26.99 for a radio. How much change should he receive from £30.00?

16. Alison received two gifts worth £2.95 and £6.75. How much are they worth together?

17. A table, together with a set of chairs, cost £356.95. If the cost of the chairs is £155.45, what is the cost of the table?

18. By investing £254.55 in a savings account a man makes £20.79 interest at the end of the year. How much will he have altogether?

19. A girl buys two books, one for £15.99 and the other for £6.99. How much does she spend?

20. A boy goes into a shop with £24.25 in order to buy paints, brushes and paper. He spends £14.85 on some paints and £2.46 on brushes. How much does he have left to spend on paper?

Exercise 13d Further addition practice. Set each sum out with the decimal points in a vertical line.

1. 32.14 + 98.7	11. 76.35 + 65.209 + 477.65
2. 5.768 + 0.56	12. Add together 3.37, 89.2 and 68.9.
3. 34.5 + 9.556	13. Find the sum of 356.5 and 87.09.
4. 4.05 + 2.1	14. Add 67.8 and 234.89.
5. 54.6 + 0.87	15. Increase 44.503 by 23.77.
6. 6.650 + 12.8	16. Add 1.67, 3.607, 3.555 and 6.753.
7. 85.38 + 9.876	17. Find the sum of 46.112, 7.008 and 87.456.
8. 1.6038 + 0.45	18. Find the total of 3.45, 6.99 and 43.8085.
9. 56.2 + 2.08	19. What is the sum of 55.705, 3.56 and 58.2?
10. 67.3 + 33.7	20. Add together 3.5673, 5.0532, 3.185 and 6.78.

From 38.62 subtract 19.473.

$$
\begin{array}{r}
38\ .620 \\
-\ 19\ .473 \\
\hline
19\ .147
\end{array}
$$

Exercise 13e Further subtraction practice

1. 18.7 − 12.4   5. 421.6 − 48.8   9. 27.35 − 1.8

2. 3.86 − 1.95   6. 5.38 − 2.1   10. 9.3 − 2.67

3. 23.42 − 8.7   7. 9.48 − 5.6   11. 14.3 − 8.627

4. 21.4 − 7.6   8. 6.2 − 2.67   12. 43 − 4.3

13. Take 1.97 from 8.3.   17. What is the difference between 28.7 and 2.87?

14. From 43.45 take 9.5.   18. What must be added to 13.87 to make 50?

15. From 2.9 subtract 0.84.   19. By how much does 1.75 exceed 0.175?

16. Subtract 14.2 from 20.   20. Find the difference between 0.7 and 0.07.

Three types of remainder

When we divide 2 into 1 there are three ways in which to express the remainder. We may say 2 into 1 is 0 remainder 1, 2 into 1 is 0.5 or 2 into 1 is $\frac{1}{2}$.

The vulgar fraction, $\frac{1}{2}$, is an attempt to divide 1 by 2. It is an incomplete division because, in fact, it is impossible to divide 1. The horizontal line used for fractions comes from the division sign, ÷, the two numbers standing in place of the dots.

In decimal arithmetic, the 0.5 also arises from trying to divide 2 into 1. The process is to call the one 10 and divide it by 2 to give 5. The decimal point signifies that the 5 is five tenths and not five units.

From the place value system it follows that,

0.1	= $\frac{1}{10}$	one tenth		0.2	= $\frac{2}{10}$	= $\frac{1}{5}$
0.01	= $\frac{1}{100}$	one hundredth		0.5	= $\frac{5}{10}$	= $\frac{1}{2}$
0.001	= $\frac{1}{1000}$	one thousandth		0.25	= $\frac{25}{100}$	= $\frac{1}{4}$
0.0001	= $\frac{1}{10000}$	one ten thousandth				

Converting decimal fractions into vulgar fractions

We can convert a decimal fraction into a vulgar fraction using a sutra which simply says, *Only by the last digit*.

125

Suppose we wish to convert 0.45 into a vulgar fraction. To find the denominator of the vulgar fraction inspect only the last digit to see which place value it has.

$$0.45 = \frac{45}{100} = \frac{9}{20}$$

The 5 of 0.45 is in the hundredths column and so 100 is the denominator. The numerator is 45 and we can then cancel to lowest terms as necessary.

Exercise 13f Write the following numbers as vulgar fractions and then reduce to lowest terms. Some are mixed numbers.

1. 0.2	**8.** 2.01	**15.** 0.205	**22.** 0.06
2. 1.25	**9.** 1.8	**16.** 0.0029	**23.** 0.36
3. 1.3	**10.** 1.7	**17.** 0.0041	**24.** 0.72
4. 0.007	**11.** 15.5	**18.** 0.17	**25.** 2.125
5. 0.0001	**12.** 8.06	**19.** 0.071	**26.** 0.15
6. 6.4	**13.** 0.73	**20.** 0.35	**27.** 0.025
7. 0.7	**14.** 0.081	**21.** 0.63	**28.** 3.85

Converting vulgar fractions into decimal fractions

To convert a vulgar fraction into a decimal fraction is very simple as long as the denominator is 10, 100, 1000, etc. We use the same sutra, *Only the last digit*.

Convert $\frac{57}{1000}$ into a decimal fraction.

$$\frac{57}{1000} = 0.057$$

The denominator is 1000. This tells us that the last digit of the numerator, 57, must be in the thousandths column. The 5 is placed to the left and any noughts required are also put in place.

Exercise 13g Write the following vulgar fractions as decimal fractions:

1. $\frac{1}{10}$	**7.** $\frac{10}{100}$	**13.** $\frac{13}{1000}$	**19.** $3\frac{82}{100}$
2. $\frac{3}{10}$	**8.** $\frac{11}{100}$	**14.** $\frac{55}{1000}$	**20.** $6\frac{44}{100}$
3. $\frac{9}{10}$	**9.** $\frac{20}{100}$	**15.** $\frac{542}{1000}$	**21.** $7\frac{8}{100}$
4. $\frac{1}{100}$	**10.** $\frac{67}{100}$	**16.** $\frac{12}{10}$	**22.** $\frac{61}{10}$
5. $\frac{5}{100}$	**11.** $\frac{1}{1000}$	**17.** $\frac{26}{10}$	**23.** $\frac{61}{100}$
6. $\frac{9}{100}$	**12.** $\frac{9}{1000}$	**18.** $2\frac{45}{100}$	**24.** $\frac{61}{1000}$

When the denominator of the vulgar fraction is a factor or multiple of 10, 100, 1000, etc, then we multiply both the numerator and denominator until the denominator is 10, 100, 1000, etc. The sutra for this is *Proportionately*.

Convert $\frac{9}{20}$ into a decimal fraction.

$$\frac{9}{20} = \frac{9 \times 5}{20 \times 5} = \frac{45}{100} = 0.45$$

$$\frac{9}{20} = \frac{9 \div 2}{20 \div 2} = \frac{4.5}{10} = 0.45$$

On inspection we see that 20 is a factor of 100 and 20 into 100 is 5. We therefore multiply the top and bottom of the fraction by 5.

Alternatively, we could use the fact that 20 is twice 10 and therefore divide both top and bottom by 2.

Exercise 13h Use *Proportionately* to convert the following into decimal fractions:

1. $\frac{4}{5}$	**7.** $\frac{6}{20}$	**13.** $\frac{13}{50}$	**19.** $3\frac{82}{50}$
2. $\frac{3}{25}$	**8.** $\frac{11}{50}$	**14.** $\frac{36}{40}$	**20.** $6\frac{42}{70}$
3. $\frac{9}{30}$	**9.** $\frac{24}{200}$	**15.** $\frac{42}{250}$	**21.** $7\frac{9}{300}$
4. $\frac{32}{50}$	**10.** $\frac{1}{25}$	**16.** $\frac{3}{20}$	**22.** $\frac{161}{250}$
5. $\frac{2}{5}$	**11.** $\frac{12}{15}$	**17.** $\frac{1}{250}$	**23.** $\frac{21}{50}$
6. $\frac{16}{40}$	**12.** $\frac{9}{25}$	**18.** $2\frac{45}{50}$	**24.** $\frac{6}{125}$

Chapter 14 - Perimeters and Areas

Perimeters

The word *perimeter* means *to measure round* and so the perimeter of any plane shape is the distance round it. The perimeter is then the total length of the boundary of a shape.

The perimeter of a rectangle is twice the sum of the length and the the width. This follows from the fact that the opposite sides of a rectangle are equal in length. If the length is called the base and the width is called the height, then we have the formula,

$$\text{Perimeter} = 2 \times (\text{base} + \text{height})$$

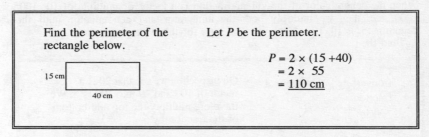

Find the perimeter of the rectangle below.

15 cm / 40 cm

Let P be the perimeter.

$P = 2 \times (15 + 40)$
$= 2 \times 55$
$= \underline{110 \text{ cm}}$

Exercise 14a Find the perimeter of these rectangles. Remember to give the units.

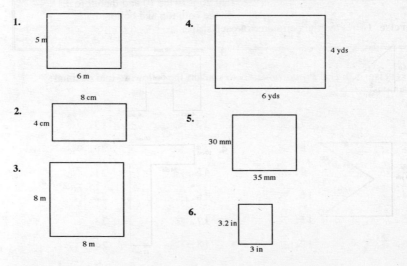

1. 5 m / 6 m

2. 4 cm / 8 cm

3. 8 m / 8 m

4. 4 yds / 6 yds

5. 30 mm / 35 mm

6. 3.2 in / 3 in

7.

8.

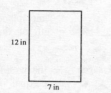

9.

10.

We can find the perimeters of other shapes just by adding up the individual lengths.

Find the perimeter.

Let P be the perimeter.

$$P = 9 + 6 + 6 + 4 + 4 + 4.5$$
$$= \underline{33.5 \text{ m}}$$

Exercise 14b Find the perimeter of each shape.

1.

3.

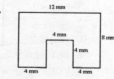

2.

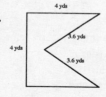

4.

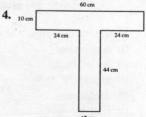

5. Measurements are in cm

8. A regular hexagon

6.4 in

6. An equilateral triangle

8.2 mm

9. A regular pentagon

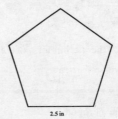

2.5 in

7. An isosceles triangle

6 cm

4 cm

10.

4 cm

6 cm

British Measures of Length

12 inches (in)	make	1 foot (ft)
3 feet	....	1 yard (yd)
22 yards	....	1 chain
10 chains	....	1 furlong
8 furlongs	....	1 mile
or 1760 yards		

Metric Measures of Length

10 millimetres (mm.)	make	1 centimetre (cm.)
10 centimetres	....	1 decimetre (dm.)
10 decimetres	....	1 METRE (m.)
10 metres	....	1 decametre (dam.)
10 decametres	....	1 hectometre (hm.)
10 hectometres	....	1 kilometre (km.)

Exercise 14c Problems

1. A rectangle measures 4 inches by 12 inches. What is its perimeter?

2. Find the distance round a house which is 52 ft long and 24 ft wide.

3. Find the width of a rectangular pond with perimeter 210 m.and length 64 m.

4. Two sides of an isosceles triangle are each 4.5 cm. If the perimeter is 22 cm, find the length of the third side.

5. What is the perimeter of a square with side length 4.8 cm?

6. A table is 3 ft 6 in wide and 6 ft long. What is its perimeter?

7. The perimeter of a gymnasium is 140 yds and it is 28 yds wide. How long is it?

8. Skirting board costs £3.55 per metre. How much will it cost to buy sufficient for a room which is 5 m long and 3 m wide?

9. In a race on a 400 m track a girl runs at an average speed of 8 m per second. How long will it take her to run three and three-quarter laps?

10. A garden consists of a rectangular lawn completely surrounded by flower beds. The total width of the garden is 60 ft and its length is 100 ft. If the flower beds are all 8 ft wide, find the perimeter of the lawn.

11. How many hurdles each 1.8 m long will be required to make a sheep fold 7.2 m long and 5.4 m wide?

12. Find, in feet, the perimeter of a strip of land 22 yds wide and 220 yds long. (This was the size of a piece of land used for strip farming in medieval times and is equal to one acre).

13. A piece of paper measures 16 cm by 30 cm. (a) What is its perimeter, (b) Find the perimeter when it is folded in half lengthways, and (c) Find the perimeter when it is folded the other way.

14. A farmer has a field which has six sides. He finds he needs 620 m of fencing to fence the field completely. The first four sides take 125 m 50 cm, 64 m 70 cm, 78 m 60 cm and 123 m 80 cm. The last two sides are of equal length. How much fencing is needed for one of these sides?

15. I make a journey by car from A to F, calling at B, C, D and E on the way. The first distance is 8.6 km, the second is twice that and the remaining ones are of equal length, and are each a half of my first journey. What is the total distance from A to F in km.

131

Area

Area is a measure of any surface.

What is a surface? A surface is the boundary of any form. For the purposes of measuring surfaces we will only consider flat or plane surfaces.

We ordinarily think of surfaces as a limit to space. Thus we say, for example, that the space of a room is limited by its walls. In fact space is not limited by walls or any other boundary. It pervades everything. It was there before any room was built and will be there long after the walls are knocked down. Such forms as rooms occupy the space while they exist.

A surface exists where one substance meets another. For example, on a table, where the wood meets the air is a surface.

To measure a plane surface requires the use of a unit. The most convenient unit to use is square in shape. The unit must also be of such a size that it is suitable for the task in hand. For example, it would be somewhat tiresome to have to measure the size of a football pitch in square millimetres. Square metres would be much more suitable.

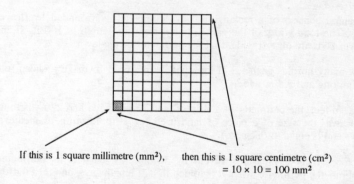

If this is 1 square millimetre (mm²),   then this is 1 square centimetre (cm²)
                                         = 10 × 10 = 100 mm²

The most common units for area in the metric system given below:-

100	square millimetres (mm²)	make	1 square centimetre (cm²)
10,000	square centimetres (cm²)	....	1 square metre (m²)
1,000,000	square metres (m²)	....	1 square kilometre (km²)
10,000	square metres (m²)	....	1 hectare

In the British system the common measures are square inches, square feet, square yards, acres and square miles. The table below shows how many of each unit is in the next one.

114	sq. inches	make	1 sq. foot (sq.ft.)
9	sq. feet	....	1 sq. yard (sq.yd.)
484	sq. yards	....	1 sq. chain
10	sq. chains	....	1 acre
640	acres	....	1 sq. mile
Also, 4840	sq. yards	make	1 acre

Areas of rectangles

The area of any rectangle may be found by multiplying the length by the breadth. If the length is called the base and the breadth is called the height then the area is given by the formula,

$$\text{Area} = \text{base} \times \text{height}$$

This is an application of *Vertically and Crosswise*.

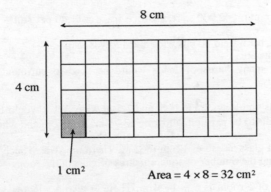

8 cm

4 cm

1 cm²   Area = 4 × 8 = 32 cm²

Exercise 14d Find the areas of the rectangles given in Exercise 14a. Remember to give the units.

Exercise 14e Problems

1. A rectangular room is 4 metres long and 3 metres wide. What is its area?

2. Find the area of a blackboard 2 m high and 4 m long.

3. Find the area of the cover of a book measuring 18 cm by 24 cm.

4. What is the area of the top of a desk measuring 42 inches by 31 inches?

5. A man measures his garden and finds that it is 70 ft long and 25 ft wide. What is its area?

6. A rectangle has an area of 55 cm². If it is 5 cm wide, how long is it?

7. If a rugby pitch is to be 60 m wide and 100 m long, what is the minimum area of land required for two such pitches?

8. A section of wall measuring 8 ft by 4 ft is to be covered with ceramic tiles each 6 in square. How many tiles are required?

9. A man's back garden is a quarter of an acre. How many square yards is this?

10. How many square feet are there in one acre?

11. Find the rent on 42,000 sq ft of office space at £1.40 per sq.ft.

12. A farmer has a field 80 yds wide and 120 yds long.
(a) Find its area
(b) How many yards of fence would he need to surround the field completely?

13. A room is 4 m long, 2.5 m high and 2.5 m wide. What would be the area of the walls to be papered, allowing 13.75 m² for doors and windows?

14. A pane of glass measures 1.5 m by 2 m. There are twelve such panes in a room. Find the number of square metres of glass in the room.

15. The wall of a room is 6 m by 4 m. There is also a window set into the wall which measures 1.2 m by 2 m. Find the remaining area of the wall.

16. My car is 3.3 m long and 1.5 m wide. My garage measures 5.4 m by 2.4 m. What area of garage floor is not covered when the car is in the garage?

17. Find the length of a field of area 8 hectares and width 200 m.

18. The total distance round a square piece of cardboard is 220 cm. Find the length of one of the four sides. Find the area of the cardboard giving your answers in cm^2.

19. A rectangular field is 350 m long and 200 m broad. What is its area in hectares?

20. A square field has a perimeter of half a mile. What is its area in acres?

21. A housing estate covers an area of 4 square miles. How many acres is this?

22. A rectangular lawn 60 ft long and 50 ft wide is surrounded by a paved footpath 2 ft wide. How many square paving stones, each side of which measures a foot, would be required to cover the path?

Compound areas

Problems in compound areas arise when the area of a certain shape may only be found by considering the areas of shapes which go to make up the total shape. The sutra for these problems is *By Addition or* Subtraction.

The next example shows how to find the area of a compound shape.

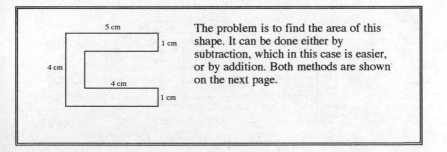

The problem is to find the area of this shape. It can be done either by subtraction, which in this case is easier, or by addition. Both methods are shown on the next page.

To find the easiest way of answering each problem the nature of the shape and the numbers involved in the calculation must first be inspected. Both of these aspects will determine the best approach.

---

* This sutra is usually translated as By Addition *and* Subtraction but these sutras are flexible in this respect and here the word *or* is more applicable.

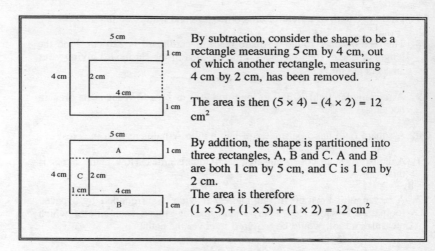

By subtraction, consider the shape to be a rectangle measuring 5 cm by 4 cm, out of which another rectangle, measuring 4 cm by 2 cm, has been removed.

The area is then $(5 \times 4) - (4 \times 2) = 12$ cm^2

By addition, the shape is partitioned into three rectangles, A, B and C. A and B are both 1 cm by 5 cm, and C is 1 cm by 2 cm.
The area is therefore
$(1 \times 5) + (1 \times 5) + (1 \times 2) = 12$ cm^2

Exercise 14f Find the areas of these shapes.

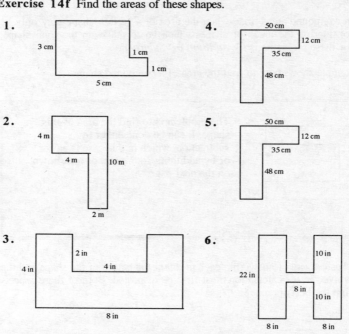

7.

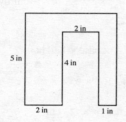

8.

9.

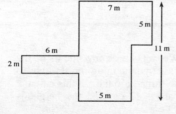

10.

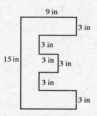

11. A rectangular piece of card has four corners removed, each measuring 2 in by 2 in.

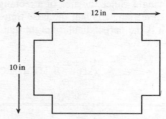

12. The shaded rectangle is 11 cm by 16 cm. Find the area of the border.

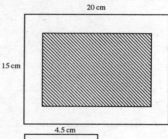

13.

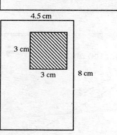

14. Each step is 8 in by 8 in

137

Areas of triangles

In section 9 of chapter 18 there is a construction to show that any triangle is half a rectangle. Since the area of a rectangle is base times height, it follows that the area of a triangle is half the base times the height. We should always remember that it is the perpendicular height that is meant.

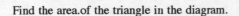

$$\text{Area of triangle} = \frac{1}{2} \times \text{base} \times \text{height}$$

Find the area.of the triangle in the diagram.

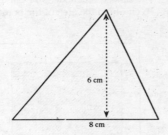

6 cm

8 cm

$$\text{Area} = \frac{1}{2} \times \text{base} \times \text{height}$$

$$= \frac{1}{2} \times 8 \times 6$$

$$= 4 \times 6 = \underline{24 \text{ cm}^2}$$

Find the area

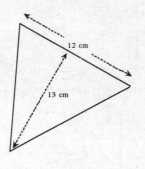

12 cm

13 cm

We can choose any side to be the base by imagining the triangle to be turned around. In this case the base is 12 cm and the height is 13 cm.

$$\text{Area} = \frac{1}{2} \times \text{base} \times \text{height}$$

$$= \frac{1}{2} \times 12 \times 13$$

$$= 6 \times 13 = \underline{78 \text{ cm}^2}$$

Exercise 14g Find the area of each triangle. You may have to turn the diagrams round to find the right line for the base.

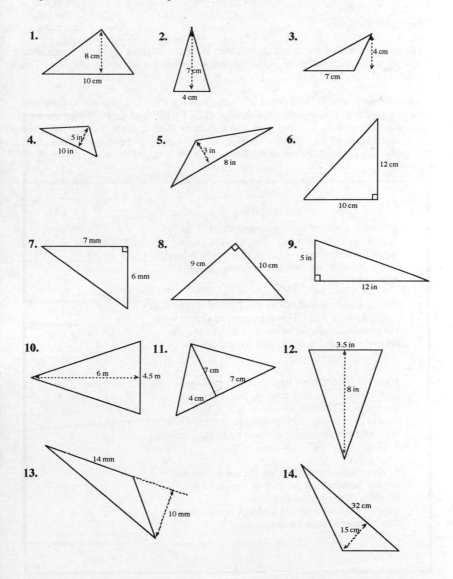

1.
8 cm
10 cm

2.
7 cm
4 cm

3.
4 cm
7 cm

4.
5 in
10 in

5.
3 in
8 in

6.
12 cm
10 cm

7.
7 mm
6 mm

8.
9 cm
10 cm

9.
5 in
12 in

10.
6 m
4.5 m

11.
7 cm
7 cm
4 cm

12.
3.5 in
8 in

13.
14 mm
10 mm

14.
32 cm
15 cm

139

Chapter 15 - Straight Division

Straight Division

The general method for dividing numbers is called Straight division. It is called *straight* because it covers all possibilities and the answer comes in one line. The sutra is *On top of the flag*.

When the divisor is written down all its digits, except for the first are hoisted into the flag position. The dividing is then only done by the first digit. With two-digit divisors there will be one flag digit and with three digit divisors there will be two flag digits, and so on. In this chapter we will take up the case of two digit divisors. The example below shows the method for Straight division.

---

337 ÷ 24

The sum is set out as shown with the 4 of 24 placed *On top of the flag*. The number of flag-digits indicates the number of digits which need to be placed after the remainder stroke, in this case one.

$$\begin{array}{c} 4 \\ 2 \quad \big| 3 \ \ 3 \ / \ 7 \end{array}$$

All the dividing is done by the 2 of 24. 2 into 3 is 1 remainder 1 and this is put down as shown with the remainder placed below and just before the second dividend digit, 3. The second dividend number is now 13.

$$\begin{array}{c} 4 \\ 2 \quad \big| 3 \ \ 3 \ / \ 7 \\ \quad \ \ _1 \\ \quad 1 \end{array}$$

From 13 subtract the first quotient digit, 1, multiplied by the flag digit, 4, and divide the answer by 2. This is 13 − (1 × 4) = 9, and 2 into 9 = 4 rem. 1. The 4 is the next quotient digit and the remainder is annexed to the 7 making it 17.

$$\begin{array}{c} 4 \\ 2 \quad \big| 3 \ \ 3 / \ 7 \\ \quad \ \ _1 \ \ _1 \\ \quad 1 \ \ 4 \ / \end{array}$$

In the remainder portion we do not divide but merely subtract the product of the previous quotient digit and the flag digit.
This is 17 − (4 × 4) = 1 and this is the remainder. The answer is then 14 remainder 1.

$$\begin{array}{c} 4 \\ 2 \quad \big| 3 \ \ 3 / \ 7 \\ \quad \ \ _1 \ \ _1 \\ \quad 1 \ \ 4 \ / \ \ 1 \end{array}$$

Exercise 15a

1. 31 | 848   9. 21 | 756   17. 22 | 738   25. 22 | 242

2. 13 | 138   10. 31 | 449   18. 22 | 221   26. 21 | 462

3. 32 | 197   11. 21 | 888   19. 33 | 441   27. 21 | 693

4. 11 | 568   12. 35 | 741   20. 14 | 289   28. 32 | 387

5. 23 | 233   13. 32 | 654   21. 21 | 441   29. 21 | 222

6. 21 | 685   14. 21 | 247   22. 31 | 341   30. 30 | 900

7. 12 | 145   15. 11 | 794   23. 31 | 651   31. 63 | 458

8. 21 | 423   16. 31 | 119   24. 41 | 451   32. 81 | 849

We can extend the Straight division method to dividends with a larger number of digits. With two-digit divisors the remainder stroke must be placed so that there is one digit after it in the dividend. The remainder may have more than one digit. The next example has two digits in the divisor and four digits in the dividend.

9774 ÷ 78

The remainder stroke placed so that the number of digits to the right of it is the same as the number of flag digits.

$$
\begin{array}{c}
\ \ \ 8 \\
7\ |9\ 7\ 7/\ 4
\end{array}
$$

7 into 9 = 1 remainder 2.

27 − (1 × 8) = 19, 7 into 19 = 2 rem. 5.

57 − (2 × 8) = 41, 7 into 41 = 5 rem. 6.

64 − (5 × 8) = 24.

The answer is 125 remainder 24.

$$
\begin{array}{c}
\ \ \ 8 \\
7\ |9\ 7\ 7/\ 4 \\
\ \ 2\ 5\ \ \ 6 \\
\hline
1\ 2\ 5/\ 2\ 4
\end{array}
$$

Exercise 15b

1. 25 ⌐5576	9. 63 ⌐3475	17. 67 ⌐6785	25. 35 ⌐1087
2. 32 ⌐4911	10. 85 ⌐9897	18. 83 ⌐9336	26. 55 ⌐1289
3. 41 ⌐1232	11. 22 ⌐5065	19. 61 ⌐9685	27. 43 ⌐5187
4. 45 ⌐6048	12. 11 ⌐4976	20. 64 ⌐8466	28. 12 ⌐2893
5. 54 ⌐7347	13. 55 ⌐1778	21. 72 ⌐2924	29. 22 ⌐3314
6. 33 ⌐4984	14. 42 ⌐4728	22. 41 ⌐1670	30. 32 ⌐9801
7. 31 ⌐4495	15. 73 ⌐9680	23. 32 ⌐1390	31. 54 ⌐1668
8. 52 ⌐2992	16. 43 ⌐4841	24. 44 ⌐1381	32. 73 ⌐9070

Exercise 15c Five-digit dividends

1. 21 ⌐89530	6. 32 ⌐81035	11. 53 ⌐59266	16. 69 ⌐85700
2. 31 ⌐87305	7. 52 ⌐81800	12. 62 ⌐85295	17. 79 ⌐96001
3. 33 ⌐80628	8. 41 ⌐89523	13. 83 ⌐97662	18. 76 ⌐86369
4. 43 ⌐96583	9. 54 ⌐66692	14. 66 ⌐95786	19. 61 ⌐72688
5. 25 ⌐53079	10. 21 ⌐74474	15. 71 ⌐93875	20. 75 ⌐91681

Exercise 15d Problems

1. King Amirkabul wishes to divide his 27469 acres of land equally amongst his thirteen sons. How much land will each son receive?

2. What is 1305 divided by 87?

3. Divide 34632 by 52.

4. How many thirty-fours are there in six thousand nine hundred and thirty-six?

142

5. If a coach holds 53 children, how many coaches will be needed to take 636 children on a school outing?

6. How many times can 24 be taken away from 5520?

7. A book is 23 mm thick, excluding the cover. If it has 483 pages, how many pages are there per mm?

8. How many 64p pens can be purchased for £11.60?

9. 4590 plums are put into boxes each containing 85. How many boxes of plums are there?

10. A decorator wishes to lay cork tiles onto a kitchen floor which is 434 cm long. If the tiles are 31 cm long, how many would be needed along the length of the floor?

11. A landscape gardener sows a single row of wall flowers each 14 inches apart. If the flower bed is 24 feet 6 inches long, how many wall flowers does he plant?

12. An engineer requires 1444 bolts for a certain task. If the bolts come in boxes of 32, how many boxes will he need?

13. Tulip bulbs are sold in packets of 24. Simon needs 338 bulbs. How many packets must he buy and how many bulbs are are left unused?

14. What is the remainder when 5530 is divided by 23?

15. How many pieces of wire, each 31 cm long, can be cut from a roll 100 m in length and what will be the remainder?

16. A bricklayer receives £924 for building a wall which took him 42 hours to complete. How much per hour did he earn

17. In one year a hotel made £702,513 from its 63 rooms. How much did it make, on average for each room?

18. The area of a certain field is 5356 m². If its width is 52 m, find the length.

19. In one year a tree plantation of 6696 acres has 93 diseased trees which have to be cut down and burnt. On average, how many acres are there for one diseased tree?

20. A sweet factory can produce 84,525 chocolates in a week. Given that the factory is working for fifteen hours a day for five days a week, how many chocolates per hour does it produce?

Altered Remainders

To the question "how many two's are there in nine?" the answer comes as 4 remainder 1. But this is not the only answer. We could also say that 2 into 9 goes 3 remainder 3 or 2 remainder 5. The chart below shows various possibilities.

$$2 \text{ into } 9 = 4 \text{ r } 1$$
$$= 3 \text{ r } 3$$
$$= 2 \text{ r } 5$$
$$= 1 \text{ r } 7$$
$$= 0 \text{ r } 9$$

In fact , we can take this further in both directions by using vinculum numbers.

2 into 9 = 7 r $\bar{5}$	Also 2 into 9 = 2 r 5
= 6 r $\bar{3}$	= 1 r 7
= 5 r $\bar{1}$	= 0 r 9
= 4 r 1	= $\bar{1}$ r 11
= 3 r 3	= $\bar{2}$ r 13, etc.

By extending this chart both upwards and downwards we can see that there is no limit to the number of possible answers. There are an infinite number of answers all of which are valid. The answer we usually give is the conventional one and is useful for most purposes but there are occasions when an altered remainder is required for Straight division.

Give the answer together with the next three altered remainders for 31 ÷ 3

3)31 = 10 r 1
= 9 r 4
= 8 r 7 ·
= 7 r 10

3 into 31 = 10 remainder 1

By repeatedly subtracting 1 from the quotient, 10, we find the next quotients, 9, 8 and 7.
With each subtraction of 1 we add the divisor 3 to the remainder, that is,
1 + 3 = 4, 4 + 3 = 7 and 7 + 3 = 10.

Exercise 15e Give the answer together with the next three altered remainders.

1. 15 ÷ 2	**5.** 28 ÷ 5	**9.** 47 ÷ 7	**13.** 59 ÷ 6	**17.** 82 ÷ 8
2. 17 ÷ 3	**6.** 23 ÷ 4	**10.** 88 ÷ 9	**14.** 43 ÷ 6	**18.** 71 ÷ 9
3. 21 ÷ 2	**7.** 39 ÷ 6	**11.** 45 ÷ 8	**15.** 81 ÷ 9	**19.** 68 ÷ 7
4. 19 ÷ 3	**8.** 35 ÷ 4	**12.** 36 ÷ 4	**16.** 65 ÷ 8	**20.** 74 ÷ 8

Straight division with altered remainders

To master Straight division there must be practice involving altered remainders. The key is to look ahead at each stage to see whether or not the remainder needs to be altered.

7818 ÷ 22

Before each answer digit is written down with its remainder, the next step of subtraction must be checked. If the subtraction leads to a minus number then an altered remainder is required at the previous step.

$$2$$
$$2 \overline{\smash{)}7\,8\,1\,/\,8}$$
$$\underline{1\,2}$$
$$3\,5$$

2 into 7 = 3 r 1, check 18 - 6, Yes! 18 - 6 = 12

2 into 12 = 6 r 0, check 1 - 12, No!
2 into 12 = 5 r 2, check 21 - 10, Yes! 21 - 10 = 11

$$2$$
$$2 \overline{\smash{)}7\,8\,1\,/\,8}$$
$$\underline{1\,2\ \ 1}$$
$$3\,5\,5\,/\,8$$

2 into 11 = 5 r 1, check 18 - 10, Yes! 18 - 10 = 8
The answer is 355 remainder 8

Exercise 15f

1. 24|3412	9. 42|9621	17. 21|5614	25. 19|371
2. 42|7943	10. 12|2917	18. 22|7818	26. 27|1173
3. 35|5972	11. 33|8218	19. 53|6712	27. 16|864
4. 22|7857	12. 28|3934	20. 28|4622	28. 17|278
5. 33|7858	13. 59|9678	21. 14|252	29. 25|2150
6. 41|9416	14. 15|1816	22. 54|5711	30. 18|4143
7. 35|8856	15. 11|4919	23. 23|1408	31. 29|1864
8. 21|9836	16. 31|8914	24. 32|1876	32. 66|15707

Exercise 15g Problems involving harder division

1. Divide 59,754 by 23
2. How many times does 21 divide into 809,712 and what is the remainder?
3. How many seventeens make 32,385?
4. Find the remainder when 25,791 is divided by 64.
5. The product of two numbers is 5092; one number is 76; find the other.
6. The petrol tank of a certain car holds fourteen gallons of petrol and travels 476 miles on a full tank. How many miles per gallon does it go?
7. How many days would ten thousand potatoes last a family consuming on average 25 daily?
8. What is the number nearest to 4000 which can be divided by 13?
9. In four days a clock loses 2208 seconds. How many seconds does it lose every hour?
10. A mobile telephone company charges calls at 26 p per minute.
    If Mr Quango is charged £35.88 for the calls he has made, for how many minutes did he use the telephone?
11. Elizabeth feeds her pet fish 14 grammes of food every day. How long will a box containing 952 grammes last?
12. An airport car-park can hold 6552 cars and there are 52 cars in each row. How many rows are there?
13. An oil tanker holds 250,040 tons of crude oil in its 28 tanks. How many tons of oil are there in each tank?
14. Alison decides to learn twenty-five new French words every day. How long will it take her to learn 9125 words?
15. A certain computer performs 211,770 operations in 65 seconds. How many operations is this per second?
16. A carnation exporter wishes to send 152,460 carnations in boxes of thirty-six. How many boxes will he require?
17. Find the remainder when 10,000 is divided by 36.
18. Jenifer finds that in making a dish for fifteen people, 3300 grammes of fish are needed. How many grammes does this give for each person?
19. A biologist discovers that for 201,600 spores produced by a fungus, on average 72 will grow into fungi. How many spores are required for one such fungus to grow?
20. A man was paid £82,488 over a two year period. How much is this per month?

Chapter 16 - Practice and Revision 2

Exercise 16a

1. Find the digital roots of, a) 3421, b) 23142, c) 6743821, d) 38576014

Addition and subtraction:

2. 67
    34
    + 82

3. 5434
    234
    + 3581

4. 46574834
    + 23106643

5. 76.23
    12.89
    + 1.32

6. 756
    – 235

7. 3287
    – 1786

8. 476874
    – 213477

9. 7680012
    – 3239987

Vertically and crosswise: check answers using digital roots:

10. 6533
     ×   3

11. 45
     × 23

12. 56
     × 11

13. 534
     × 272

All from nine and the last from ten (below the base and above the base)

14. 98
     × 95

15. 998
     × 997

16. 1002
     × 1005

17. 114
     × 103

Simple division

18. 2) 1764

19. 5) 4785

20. 6) 34253

21. 8) 627014

Division by *All from nine and the last from ten*

22. 98) 12110

23. 89) 21002

24. 989) 112312

25. 878) 11012

Division by *Transpose and adjust*

26. 12) 1468

27. 13) 15759

28. 112) 1344

29. 1013) 122974

Straight division by *On top of the flag*

30. 21) 346

31. 32) 5248

32. 53) 7182

33. 31) 562481

Exercise 16b Which of the following are divisible by the first number:-

1. 2; 6574, 1001, 453232, 7700, 50673
2. 3; 546, 3677, 12121, 222, 1011, 81453
3. 4; 724, 567, 882, 1265734, 768548
4. 5; 5675, 987600, 23410554, 76865456, 87567435
5. 8; 785, 1000, 5642, 79152, 73421210534
6. 9; 637, 33321, 61287409, 7112048571, 678234170234
7. 10; 2500, 450, 453625, 20025, 5060
8. 6; 876, 123, 4584, 37465874, 342612
9. 12; 785, 348, 1428, 87596, 904632876
10. 15; 315, 460, 68775, 1765855, 8088962430

Exercise 16c Remember to inspect the denominators first.

1. $\frac{5}{16} + \frac{3}{16}$
2. $\frac{11}{15} + \frac{8}{15}$
3. $1\frac{2}{3} + 4\frac{2}{3}$
4. $6\frac{4}{5} - 3\frac{1}{5}$
5. $2\frac{5}{12} + 3\frac{11}{12}$

6. $3\frac{1}{4} + 1\frac{5}{12}$
7. $2\frac{1}{2} + 1\frac{3}{8}$
8. $2\frac{1}{8} + 4\frac{9}{16}$
9. $7\frac{3}{4} - 3\frac{7}{16}$
10. $5\frac{1}{6} + \frac{2}{3}$

11. $1\frac{1}{5} + 2\frac{1}{3}$
12. $6\frac{5}{8} - 3\frac{2}{5}$
13. $5\frac{3}{8} + 4\frac{2}{9}$
14. $1\frac{7}{9} + \frac{3}{10}$
15. $4\frac{2}{3} - 1\frac{3}{7}$

16. $1\frac{1}{6} + 2\frac{5}{8}$
17. $6\frac{9}{16} - 2\frac{1}{12}$
18. $4\frac{3}{4} - 3\frac{1}{6}$
19. $6\frac{9}{10} - 2\frac{4}{15}$
20. $5\frac{4}{15} + 8\frac{3}{20}$

Exercise 16d Multiplying and dividing fractions

1. $4 \times \frac{5}{8}$
2. $\frac{2}{3} \times 15$
3. $\frac{5}{6} \times \frac{7}{10}$
4. $\frac{2}{3} \times \frac{9}{16}$
5. $\frac{3}{4} \div \frac{5}{7}$

6. $\frac{4}{5} \div \frac{5}{8}$
7. $2\frac{1}{2} \times \frac{4}{5}$
8. $3\frac{7}{8} \div \frac{3}{8}$
9. $\frac{15}{17} \div 5$
10. $4\frac{3}{4} \times 2\frac{2}{3}$

11. $\frac{5}{12} \div 1\frac{3}{4}$
12. $5\frac{1}{3} \times 1\frac{11}{16}$
13. $2\frac{2}{9} \times 1\frac{1}{2}$
14. $4\frac{1}{5} \div 1\frac{1}{3}$
15. $15 \times 1\frac{1}{5}$

16. $\frac{11}{16} \times 2\frac{10}{11}$
17. $8\frac{1}{8} \div 1\frac{6}{7}$
18. $7\frac{1}{12} \times 7\frac{1}{5}$
19. $3\frac{1}{2} \div \frac{5}{21}$
20. $6\frac{3}{5} \times 7\frac{1}{22}$

Exercise 16e Adding and subtracting decimals

1. 23.4 – 19.6
2. 3.81 – 1.95
3. 23.42 + 54.1
4. 10.1 – 2.4

5. 87.1 + 2.56
6. 9 – 3.4
7. 12.5 – 7.23
8. 34.5 + 26.8 + 61.09

9. 213.76 – 67.9
10. 0.756 – 0.3011
11. 9.1 + 2.456 + 0.865
12. 100 – 9.99

13. Take 46.3 from 97.1

14. Add 113.67 and 43.2

15. 120 take away 56.34

ⅰ. Subtract 0.2536 from 1.0132

17. What must be added to 4.67 to make 10?

18. Find the total of 3.021, 0.87 and 0.099

19. What is the difference between 76.25 and 68.08?

20. Add together 5.29 and 6.24 and subtract 9.264 from your answer.

Exercise 16f

Write the following numbers as vulgar fractions and reduce to lowest terms.

1. 0.3
2. 0.85

3. 0.5
4. 0.45

5. 0.001
6. 0.02

7. 0.68
8. 0.75

9. 0.05
10. 0.004

Write the following vulgar fractions as decimal fractions:

11. $\frac{3}{10}$
12. $\frac{7}{10}$

13. $\frac{2}{5}$
14. $\frac{3}{100}$

15. $\frac{13}{100}$
16. $\frac{81}{100}$

17. $\frac{1}{1000}$
18. $\frac{11}{1000}$

19. $\frac{237}{1000}$
20. $\frac{2}{10000}$

Use *Proportionately* to convert the following into decimal fractions:

21. $\frac{3}{5}$
22. $\frac{7}{25}$

23. $\frac{24}{30}$
24. $\frac{22}{50}$

25. $\frac{2}{5}$
26. $\frac{32}{40}$

27. $\frac{7}{20}$
28. $\frac{29}{50}$

29. $\frac{38}{200}$
30. $\frac{3}{25}$

Exercise 16g Mixed practice

1. 1.2 + 5.6
2. 7.8 + 9.7
3. 12.4 – 8.2

4. 34.6 – 17.9
5. 234.65 + 129.7
6. 8.98 – 4.73

7. 82.115 + 9.98
8. 104.7 – 67.48
9. 657.12 – 289.7

10. Solve the equation, $3x - 5 = 34$

149

11. Simplify $4a + 8b - 3a - 2b$

12. Given that $x = 6$, find the value of $2x^2 + 2x$

13. A boy buys a pair of shoes and a pair of trainers. If the shoes cost £37.50 and the trainers cost £19.85, how much did he spend altogether? How much change should he have left from £70.00?

14. A carpenter measures a piece of wood and finds that it is 3.65 m long. If he cuts a 1.86 m off this, how much will be left?

15. A rectangular field measures 35 m by 68 m. (a) What is its perimeter? (b) What is its area?

16. A boy spends one half of his pocket money and then spends one third of the remainder. What fraction of the original amount does he have left?

Exercise 16h Find the perimeter of each shape

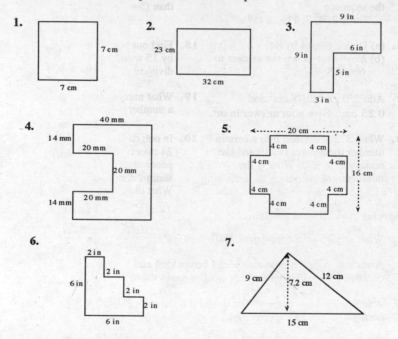

Exercise 16i Find the area of each shape in the previous exercise

150

Exercise 16j Problems. Set each sum out as appropriate for the calculation.

1. Multiply 57 by 12.

2. Add 37 to the difference between 75 and 52.

3. Add £8.79 to £2.46.

4. Divide 3285 by 9.

5. How many seconds are there in $\frac{3}{4}$ of an hour?

6. Divide 29271 by 11.

7. What are the next two numbers in the sequence
   1, 2, 4, 7, 11, ..., ...?

8. (a) Divide 60648 by 84.
   (b) Now write down the answer to 60648 ÷ 42.

9. Add 250 cm², 0.75 cm² and 0.25 cm². Give your answer in m².

10. When 372 is divided into a certain number the answer is 218 and the remainder is 270. What is the number?

11. What is 0.2 as a vulgar fraction?

12. Convert 0.36 into a vulgar fraction.

13. Convert $\frac{55}{100}$ into a decimal fraction.

14. Convert $\frac{42}{250}$ into a decimal fraction.

15. Use straight division, 81035 ÷ 32

16. Write in words: 5,407,068.

17. By how much is 5(7 + 4) greater than (5 + 7)4?

18. Find out whether 91365 is divisible by 15 without actually doing the division.

19. What number added to 30 will give a number 4 times as big as 9?

20. In one day an office used:-
    24 twenty-pence stamps, 136 thirty-pence stamps, 27 thirty-five-pence stamps and 10 one pound stamps. What did the stamps cost?

Exercise 16k Harder problems

1. What are the prime factors of 180?

2. A stack of boxes is 3 boxes wide, 4 boxes long and 5 boxes high. Each box contains 12 candles. How many candles are in the stack?

3. A box contains 6 jars, each jar contains a quarter of a litre of jam, and jam costs £2.40 for a litre. How much does half a boxful cost?

4. Take two square metres from a square whose sides are two metres long. How many square centimetres are left?

5. A field is 210 metres long and 180 metres wide. If a man walks 3 metres in a second, how long will it take him to walk round the field?

6. A father is 50 kg 500 g heavier than his son. Together they weigh 130 kg. Find the weight of each.

7. What is the smallest number which, multiplied by £1.15, gives a whole number of pounds?

8. William and John saved £32.40 between them. John saved £6.00 more than William. How much did John save?

9. I bought $\frac{3}{4}$ kg of butter and 2 dozen eggs for £6.66. If the butter is £4.08 per kg, how much does an egg cost?

10. Of £15000 prize money, the 1st prize is one-half, the 2nd one-quarter and the 3rd one-fifth. The remainder is divided into 75 equal consolation prizes. What is the value of a consolation prize?

11. In how many different ways can you arrange three boys in a row?

12. Petrol this year is dearer by one-tenth than last year, and last year it was dearer by one-tenth than the year before. Two years ago it cost 50p per litre. What does a litre cost today?

13. Divide £27.81 between two people so that one receives half of what the other receives. How much do you give to the one who receives more?

14. The total distance round a square piece of cardboard is 220 cm. Find the length of one of the four edges. Now find the area of the cardboard.

15. How many pieces of wire, each 31 cm long, can be cut from a coil of wire containing 10 metres, and what will be the length of the piece left over?

16. The rungs of a 21-rung ladder are 40 cm apart, and the top and bottom rungs are 30 cm from the ends. Find the length of the ladder in metres.

17. Express 10000 seconds in hours, minutes, seconds.

18. Five children have ten pens between them; each has at least one pen, and one has five pens. How many have two pens?

19. As nearly as I can measure it, the distance between two places on a map is 2.7 cm. Every cm on the map represents 800 m. What is the real distance between the two places in km?

Chapter 17 - Working Base Multiplication

Using a working base

Having used the *All from nine and the last from ten* rule, in Chapter 1, for multiplying numbers which are both close to a base of 10, 100, 1000, etc., we shall now go on to consider using the same method for working bases. A working base is a base which can be related to a power of ten by ratio. For example, if we wish to multiply 51 and 53 together, we may use a base of 50 since 50 is five times ten. There is one new step to the method.

To use a working base we employ the *Proportionately* rule.

---

203 × 207

Taking 100 as the real base and 200 as a working base the sum is set out with 200 = 100 × 2 set out above.

$$
\begin{array}{r}
(200 = 100 \times 2) \\
203 + 03 \\
\times\ 207 + 07 \\
\hline
210\ /\ 21
\end{array}
$$

The surplus amounts are put down on the right in the usual fashion and these are multiplied together to give the right-hand part of the answer, that is, 3 × 7 = 21.

The left-hand part of the answer is then found by cross-addition, 207 + 3 = 210.

Finally we take the number which is used to obtain the working base from the real base, that is 2, and multiply the left-hand part of the answer by that 2 to give 420.

$$
\begin{array}{r}
(200 = 100 \times 2) \\
203 + 03 \\
\times\ 207 + 07 \\
\hline
2 \times\ 210\ /\ 21 \\
\hline
420\ /\ 21
\end{array}
$$

The right-hand part of the answer is left alone and so the final answer is 42021.

Exercise 17a The real and working bases are placed in brackets after the first ten questions.

1. 21 × 22 (20 = 10 × 2)
2. 22 × 24 (20 = 10 × 2)
3. 31 × 32 (30 = 10 × 3)
4. 41 × 43 (40 = 10 × 4)

5. 33×32 $(30 = 10 \times 3)$

6. 51×52 $(50 = 10 \times 5)$

7. 32×32 $(30 = 10 \times 3)$

8. 203×204 $(200 = 100 \times 2)$

9. 403×411 $(400 = 100 \times 4)$

10. 306×312 $(300 = 100 \times 3)$

11. 42×44

12. 23×22

13. 44×41

14. 201×206

15. 304×307

16. 202×234

17. 413×403

18. 508×511

19. 3004×3005

20. 2001×2008

21. 33×31

22. 62×61

23. 53×52

24. 305×310

25. 412×408

26. 504×509

27. 2003×2011

28. 5004×5009

29. 3111×3008

30. 2134×2007

Exercise 17b Further practice

1. 51×53

2. 57×55

3. 59×53

4. 55×33

5. 25×22

6. 63×67

7. 47×44

8. 22×28

9. 605×607

10. 504×512

11. 208×210

12. 217×205

13. 426×403

14. 275×209

15. 358×309

16. 349×309

17. 555×505

18. 622×612

19. 536×520

20. 2132×2002

21. 2111×2007

22. 3212×3004

23. 3512×3005

24. 526734×500002

The following is an example where the two numbers are below a working base.

38×36

$(40 = 10 \times 4)$

Taking a working base of $40 = 10 \times 4$, the deficiencies are 2 and 4 respectively.

$$
\begin{array}{r}
38 - 2 \\
\times\ 36 - 4 \\
\hline
4 \times\quad 34 / 8 \\
\hline
136 / 8 \\
11
\end{array}
$$

The right-hand part is the product of the two deficiencies, that is, $2 \times 4 = 8$.

On cross-subtracting we arrive at 34 for the left-hand part. This has to be multiplied by 4 to give the answer, 1368.

Where there are carry digits from the right-hand portion these are not involved with the proportionality and so should be carried at the end.

37×36 $(30 = 10 \times 3)$
$$\begin{array}{r} 37 + 7 \\ \times 36 + 6 \\ \hline 43 \ / 2 \\ 4 \end{array}$$

In this example, the cross-addition gives 43 and the product on the right gives 42.

43 is multiplied by 3 before the carry 4 is added on.

$43 \times 3 = 129, \ 129 + 4 = 133$ $(30 = 10 \times 3)$
$$\begin{array}{r} 37 + 7 \\ \times 36 + 6 \\ \hline 3 \times 43 \ / 2 \\ 129 \quad 4 \\ \hline 133 \ / 2 \end{array}$$

The answer is 1332.

Exercise 17c The real and working bases are placed in brackets after the first ten questions.

1. 19×18 $(20 = 10 \times 2)$
2. 17×18 $(20 = 10 \times 2)$
3. 29×28 $(30 = 10 \times 3)$
4. 49×47 $(50 = 10 \times 5)$
5. 48×48 $(50 = 10 \times 5)$
6. 57×58 $(50 = 10 \times 5)$
7. 27×27 $(30 = 10 \times 3)$
8. 38×39 $(40 = 10 \times 4)$
9. 398×396 $(400 = 100 \times 4)$
10. 289×295 $(300 = 100 \times 3)$

11. 16×19
12. 29×27
13. 38×37
14. 58×59
15. 49×48
16. 299×298
17. 195×196
18. 593×597
19. 694×695
20. 398×391

21. 29×24
22. 37×36
23. 48×45
24. 23×29
25. 267×297
26. 485×492
27. 173×196
28. 512×599
29. 3998×3995
30. 7994×7887

A working base may also be a sub-multiple of the real base. For example, $25 = 100 \div 4$ or $500 = 1000 \div 2$. The next example illustrates using a working base in this way and dividing the left-hand part of the answer by the proportionality.

52×56 $\qquad$ $(50 = 100 \div 2)$
$\qquad\qquad\qquad\qquad\qquad\qquad\qquad$ $52 + 02$
Since the real base is 100, with two noughts, each $\qquad$ $\times\ 56 + 06$
surplus has two digits, that is, 02 and 06. $\qquad\qquad$ $58\ /\ 12$

The cross-addition gives 58 and the product on
the right gives 12. $\qquad\qquad\qquad\qquad\qquad$ $(50 = 100 \div 2)$
$\qquad\qquad\qquad\qquad\qquad\qquad\qquad$ $52 + 02$
28 is divided by 2 to give the answer as 2912. $\qquad$ $\times\ 56 + 06$
$\qquad\qquad\qquad\qquad\qquad\qquad\qquad$ $\div\ 2\ \ \underline{58\ /\ 12}$
$\qquad\qquad\qquad\qquad\qquad\qquad\qquad\qquad$ $\underline{29\ /\ 12}$

Exercise 17d   Use a working base of 50 (= 100 ÷ 2) for each one

1. 49×47	**16.** 38×38	**31.** 47×59
2. 48×48	**17.** 41×37	**32.** 42×58
3. 49×45	**18.** 39×37	**33.** 44×54
4. 48×46	**19.** 32×44	**34.** 52×46
5. 49×37	**20.** 42×36	**35.** 48×58
6. 41×39	**21.** 51×51	**36.** 71×49
7. 31×49	**22.** 53×55	**37.** 68×48
8. 12×48	**23.** 55×57	**38.** 47×61
9. 46×26	**24.** 61×59	**39.** 38×52
10. 48×14	**25.** 61×61	**40.** 37×55
11. 52×54	**26.** 51×49	**41.** 45×57
12. 52×56	**27.** 53×47	**42.** 67×47
13. 54×54	**28.** 55×45	**43.** 75×47
14. 52×52	**29.** 43×57	**44.** 48×82
15. 58×52	**30.** 43×53	**45.** 23×51

Exercise 17e Use a sub-multiple working base. The real and working bases are
placed in brackets after the first ten questions.

1. 52×54 $(50 = 100 \div 2)$ $\qquad$ **4.** 29×27 $(25 = 100 \div 4)$

2. 53×51 $(50 = 100 \div 2)$ $\qquad$ **5.** 48×46 $(50 = 100 \div 2)$

3. 54×58 $(50 = 100 \div 2)$ $\qquad$ **6.** 23×22 $(25 = 100 \div 4)$

7. 505 × 511 (500 = 1000 ÷ 2)	**15.** 47 × 41	**23.** 249 × 245
8. 498 × 496 (500 = 1000 ÷ 2)	**16.** 506 × 512	**24.** 5123 × 5003
9. 252 × 254 (250 = 1000 ÷ 5)	**17.** 578 × 502	**25.** 511 × 503
10. 121 × 116 (125 = 1000 ÷ 8)	**18.** 464 × 496	**26.** 201 × 204
11. 52 × 58	**19.** 409 × 495	**27.** 4994 × 4800
12. 55 × 53	**20.** 492 × 466	**28.** 2501 × 2503
13. 49 × 47	**21.** 253 × 257	**29.** 51324 × 50004
14. 48 × 44	**22.** 254 × 260	**30.** 240 × 238

In the case where the division of the left-hand portion has a remainder this should be carried to the next column on the right and the division can then continue.

---

512 × 507

Note that since the real base has three
noughts, each surplus must have three digits.

$$(500 = 1000 \div 2)$$
$$512 + 012$$
$$\underline{\times\ 507 + 007}$$
$$519\ /\ 084$$

On obtaining 519 as the left-hand part this
must now be divided be 2. It should be
remembered that the 519 is actually 519000
and so when dividing by 2 we have 259500.
The answer is therefore 259584.

$$(500 = 1000 \div 2)$$
$$512 + 012$$
$$\underline{\times\ 507 + 007}$$
$$\div 2\ \underline{519\ /\ 084}$$
$$259\ /\ 584$$

Exercise 17f The real and working bases are placed in brackets after the first ten questions.

1. 56 × 51 (50 = 100 ÷ 2)	**11.** 53 × 58
2. 53 × 54 (50 = 100 ÷ 2)	**12.** 46 × 43
3. 49 × 46 (50 = 100 ÷ 2)	**13.** 28 × 27
4. 26 × 29 (25 = 100 ÷ 4)	**14.** 488 × 495
5. 503 × 504 (500 = 1000 ÷ 2)	**15.** 511 × 504
6. 497 × 496 (500 = 1000 ÷ 2)	**16.** 202 × 204
7. 505 × 510 (500 = 1000 ÷ 2)	**17.** 249 × 244
8. 199 × 193 (200 = 1000 ÷ 5)	**18.** 1998 × 1989
9. 21 × 23 (20 = 100 ÷ 5)	**19.** 50004 × 50007
10. 247 × 242 (250 = 1000 ÷ 4)	**20.** 248 × 223

Exercise 17g Choose your own working base.

1. 52×54	11. 27×24	21. 253×257
2. 53×51	12. 48×38	22. 254×260
3. 54×58	13. 49×47	23. 249×245
4. 29×27	14. 48×44	24. 5123×5003
5. 48×46	15. 47×41	25. 511×503
6. 23×22	16. 506×512	26. 201×204
7. 505×511	17. 397×372	27. 4994×4800
8. 498×496	18. 464×496	28. 2501×2503
9. 252×254	19. 409×495	29. 51324×50004
10. 121×116	20. 492×466	30. 240×238

Chapter 18 - Ratio and Proportion

The sutra governing all aspects of ratio and proportion is *Proportionately.*

Ratio

A ratio is a relation of quantity in respect of size within a given unity.

The ratio, for example, of 3 kg of tea to 5 kg of tea may expressed as 3 : 5 (read as *three to five*). The unity in this case is 1 kg of tea because it is through this unit that both quantities are related. Again, if in a field there are 12 horses and 20 cattle the ratio of the number of horses to that of cattle is 12 : 20. The given unity is *animals in the field.*

Ratio may also be described as the multiple which one quantity is of another or the part which one quantity is of another. For example, if one pupil scores 30% in an examination and another scores 90% then the higher mark is three times the lower mark. The ratio of the lower mark to the higher mark is 1 : 3.

Another way of expressing a ratio is as a vulgar fraction, so 3 : 5 may be expressed in the form $\frac{3}{5}$.

To bring a ratio to its simplest form we divide both parts of the ratio by their highest common factor (HCF). This is the same as reducing fractions to lowest terms. The highest common factor of two numbers is the highest number which can divide into those numbers exactly.

For example, with the ratio, 6 : 9, the HCF of 6 and 9 is 3. Dividing 6 and 9 by 3 gives 2 and 3, and so the simplest form of the ratio 6 : 9 is 2 : 3.

Exercise 18a Bring each ratio to its simplest form.

1. 4 : 6	**9.** 6 : 36	**17.** 8 : 32	**25.** 48 : 60
2. 6 : 10	**10.** 100 : 88	**18.** 12 : 16	**26.** 96 : 24
3. 8 : 12	**11.** 32 : 100	**19.** 200 : 300	**27.** 20,000 : 1000
4. 10 : 15	**12.** 10 : 100	**20.** 32 : 24	**28.** 16 : 88
5. 20 : 15	**13.** 63 : 9	**21.** 20 : 24	**29.** 125 : 400
6. 50 : 60	**14.** 35 : 65	**22.** 32 : 16	**30.** 27 : 54
7. 100 : 25	**15.** 60 : 40	**23.** 50 : 550	**31.** 64 : 96
8. 16 : 20	**16.** 80 : 70	**24.** 16 : 36	**32.** 19 : 57

Exercise 18b Problems

1. A theatre has 450 seats in the stalls and 150 seats in the dress circle. What is the ratio of the number of seats in the stalls to that in the dress circle?

2. A school has 360 pupils and 30 teachers. What is the pupil/teacher ratio?

3. A school contains 60 girls and 90 boys
   (a) What is the ratio of the number of girls to the number of boys?
   (b) How many pupils are there in the school?
   (c) What fraction of the whole school are boys?

4. A train travels 270 miles in 3 hours and a car travels 120 miles in 2 hours.
   (a) How many miles will the train go in one hour? (The units are mph)
   (b) How many miles will the car go in one hour?
   (c) What is the ratio of the speed of the car to the speed of the train?

5. The sides of two squares are 6 cm and 8 cm.

   (a) What is the perimeter of the first square?
   (b) What is the perimeter of the second square?
   (c) Find the ratio of the perimeter of the first square to that of the second.
   (d) What is the area of the first square?
   (e) Find the area of the second square.
   (f) What is the ratio of the areas?

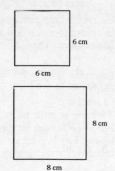

6 cm

6 cm

8 cm

8 cm

6. If you sleep for 6 hours at night,
   (a) For how many hours are you awake during the day?
   (b) What is the ratio of hours sleeping to hours awake?
   (c) What is the ratio of hours awake to hours sleeping?

7. Mrs Beaton makes a pie for six people by following a recipe for 4 people. How many ounces of pastry will she need if the recipe says use 12 ounces?

8. A newspaper shop manager finds that William can deliver 50 newspapers in the same time that it takes Simon to deliver 30 papers. If he pays Simon £15 a week, how much should he pay William?

9. Laura shares her 36 chocolates with her friend, Lisa, so that Lisa receives twice as many as she does. How many sweets will each girl have?

10. At a Chinese puppet show the ratio of adults to children is 2 : 15. If there are eight adults, how many children are there?

Proportion

Proportion is an equality of ratios.

The ratio 12 to 20 is the same as the ratio of 3 to 5 for by dividing both 12 and 20 by 4 we obtain 3 and 5. 12 : 20 and 3 : 5 are in proportion.

This may be written as 12 : 20 :: 3 : 5 and read as *twelve is to twenty as three is to five.*

Find the value of x in, 32 : 8 :: x : 15

We look for a multiplying or dividing number connecting a pair of numbers on one side of the proportion and apply that to the pairs of numbers on the other side. In the ratio 32 : 8, we see that 32 is 4 times as much as 8. So x is 4 times 15. Therefore $\underline{x = 60}$.

Exercise 18c Find the missing number in each proportion.

1. 4 : 8 :: __ : 12	**11.** 15 : 3 :: 100 : __	**21.** 20 : __ :: 5 : 15
2. 1 : 3 :: 4 : __	**12.** 12 : 48 :: 1 : __	**22.** __ : 27 :: 27 : 81
3. 5 : 30 :: 1 : __	**13.** 15 : 15 :: __ : 14	**23.** 14 : __ :: 2 : 6
4. 4 : 20 :: 3 : __	**14.** 3 : $\bar{3}$ :: 1 : __	**24.** 15 : __ :: 45 : 3
5. 2 : 6 :: __ : 9	**15.** 5 : 25 :: __ : 25	**25.** 25 : __ :: 18 : 36
6. 1 : 5 :: __ : 25	**16.** __ : 4 :: 5 : 20	**26.** 20 : 100 :: __ : 500
7. 4 : 2 :: 6 : __	**17.** 8 : __ :: 16 : 2	**27.** 35 : 70 :: __ : 2
8. 8 : 1 :: 32 : __	**18.** 3 : __ :: 4 : 16	**28.** 3 : __ :: 1 : $\bar{2}$
9. 9 : 3 :: 6 : __	**19.** __ : 24 :: 40 : 80	**29.** __ : $\bar{4}$ :: $\bar{3}$: $\bar{6}$
10. 12 : 3 :: __ : 4	**20.** 6 : __ :: 1 : 3	**30.** 5 : __ :: 24 : 12

In the examples of this exercise one number in each ratio is a factor of the other number. The missing number may easily be found *By inspection.* For example, in

5 : 15 :: x : 30, 15 is three times 5 and so we just have to find what number multiplied by 3 gives 30. The answer is 10.

In some ratios, one number is not a factor of the other and we must look at another relationship to find the answer. Up until now we have been using the fact that when two ratios are equivalent if the first number is a factor of the second number then the third number is the same factor of the fourth number. But in proportion, it is also true that if the first number is a factor of the third number then the second number will be the same factor of the fourth number.

For example, in the proportion 3 : 4 :: 9 : 12, we can see that 3 is not a factor of 4 and 9 is not a factor of 12. However, 3 is a factor of 9 and 4 is a factor of 12.

---

5 : 6 :: 15 : x Here, 5 does not go into 6 an exact number of times but it does go into 15 three times. Therefore 6 goes into x three times and so x is 18.

5 : 6 :: 15 : x

$\underline{x = 18}$

Exercise 18d Find the missing number *By inspection.*

1. 2 : 3 :: 4 : x

2. 3 : 4 :: 9 : x

3. 5 : 7 :: 10 : x

4. 4 : 5 :: 20 : x

5. 6 : 7 :: 18 : x

6. 12 : 5 :: 24 : x

7. 6 : 9 :: 12 : x

8. 32 : 12 :: 8 : x

9. 20 : 16 :: 5 : x

10. 12 : 10 :: 6 : x

11. 6 : 9 :: x : 3

12. 35 : 14 :: x : 2

13. 3 : 4 :: x : 20

14. 15 : 100 :: 3 : x

15. x : 4 :: 12 : 16

16. x : 80 :: 24 : 40

17. 5 : x :: 20 : 16

18. 3 : x :: 6 : 14

19. x : 8 :: 14 : 16

20. x : 9 :: 18 : 27

21. 6 : x :: 24 : 20

22. x : 19 :: 6 : 38

23. 12 : x :: 51 : 51

24. 1 : x :: 7 : 49

25. x : 3 :: 18 : 27

26. x : 6 :: 63 : 42

27. 56 : 80 :: 7 : x

28. x : 35 :: 10 : 7

29. 9 : 16 :: x : 64

30. 1.2 : 5 :: x : 15

Solving Ratio Equations

When the ratio equation cannot be solved *By Inspection* then we can use the general method. This uses the sutra, *The product of the means equals the product of the extremes.* In a proportion, by the word *means* is meant the middle two numbers and by the word *extremes* is meant the outer two numbers.

For example, in the proportion, $3 : 4 :: 9 : 12$, the middle two numbers are 4 and 9 and their product is 36. The outer two numbers are 3 and 12 and their product is also 36. This is what the sutra tells us and can be used to solve ratio equations.

$2 : 3 :: x : 45$ Multiplying 3 by x gives $3x$. and the product of the extremes is $2 \times 45 = 90$.

$3x = 90$

$\underline{x = 30}$ The equation $3x = 90$ is solved by transposing the 3 so that x is equal to $90 \div 3 = 30$.

$3 : 7 :: 2 : x$ Fractions can also be involved as with this example.

$14 = 3x$

$\frac{14}{3} = x$ On arriving at $14 = 3x$, the 3 needs to be transposed by dividing 14 by 3. This is expressed as a *top heavy* fraction. The answer is left as a mixed number.

$x = 2\frac{2}{3}$

Exercise 18e Solve the following setting them out as shown in the example.

1. $2 : 3 :: x : 48$ 8. $3 : 5 :: x : 6$ 15. $5 : 25 :: x : 1$

2. $1 : x :: 4 : 8$ 9. $x : 12 :: 7 : 4$ 16. $6 : 15 :: x : 1$

3. $3 : 4 :: x : 20$ 10. $3 : 5 :: x : 105$ 17. $1 : \frac{3}{5} :: 1 : x$

4. $2 : x :: 5 : 3$ 11. $2 : 3 :: 40 : x$ 18. $7 : 21 :: x : 1$

5. $3 : x :: 4 : 6$ 12. $36 : 48 :: 3 : x$ 19. $11 : 15 :: x : 1$

6. $5 : x :: 7 : 4$ 13. $3 : 12 :: x : 1$ 20. $x : 4 :: 3 : 8$

7. $2 : 9 :: x : 10$ 14. $7 : 2 :: x : 3$ 21. $5 : 6 :: x : 4$

22. $1 : x :: 10 : 13$ **25.** $x : 1 :: 3 : 5$ **28.** $x : 35 :: 10 : 7$

23. $0.6 : 0.2 :: x : 1$ **26.** $60 : 50 :: x : 1$ **29.** $9 : 16 :: x : 64$

24. $35 : 6 :: 5 : x$ **27.** $56 : 80 :: 7 : x$ **30.** $1.2 : 5 :: x : 15$

Problems in Direct Proportion

The following problems involve what is called *Direct Proportion*. This is where when one quantity is increased the other quantity is increased in the same ratio. For example, if two bags of cement cost £10 then we would expect four bags of cement to cost £20. As the number of bags increases the cost increases in the same ratio.

If five bags of sugar cost £1.20, how much do two bags cost?

Let x be the cost of 2 bags of sugar.

$5 : 120 :: 2 : x$	Always begin with a statement of letting x be the unknown quantity which is to be found.
$240 = 5x$	
	Costs in pounds are converted to pence for ease of calculation.
$x = \frac{240}{5} = 48$	In dividing 240 by 5 we can divide by 10 and multiply by 2.
Two bags cost 48p	

Exercise 18f

1. a) If 6 pieces of fence cost £72 how much will 10 pieces cost?
   b) What is the ratio of the numbers of pieces of fence
   c) What is the ratio of the costs
   d) What do you notice about your answers to b) and c)?

2. a) If 60 newspapers cost £18, how much will 3 newspapers cost?
   b) What is the ratio of the numbers of newspapers?

3. 3 kg of sugar cost £1.62. What quantity of sugar would cost £1.08?

4. 5 pens cost £1.20. What is the cost of 8 such pens?

5. The ratio of the area of two classroom floors is 4 : 5. If the smaller classroom has a floor area of 30 m², find the area of the larger classroom floor.

6. A recipe for 6 people requires 900 g of aubergines. How many grammes of aubergines are required for 4 people?

7. The ratio of the numbers of pints of water and milk drunk at lunch in a school is 5 : 2. If 60 pints of water are drunk, how many pints of milk are consumed?

8. 3000 kg of coal cost £54. Find the cost of 8000 kg.

9. Mark cycles 24 km in 3 hrs. How far would he cycle in 5 hrs at the same speed?

10. A train travels 36 miles in 21 minutes. Find how long it takes to travel 60 miles at the same speed.

11. The train fare for a journey of 110 km is £20. Find the fare for a trip of 165 km assuming that the cost and the distance are directly proportional.

12. If twelve bottles of water cost £7.20, how many bottles can be bought for £9.00?

13. If three litres of petrol have a mass of 2.5 kg, find the mass of 15 litres of petrol.

14. A train travels at 60 km/h. Find the distance travelled in $2\frac{1}{2}$ hours.

15. If four people can stay at a hotel for one night for £420, how much will it cost for three people to stay for two nights?

16. £150 invested brings £6 interest per year. Find the interest on £400 for one year with the same rate of interest.

17. To insure a house valued at £300,000 costs £750 per year. Find the cost of insuring a house valued at £200,000 for a period of five years.

Problems in Indirect Proportion

Where one quantity increases in the same ratio as another quantity decreases then the proportion is inverse. For example, if it takes four men three days to build a wall, how long will it take six men working at the same rate? Clearly if the number of men working increases then the time it takes must decrease.

165

Such problems come under the heading of *Indirect Proportion*. and are solved using the sutra, *The first by the first and the last by the last.*

In the example above, there are two situations, as it were. One where there are four men working for three days and the other in which six men work for an unknown, or x, number of days. The sutra is based on the fact that the product of the two numbers in the first situation is equal to the product of the two numbers in the second situation. This gives $4 \times 3 = 6x$ and therefore $x = 2$ days. So we can use *The first by the first and the last by the last* for this type of problem.

When Timothy cycles to school at a speed of 16 km/h he takes 24 minutes. How long does it take him at a speed of 20 km/h?

Let x be the time taken at 12 km/h

$16 \times 24 = 20 \times x$

$x = \dfrac{16 \times 24}{20} = \dfrac{4 \times 24}{5} = \dfrac{96}{5}$

$\therefore x = 19\frac{1}{5}$ minutes

The *first by the first* gives 16×24 and *the last by the last* gives $20x$.

It is often easier to cancel down to lowest terms before multiplying or dividing.

Exercise 18g

1. A train takes twenty minutes to cover a certain distance at a constant speed of 60 km/h. How long will it take to cover the same distance at a speed of 40 km/h?

2. 16 men complete a piece of work in 15 days. How long would it take 24 men working at the same rate?

3. If four taps fill a tank in 12 minutes, how long does it take three taps running at the same rate?

4. I have a certain sum of money which would last eight weeks if I spend £70 a week. How long will it last if I spend £80 a week?

5. A man packs 20 boxes of peaches with 18 in each box; how many boxes are needed if only 12 are put in each box?

6. If 14 men can dig a trench in four and a half hours, how long will it take 18 men?

7. A haystack is large enough to feed 12 horses for 15 days; how long will it last 20 horses?

8. A train takes 15 minutes to cover a certain stretch of line when it travels at 40 km/h. How long would it take to go the same distance at a speed of 30 km/h?

9. 15 men can mend a road in 24 days; how long will it take 9 men to mend it?

10. A nursery gardener makes up 54 bunches of flowers with 10 in each bunch. How many bunches would there be if he put 12 in each bunch?

11. When George buys some first class stamps he receives a block of 12 rows with 18 in each row. How many rows would there be if there are 8 in each row?

12. A swimming pool can be filled in 10 hours by six pumps working together. How many pumps are required to fill the pool in 15 hours?

13. I have enough money to spend £18 a day for 40 days. How long will the money last if I spend £15 a day?

14. A farm employs fifteen labourers each working 44 hours a week. If four men are ill for a whole week, how many hours would the rest have to work to make up the time lost?

15. Twenty soldiers are surrounded and cut off by the enemy and have enough food to last them 32 days. If four of them die, for how long would the food now last?

16. The greatest safe load for a lift is 12 men each weighing 15 stone. How many people, each weighing 10 stone, can it take safely?

17. A bicycle wheel with a circumference of 6 ft makes 120 revolutions in going from A to B. How many revolutions does a wheel with circumference 4 ft make in going from A to B and back again?

18. A man can pay off a loan at £4800 a year for twenty-five years; how long will it take him to pay off the loan if he pays £6000 a year?

Chapter 19 - Geometry 2 - The Rectangle Propositions

1 A rectangle is a form of knowledge with the following characteristics:

It is a plane figure with four straight sides

Opposite sides are equal

Opposite sides are parallel

At each corner is a right angle

The diagonals are equal

The diagonals intersect one another at their centre and at the centre of the rectangle.

2 Triangles in Semicircles

Draw a large circle with a horizontal diameter. Let the ends of the diameter be P and Q.

Mark a point anywhere on the top half of the circumference and label it A.

We are going to use the diameter as the base of the triangle and use the point A as the top corner.

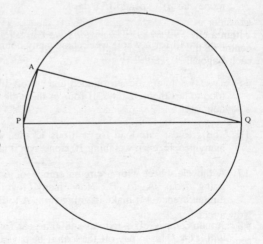

Draw in the triangle with PQ as the base and A as the top corner.

By choosing another four points, B, C, D and E, somewhere round the circumference, draw another four triangles using the diameter PQ as the base of each one.

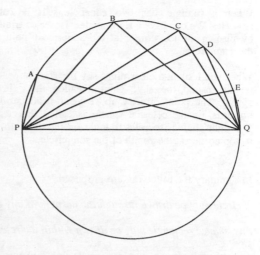

Having drawn five triangles, the question is what do these triangles have in common? The first thing that is the same about these triangles is that the base PQ is the same for each. What else do these triangles have in common? Measure the top angles of each one, that is, the angles at A, B, C, D and E. They are all right angles. And the triangles are right-angled triangles.

Is it always true that triangles in semicircles are right-angled?

Consider a rectangle, together with its diagonals, drawn within a circle. *By mere observation* we can see that the centre of the rectangle is at the centre of the circle and each diagonal is a diameter.

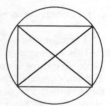

Any such rectangle drawn within a circle will have the same symmetry. We can draw any shaped rectangle within a circle. Its diagonals will always be diameters.

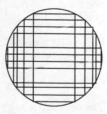

Now a rectangle has right angles at the corners.
Half of the rectangle is a right-angled triangle in a semicircle. So all triangles in semicircles, that is with the diameter as base, are right-angled triangles.

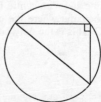

169

When a triangle has two equal legs it is called isosceles. We can have a right-angled isosceles triangle by placing the top corner at the uppermost point on the semicircle.

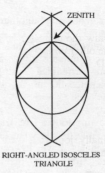

When you look at a clear night sky the stars appear to be all around the sky. This is called the celestial sphere. The point directly above your head, straight upwards, on the celestial sphere is called the *zenith*. The right-angled isosceles triangle on the diagram has its top corner at the zenith of the semicircle.

RIGHT-ANGLED ISOSCELES
TRIANGLE

In summary the following are proposed:

A circle may be drawn through the corners of any rectangle.

Any shaped rectangle may be drawn within a circle.

Any triangle drawn in a semicircle and touching the circumference is a right-angled triangle.

3 To construct a perpendicular at a given point on a straight line.

This is a construction which has been done before but here is a new way of doing it. This construction uses what was discovered concerning the angle in a semicircle. We drew a circle with a diameter and used that as a base for a triangle. The top corner of the triangle is always a right angle. We are going to use this fact to construct a perpendicular. Up until now, all the constructions for drawing perpendiculars have involved quite a few circles and then getting an intersection point and drawing. This construction requires just one point, one circle and one line.

Begin with a straight line with a point marked on it. Let this point be A.

The next step is to choose a point B, anywhere above the line and with centre B and radius AB draw a circle. Let the point where the circle cuts the straight line again be C. This is the only circle we need for the construction.

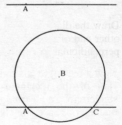

Draw the diameter of the circle through B and C. Let the other end of the diameter be D. The diameter is then CD.

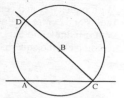

Finally join AD. AD is perpendicular to the straight line.

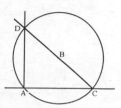

You can see the triangle in a semicircle in the diagram and that, of course, has a right angle at A. This is the simplest construction for a right angle. As to whether or not your line AD is perpendicular depends upon the accuracy of the drawing. You can tell whether it is by looking to see if it is upright and true.

The general principle of accuracy is this: the fewer the lines and circles which have to be drawn in order to complete the construction the more accurate the construction is likely to be. It should be possible to get this one quite accurate.

We are going to use this construction to draw a square.

4 To construct a square on a given base.

Choose a base AB.

Choose a point C above the base and draw a circle with radius AC and centre C. Let this circle also cut the line AB at the point D. This may require AB to be extended.

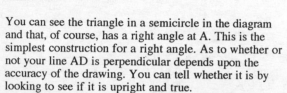

Draw the diameter through D and C and let the other end of the diameter be E. Draw the perpendicular at A through E.

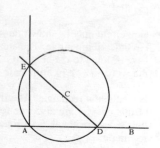

171

With radius AB and centre A draw a circle which cuts AE at F. With the same radius and centre B draw another circle. Again, with the same radius, but with centre F draw another circle cutting the circle just drawn at G. Join FG and BG to complete the square.

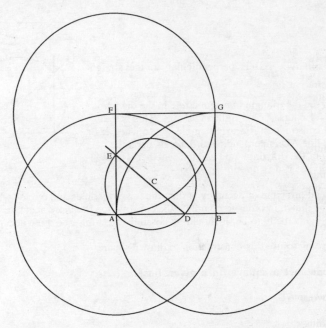

What are the qualities of a square? It has four sides, four corners and at each corner is a right angle. Each side is equal in length and opposite sides are parallel.

One circle may be drawn through all four corners and this is called the circumscribing circle. The area is equal to the base times the height but since the base is equal to the height it is just that length squared. This is where the use of the word *square* in arithmetic comes from.

Is a square a rectangle? The five properties of a rectangle given at the beginning of this chapter are also true for a square. A square has another characteristic - all four sides are equal. So a square is a rectangle but it is a particular type of rectangle.

A square also has many aspects of equality about it. The sides are equal in length, the angles are equal and right, the diagonals are equal in length and both cut each other in half and at right angles.

172

5 To draw a rectangle within a circle.

Draw a circle and within it draw any two diameters. Join the ends of the diameters to give a rectangle.

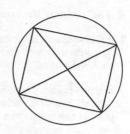

6 To draw a rectangle with a given base.

Let the straight line AB be the given base. Draw a circle with diameter larger than AB and label the centre O. Mark a point on the circumference and label it C.

With centre C and radius AB, draw an arc cutting the circle at D. Join CD. CD is the same length as AB and this is the base of the rectangle.
From C draw the diameter through the centre O, and let the other end be E. Similarly, from D draw the diameter through O, and let the other end be F. Join D to E, C to F and E to F. The rectangle is CDEF.

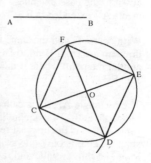

7 To draw a rectangle with a given base and a given height.

Let the two straight lines AB and CD be the given base and height.

With radius more than half AB draw a circle and label the centre E. Mark any point F on the circumference. With the same radius and with centre F make an arc cutting the first circle at G. join F to G.

From F draw the diameter of the first circle through E and let the other end be called H. In like manner, from G draw the diameter through E and label the other end I. Join G to H and F to I.

With radius CD and centres F and G draw two arcs cutting FI at J and GH at K. Join J to K and F to G. The required rectangle is FGKJ.

173

8 The Golden Rectangle

For this we can use squared paper to make the construction of right-angles easier. Begin with a square which has an edge length of 12 cm. Let the square be ABCD with AB the base.

Mark two points which are half way along AB and CD. These are E and G. Open the compasses to a radius EC and draw an arc centred at E starting at C down to the base extended. Where it meets AB extended is F.

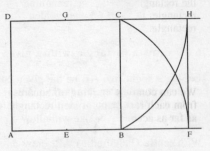

With centre G and the same radius draw an arc from B up to DC extended and let the point where it meets be H. Join FH.

The rectangle AFHD is called a golden rectangle. The special property of this rectangle is that if a square is cut away from it the rectangle that remains has the same shape as the original rectangle. It will be smaller but will have the same shape. There is only one shape of rectangle which has this property. If it were too long and thin or wide and fat then the remaining rectangle would be a different shape.

With the golden rectangle, the ratio of the long side to the short side is about 1.618033989...to one. This ratio is called the golden ratio and is given the symbol, ϕ, the Greek letter *phi*. The golden ratio has been used for harmonising effects in Greek and Renaissance Art and Architecture. This ratio embodies a natural law of growth and form. It is one of the most fundamental aspects of growth and form in the creation.

On the diagram we already have one square cut away from the rectangle. The smaller rectangle, BFHC, is also a golden rectangle. From this we shall mark off another square.

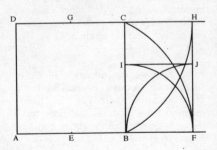

With centre B and radius BF, draw an arc from F cutting BC at I. With the same radius and centre F draw an arc from B cutting FH at J. Join IJ. The square is BFJI. The remaining golden rectangle is IJHC.

With centre J and radius JH draw an arc from H cutting JI at K. With the same radius and centre H draw an arc from J cutting HC at L. Join LK. The square JHLK has now been marked off the rectangle, JHCI. The remaining rectangle, LCIK is another golden rectangle.

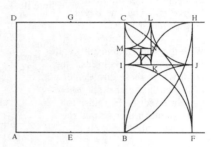

We can continue marking off squares from each remaining golden rectangle as far as accuracy or size will allow.

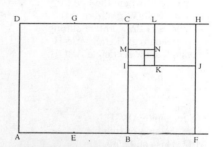

This diagram is the basis of a golden spiral. This spiral is found in some creatures and plants.

Below is a picture of an X-ray of a giant nautalus shell. The curves are all close to golden spirals.

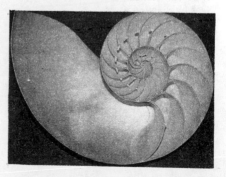

9 Any triangle is half a rectangle

Draw any triangle with the longest side as the base. Let the triangle be ABC as shown.

With centre C and radius CB draw a circle. Let the point where this circle cuts the line AB again be D. Draw the diameter of the circle from D through C and let the other end of the diameter be E. Join BE. The line BE is perpendicular to AB.

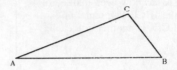

With the same radius and centres B and E draw two circles. One point where these circle intersect is C. Let the other point where they intersect be F. Join F to C and extend further so that the line passes above A.

Let the point where the line FC cuts BE be G. With radius AB and centre G draw an arc cutting FC (extended) at H. Join A to H to complete the rectangle ABGH.

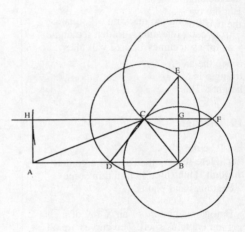

The rectangle ABGH has twice the area of triangle ABC. This can be made clear by drawing a perpendicular from C down to AB.

To do this, draw two arcs of equal radius, centred at D and B, which intersect below AB at I. Join C to I and let the point where CI cuts AB be J.

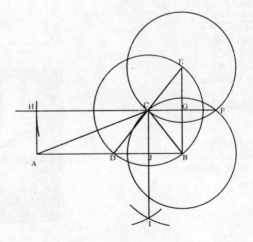

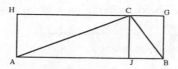

Now look at the rectangle AJCH.

The line AC cuts this rectangle in half. Therefore the triangle AJC is equal to half the rectangle AJCH. Similarly, triangle BJC is equal to half the rectangle BJCG. But the two triangles AJC and BJC taken together make the triangle ABC. Also, the two rectangles AJCH and BJCG taken together make the rectangle ABGH. Therefore the triangle ABC is half of the rectangle ABGH.

Since the area of a rectangle is base times height, it follows that the area of a triangle is half of the base times the height. (The height must be the perpendicular height). This gives the formula for finding the area of any triangle.

10 Through a given point to draw a line parallel to a given line.

Let P be the given point and AB the given line. Here the problem is to draw a line through P which is parallel to AB.

Choose any point on the straight line and label it C. With centre C and radius CP make a circle cutting the line AB at M and N. With radius NP but with centre M draw an arc cutting the circle at Q. Draw a straight line from P through Q.

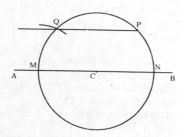

PQ is parallel to AB.

In a plane, lines which do not meet are parallel to one another. The distance between them always remains the same. Can you think of examples of parallel lines?

11 To draw a square twice as large as a given square.

Let ABCD be the given square. Draw the diagonals and let the centre of the square, where the diagonals intersect, be O.

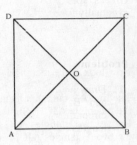

With radius AO and centre A draw a circle. With the same radius and centres B, C and D draw three more circles. Let the points where these circles intersect outside of the square be P, Q, R and S. Join P to Q, Q to R, R to S and S to P.

The square PQRS is twice the area of the square ABCD.

Why is it twice the area? Consider the square ABCD. The diagonals form the four triangles AOB, BOC, COD and DOA and these triangles are equal to one another and equal to the four triangles outside the square. Since eight equal triangles make up the square PQRS, four of which make up the square ABCD, then PQRS is twice the area of ABCD.

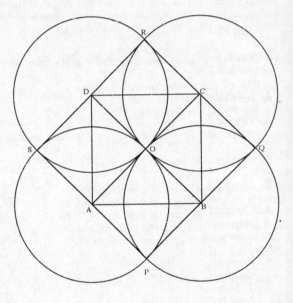

The problem of making a square twice as large a given square is similar, but easier than, the problem of doubling a cube. There is an ancient story about the doubling of a cube. In 430 BC the Athenians found themselves suffering from a plague of eruptive typhoid fever. They sent a representation to the oracle at Delos to find out how they could stop it. Apollo replied that they must double the size, by volume, of his altar which was in the form of a cube. Nothing seemed more easy and the Athenians made a cube with its edges twice as long. Alas, this cube was eight times the size! Whereupon, according to the legend, Apollo became angry and made the plague even worse than before. The Athenians then went to their geometers to try to find the answer. This problem became known as the Delian problem and the ancient Greeks spent much time and effort in trying to solve it. The solution was eventually found by Menaechmus, a follower of Plato, some hundred years later.

Problems

1. Draw a circle with a radius of 5 cm. Draw a diameter and label the ends A and B. With radius 8 cm and centre A draw an arc cutting the circumference at C. Join A to C and B to C. Measure and write down the lengths of AB, AC and BC. What type of triangle is ABC?

2. Draw a circle with radius 4 cm. Draw a diameter and label the ends P and Q. With centre P and radius 7 cm draw an arc above the diameter cutting the circumference at R. Join PR and QR. With the same radius but with centre Q draw an arc below the diameter cutting the circumference at S. Join PS and QS. What is the shape of PRQS?

3. Draw a straight line and mark on it any point P. Construct, using the method in section 3, a perpendicular and make it 2 in long.

4. Using the method in section 4, make a square with a base of 6 cm.

5. Draw a straight line and mark a point P about 2 in above this line. Construct the perpendicular to the line which passes through the point P.

6. Accurately draw any rectangle with a base of 4 cm.

7. Construct the rectangle ABCD which has AB = 5 cm and AD = 8 cm.

8. Construct the rectangle PQRS with PQ = 3 in and QR = 2 in. Draw the diagonals QS and PR and label the centre T. With centre T and radius TP draw a circle which passes through the four corners of the rectangle.

9. Construct the rectangle PQRS which has PQ = 3 in and QR = 4 in. Draw the diagonals by joining Q to S and P to R and label the point where they cut as T. Measure and write down the length of PR. With centre T and radius QT draw the circumscribing circle of the rectangle.

10. Construct a square with side 6 cm. Use the construction in section 11 to draw a square twice as large as the square you have drawn.

Chapter 20 - Order of Operations

Multiple products

Consider the triple product, $7 \times 2 \times 9$. There are three ways in which this may be done but by inspecting the numbers first we can choose the easiest method. This comes under the sutra, *By inspection*.

$$7 \times 2 \times 9$$

14×9	63×2	7×18
$90 + 36 = 126$	126	$70 + 56 = 126$

In the first case, the product of 7 and 2 is 14 and we then have to multiply this by 9. We might do this by finding 10×9 and adding 4×9 to give 126. The second case takes $7 \times 9 = 63$ and then multiplies the answer by 2 to give 126. Thirdly, the answer is found by multiplying 2×9 to give 18 and then multiplying this by 7, which is 7×10 added to 7×8. The answer is the same in all three cases but the question is which is easiest? With triple products such as this the easiest method is usually to multiply the two larger numbers together and finally multiply the answer by the smallest. The middle column above shows this.

In practice we can use the sutra, *By Elimination and Retention*. This means that we mentally *cover up* one of the numbers, multiply the other two and then multiply the answer to this by the number which was covered up.

$6 \times 3 \times 12$

Cover up the 3, $6 \times 12 = 72$, $72 \times 3 = 216$

Exercise 20a Write answers only - no rough working

1. $2 \times 3 \times 6$
2. $2 \times 14 \times 3$
3. $5 \times 30 \times 2$
4. $4 \times 10 \times 3$

5. $9 \times 2 \times 6$
6. $2 \times 8 \times 4$
7. $10 \times 5 \times 6$
8. $5 \times 2 \times 7$

9. $5 \times 10 \times 3$
10. $15 \times 2 \times 5$
11. $6 \times 5 \times 6$
12. $8 \times 3 \times 6$

13. $4 \times 12 \times 2$ 19. $5 \times 20 \times 7$ 25. $2 \times 6 \times 5 \times 5$

14. $7 \times 9 \times 3$ 20. $9 \times 5 \times 8$ 26. $4 \times 4 \times 2 \times 2$

15. $6 \times 3 \times 11$ 21. $2 \times 7 \times 3 \times 4$ 27. $3 \times 4 \times 3 \times 5$

16. $9 \times 7 \times 4$ 22. $3 \times 5 \times 2 \times 5$ 28. $6 \times 3 \times 2 \times 9$

17. $11 \times 12 \times 2$ 23. $6 \times 4 \times 2 \times 7$ 29. $5 \times 3 \times 6 \times 7$

18. $4 \times 7 \times 8$ 24. $4 \times 3 \times 5 \times 10$ 30. $8 \times 9 \times 3 \times 2$

Mixed multiplying and dividing with brackets

Where there is multiplication and division it is usually easiest to convert the expression into a fraction and then cancel down to lowest terms in the usual manner. Brackets are used to indicate that what is inside should be treated as a single term.

$$(19 \times 4) \div 2 \qquad \frac{19 \times 4}{2} = \frac{19 \times 2}{1} = 38$$

$$(24 \div 2) \times 3 \qquad \frac{24}{2} \times 3 = \frac{12 \times 3}{1} = 36$$

$$24 \div (2 \times 3) \qquad 24 \div (2 \times 3) = \frac{24}{2 \times 3} = 4$$

Exercise 20b

1. $6 \times (14 \div 2)$ 9. $(28 \div 7) \times 11$ 17. $(80 \div 20) \times 5$

2. $5 \times (18 \div 9)$ 10. $(64 \div 8) \times 3$ 18. $(24 \div 8) \times 12$

3. $4 \times (26 \div 13)$ 11. $53 \times (32 \div 16)$ 19. $(150 \div 3) \times 7$

4. $9 \times (15 \div 5)$ 12. $(48 \times 2) \div 3$ 20. $(200 \div 4) \div 2$

5. $6 \times (24 \div 6)$ 13. $(50 \div 10) \times 3$ 21. $(16 \times 9) \div 12$

6. $7 \times (21 \div 3)$ 14. $6 \times (18 \div 3)$ 22. $(42 \div 3) \times 2$

7. $(20 \div 5) \times 8$ 15. $14 \times (15 \div 5)$ 23. $24 \div (6 \div 2)$

8. $(16 \div 4) \times 7$ 16. $(64 \div 2) \div 8$ 24. $(24 \div 6) \div 2$

181

Mixed additions and subtractions

Where there are mixed additions and subtractions we should look for the grouping of numbers so that the number to be added or subtracted is as small or easy as possible.

$24 - 84 + 62 + 18 = 20$

By inspecting the numbers we can see that the 2 of 62 and 8 of 18 add up to 10. The sum of 62 and 18, 80, will then be an easy number to use. Subtracting 84 and adding 80 is equivalent to subtracting 4. The answer is then $24 - 4 = 20$.

Exercise 20c Write answers only

1. $58 + 24 - 23$	**11.** $26 + 17 - 3 - 4$	**21.** $0.45 + 0.25 - 0.2$
2. $32 + 58 - 48$	**12.** $58 - 39 + 6 + 3$	**22.** $1.64 - 0.32 + 0.7$
3. $43 - 27 + 25$	**13.** $648 + 131 - 1 - 30$	**23.** $3.28 - 1.78 + 0.5$
4. $100 - 64 + 265$	**14.** $6577 - 75 - 24 - 1$	**24.** $69.7 - 4.5 + 0.3$
5. $89 - 243 + 250$	**15.** $24 + 76 + 287 + 13$	**25.** $9.85 + 0.15 - 6.4$
6. $34 + 72 - 70$	**16.** $68 - 47 + 39 + 8$	**26.** $24.6 - 12.2 + 11.8$
7. $50 - 17 - 23$	**17.** $348 - 328 - 18 - 2$	**27.** $65.3 - 19.8 - 0.4$
8. $86 - 19 - 11$	**18.** $150 + 350 - 120$	**28.** $32.4 + 16.9 - 1.9$
9. $62 - 28 - 12$	**19.** $288 + 12 - 150$	**29.** $98.4 - 0.8 + 1.2$
10. $143 - 15 - 5$	**20.** $645 - 250 + 5$	**30.** $3.8 + 1.5 + 0.5 - 1.9$

Collecting like terms

When collecting like terms in algebra we may use whichever order is most convenient. Sometimes it is easiest to collect all the positive terms together, collect all the negative terms together and then subtract.

$7x - 5x + 3x - 4x = x$

$15y + 28y - 26y + 4y = 15y + 2y + 4y = 21y$

Exercise 20d

1. $9d - 3d - 3d$ 11. $5a + a - 3a + a - 2a$ 21. $-m - 9m + 11m + 19m$

2. $8e - 4e - 4e$ 12. $2b + 8b - 4b - b + 2b$ 22. $-7cd - 3cd + 4cd - 5cd$

3. $6f - 2f - 3f$ 13. $c + 7c - 2c - 3c + c$ 23. $-xy + 5xy - 10xy + 6xy$

4. $7g + 2g - 3g$ 14. $8d - 2d - 3d + 4d - 7d$ 24. $7p - 11p + 5p - 3p + 9p$

5. $h + 7h - 8h$ 15. $3a + 2a - a - 5a + 9a$ 25. $8x - 10x + 3x - 5x - 6x$

6. $16k - 4k - 4k$ 16. $2ab - 4ab - 6ab + 7ab$ 26. $-7c^2 + c^2 + 4c^2 - 8c^2$

7. $8n - 2n + n$ 17. $-2y - 4y + 8y + 10y$ 27. $3b^3 - 2b^3 - 6b^3 + 4b^3$

8. $5m - 4m + m$ 18. $-b + 2b + b - 6b - 2b$ 28. $4x^2y - 6x^2y + 10x^2y$

9. $6p - 2p + 3p$ 19. $pq + 3pq - 5pq + 7pq$ 29. $68ab - 34ab + 20ab$

10. $10r - 5r + 5r$ 20. $-25c - 7c - c - 21c$ 30. $8yz - 14yz - 13yz + 16yz$

Mixed operations

Where there is more than one operation to carry out, such as $32 + 16 - 8$ or $64 \div 4 \times 2$ or $3 + 4 \times 2$, we must consider the question of which operation to do first and which to do second. There are two features to this. The first is where the signs are of the same type, such as $+$ and $-$ or $\times$ and $\div$. In this case we can choose the most convenient operation first. This is what has been practised in the first four exercises of this chapter. The second case is where there are a mixture of types of operation, such as $\times$ with $+$, etc. When this is the case there are rules for the order of operation.

Numbers or terms connected together by $\times$ or $\div$ are worked out before those connected by $+$ or $-$.

This rule is necessary because otherwise more than one answer would be possible and this could cause confusion. For example, consider $3 \times 4 + 2$. There appear to be two possible answers, $12 + 2 = 14$ and $3 \times 6 = 18$. Which one is correct? The correct answer is 14. The above rule tells us to perform the multiplication first and then the addition.

$2 \times 3 + 4 \times 7 = 34$	The multiplications are done first giving $6 + 28 = 34$.
$36 - 6 \times 5 = 6$	
$4 + 3 \times 5 - 3 = 16$	$3 \times 5 = 15$ comes first and then $4 + 15 - 3 = 16$.

Exercise 20e Simplify:

1. $2 + 4 \times 5$	11. $2 \times 3 + 4 \times 6$	21. $2 \times 13 - 4 \times 6$
2. $6 - 2 \times 2$	12. $6 \times 7 - 3 \times 4$	22. $60 \div 4 + 20 \div 4$
3. $8 + 12 \div 3$	13. $8 \times 7 + 4 \times 2$	23. $6 \times 8 - 24 \div 3$
4. $4 \times 5 - 17$	14. $20 \div 4 + 36 \div 12$	24. $45 \div 15 + 90 \div 30$
5. $5 + 2 \times 7$	15. $63 \div 9 + 2 \times 7$	25. $56 - 81 \div 9 + 28$
6. $56 - 5 \times 6$	16. $84 \div 12 - 15 \div 3$	26. $72 - 72 \div 8 - 63$
7. $7 \times 8 - 24$	17. $6 \times 9 + 27 \div 9$	27. $105 \div 5 + 120 \div 20$
8. $4 \times 9 - 16$	18. $8 \times 6 - 25 \div 5$	28. $105 \div 5 - 120 \div 20$
9. $12 - 3 \times 4$	19. $40 - 4 \times 7 + 16$	29. $105 \times 5 + 120 \times 20$
10. $5 \times 7 + 18$	20. $13 + 8 \times 3 - 21$	30. $60 \times 5 - 40 \times 3$

Brackets

Brackets are used to group expressions together. Whatever is inside the brackets should be treated as a single entity although it may consist of many parts.

In the order of operations the contents of brackets is dealt with before multiplication or division even though they may contain + or − signs. The order of operations is summarised below.

First .... Brackets

Second........ Multiplication and Division

Third.......... Addition and Subtraction

Simplify $3 \times (6 + 2) - (18 - 12)$ The numbers inside the brackets are dealt with first, $6 + 2 = 8$

$= 3 \times 8 - 6 = 24 - 6 = 18$ and $18 - 12 = 6$.

Following this is $3 \times 8 = 24$

Finally, $24 - 6 = 18$

Exercise 20f Simplify:

1. $(2 + 3) \times 5$
2. $3 \times (4 + 2)$
3. $7 \times (17 - 11)$
4. $18 \div (4 + 5)$
5. $(16 + 24) \div 8$
6. $(18 - 11) \times 9$
7. $36 \div (14 - 5)$
8. $14 - (6 - 2)$
9. $10 + (3 - 4)$
10. $9 + (4 - 7)$

11. $7 + (3 - 9)$
12. $14 - (15 - 11)$
13. $28 - (3 + 4) \times 2$
14. $(9 - 5) \div (3 - 1)$
15. $(8 + 1) \times (3 + 4)$
16. $(9 - 1) \div (12 - 8)$
17. $2 + 4 \times (3 + 2)$
18. $24 - 3 \times (5 - 3)$
19. $18 - 5 + 2 \times (4 + 5)$
20. $30 - 36 \div (1 + 11)$

21. $5 \times (3 + 4) - (12 + 1)$
22. $(32 - 14) \div 2 \times 9$
23. $2 \times (3 \times 6 - 15) + 7$
24. $(101 + 19) \div (28 - 8)$
25. $(3 + 7 - 8) \times 3 - 6$
26. $6 \times (65 - 54) \div 66$
27. $72 \div (3 \times 5 - 12 + 5)$
28. $(4 + 6 - 2) \times (72 - 64)$
29. $(5 + 4) \times 2 + 10 \div 5$
30. $(16 + 4) \times (8 - 10)$

Chapter 21 - Multiplication and Division of Decimals

Multiplication and division by powers of ten

Multiplying and dividing numbers by 10 is very easy because essentially 10 is the same as one. When multiplying or dividing any number by one that number remains unchanged. This demonstrates that one, the Absolute, is completely independent. The nought on the end of ten does have an effect. For example, when multiplying 6 by 10 we place a nought on the end of 6 making 60. So when we multiply by 10 there are two aspects: one aspect which is unchanging and the other aspect which is changing. This is how creation works, the Absolute remains unchanging and everything else changes.

To multiply 3.85 by 10, move the decimal point one place to the right making 38.5. Similarly when multiplying by 100 the decimal point moves two places to the right. Whenever a decimal number is multiplied by a power of ten the answer has the same digits but with the decimal point moved to the right the same number of places as there are noughts in the multiplier.

3.54601×100
$= 354.601$

100 has two noughts and so we move the decimal point two places to the right.
Where there are not enough digits in the number then noughts should be added.

$2.35 \times 10,000$
$= 2.3500 \times 10,000$
$= 23500$

2.35 has two digits after the decimal point whilst 10,000 has four noughts. Two noughts must therefore be added.

	×10	×100	×1000
0.36	3.6	36	360

Exercise 21a Under the three headings of ×10, ×100 and ×1000 as shown above, set out a table and multiply the following:

1. 4.637	6. 123.4443	11. 12.95	16. 322.75
2. 8.643	7. 7.4	12. 0.0376	17. 0.00944
3. 86.005	8. 132.64	13. 4.3234	18. 0.02601
4. 0.5	9. 0.8723	14. 56.182	19. 0.00045
5. 14.62	10. 27.6	15. 4565.8	20. 3.020765

When dividing by a power of ten move the decimal point to the left. The number of places through which the point must be moved is the same as the number of noughts in the divisor.

$34.6 \div 1000$
$= 0.00346$

Since 1000 has four noughts the point must be moved four places to the left. Noughts must be used to fill the vacant places.

	÷10	÷100	÷1000
361	36.1	3.61	0.361

Exercise 21b Under the three headings of ÷10, ÷100 and ÷1000, as shown in the example above, divide the following:

1. 2000	**6.** 8765	**11.** 4.55	**16.** 0.45
2. 500	**7.** 7	**12.** 17.6	**17.** 3450
3. 70	**8.** 67.3	**13.** 868.9	**18.** 65700
4. 567	**9.** 68.003	**14.** 53	**19.** 0.05
5. 83	**10.** 2.3	**15.** 0.1	**20.** 6.001

Factors and multiples of powers of ten

Clearly it is very easy to multiply and divide by powers of ten because all that has to be done is for the decimal point to be moved. We can also use this method for multiplying and dividing by multiples and factors of ten using the *Proportionately* sutra. The key is to relate the multiplying or dividing number to the powers of 10, that is, 10, 100, 1000, and so on.

6.846×50
$\qquad = 342.3$

The easiest method would be to multiply by 100 and divide by 2. This gives $684.6 \div 2 = 342.3$

$657.3 \div 30$
$\qquad = 21.91$

To divide by 30, divide by 10 and then by 3.
$657.3 \div 10 = 65.73$
$65.73 \div 3 = 21.91$

Exercise 21c

1. 2.3×20	9. 132.4×30	17. $234.6 \div 50$	25. $6800 \div 400$
2. 36.4×50	10. 64.8×50	18. $28.4 \div 40$	26. 0.045×2000
3. 1.28×40	11. $4.6 \div 20$	19. $36.4 \div 200$	27. 0.842×500
4. 4.1×200	12. $23.1 \div 50$	20. $68480 \div 5000$	28. 0.065×20
5. 12.3×300	13. $6.6 \div 30$	21. 1.8×5	29. $6.624 \div 60$
6. 4.3×2000	14. $42.4 \div 200$	22. $3.6 \div 20$	30. 0.064×25
7. 5.5×500	15. $1.2 \div 60$	23. $456 \div 500$	31. $340 \div 250$
8. 32.624×5	16. $84.2 \div 500$	24. 2.4×0.5	32. 9.6×250

Single digit multipliers and divisors

For the multiplication and division of decimal numbers by a single digit number the decimal point is carried straight down into the answer.

2.34×3 $\qquad$ $82.16 \div 4$

$$
\begin{array}{r}
2.34 \\
\times \quad 3 \\
\hline
7.02 \\
\hline
1\ 1
\end{array}
\qquad
\begin{array}{r}
4\lfloor 82.16 \\
\quad\ \ 2\ 1 \\
\hline
20.54
\end{array}
$$

Exercise 21d

1. 14.6×2	9. 132.05×6	17. $283.8 \div 2$	25. $3.059 \div 7$
2. 0.35×3	10. 34.642×7	18. $6.065 \div 5$	26. 9.12×8
3. 48.1×7	11. $18.4 \div 4$	19. $248.76 \div 9$	27. $0.1572 \div 3$
4. 62.04×3	12. $4.6 \div 2$	20. $2.85 \div 3$	28. $0.0476 \div 7$
5. 2.12×9	13. $3.69 \div 3$	21. 76421.21×4	29. 3.651×9
6. 1.4×8	14. $6.88 \div 4$	22. $0.435 \div 5$	30. $0.333 \div 9$
7. 5.67×2	15. $64.8 \div 8$	23. 646.007×2	31. $67.305 \div 3$
8. 678.2×4	16. $456.24 \div 6$	24. $2.148 \div 6$	32. $992.16 \div 8$

With division, if there is no decimal point in the dividend we may need to put a point with following noughts after the units digit in order to complete the division.

$573 \div 4$

4 into 5 = 1 r 1, 4 into 17 = 4 r 1, 4 into 13 = 3 r 1.
A nought is now added after the decimal point so that the division may continue.
4 into 10 = 2 r 2.
There is still a remainder so another zero must be placed.
4 into 20 = 5. There is no remainder and so the division is complete.

$$4 \overline{)573.}$$
$$\quad \overline{1\ 1\ \ 1}$$
$$\quad 143.$$

$$4 \overline{)573.00}$$
$$\quad \overline{1\ 1\ \ 12}$$
$$\quad 143.25$$

Exercise 21e

1. $5 \div 2$	**4.** $23 \div 2$	**7.** $1.34 \div 5$	**10.** $5 \div 8$	**13.** $67.2 \div 5$
2. $10 \div 4$	**5.** $535 \div 4$	**8.** $34.56 \div 5$	**11.** $27 \div 6$	**14.** $3469 \div 4$
3. $12 \div 5$	**6.** $65670 \div 4$	**9.** $621.1 \div 4$	**12.** $435 \div 8$	**15.** $94387 \div 8$

Multiplication of decimals by Vertically and Crosswise

When multiplying two decimal numbers together the decimal point does not usually go straight down into the answer. The sutra which tells us where to place the point in the answer is *Only the last (whole) numbers*. This sutra tells us to place the decimal point immediately after the multiplication of the two units digits. To see how this sutra works follow through the examples below.

4.2×7.6

$4 \times 7 = 28$, and since these are the last whole numbers, the point is placed after 28.
$(4 \times 6) + (2 \times 7) = 38$
$2 \times 6 = 12$
The answer is 31.92.

$$\begin{array}{r} 4.2 \\ \times\ 7.6 \\ \hline 28.82 \\ 3\ \ 1 \\ \hline 31.92 \end{array}$$

3.61×14.2

From the left, $3 \times 1 = 3$
$(3 \times 4) + (6 \times 1) = 18$ and since 3 and 4 are the last
whole numbers the point is placed after the 18.
$(3 \times 2) + (6 \times 4) + (1 \times 1) = 31$
$(6 \times 2) + (1 \times 4) = 16$
$1 \times 2 = 2$
The answer is 51.262

```
      3.6 1
   ×  1 4.2
   ─────────
     3 8.1 6 2
       1 3 1
   ─────────
     5 1.2 6 2
```

There is a very simple way in which to check that the decimal point in the answer is in the correct position. This method comes under a sutra which has a large number of uses but here it means, *the total number of decimal-fraction digits in the factors is equal to the number of decimal-fraction digits in the product.*

In the last example, the factors are 3.61 and 14.2, and the total number of digits after the decimal points is three. This means that the number of digits after the decimal point in the answer must also be three. This in itself may be used as a method for obtaining the correct position for the decimal point, particularly when working from the right-hand end of the sum.

Another method for finding the correct place for the decimal point is to first ignore the decimal points, work out the answer digits, and then to place the point by inspecting the *size* of the answer. In the example above, in obtaining 51262, look at 3.61 and 14.2, and conclude that the answer must be about 50. It certainly could not be about 5 or 500 and therefore 51.262 is the correct answer.

Exercise 21f

1. 2.4×1.8	9. 7.6×1.8	17. 2.61×2.3	25. 3.4×24.7
2. 5.6×7.2	10. 7.0×8.2	18. 4.11×5.11	26. 31.5×0.5
3. 8.9×1.1	11. 0.2×0.5	19. 6.09×5.4	27. 0.4×23.1
4. 4.3×5.2	12. 1.0×0.7	20. 3.22×1.34	28. 0.42×0.12
5. 6.5×0.4	13. 0.1×5.3	21. 34.2×16.8	29. 0.13×1.57
6. 0.3×1.7	14. 6.4×0.1	22. 21.3×32.1	30. 6.23×0.85
7. 6.3×0.5	15. 0.3×0.3	23. 10.5×20.4	31. 62.3×0.085
8. 1.2×1.2	16. 1.23×4.01	24. 62.3×1.2	32. 0.623×8.5

Problems

Find the cost of 3.5 m of wire at £1.18 per metre.

Cost = £4.13

$$\begin{array}{r} 3.5 \\ \times\ 1.18 \\ \hline 3.890 \\ 24 \\ \hline 4.130 \end{array}$$

Exercise 21g

1. Find the cost of 2.5 kg of butter at £1.30 per kg.

2. Curtain material costs £6.30 per metre. How much does 8.2 m cost?

3. A car petrol tank holds 34 litres. If the car averages 9.5 miles per litre, how many miles can it travel on one full tank?

4. Find the cost of 34 litres of petrol at 51.2p per litre.

5. What is the product of 0.47 and 2.8?

6. Sections of fence are 2.2 m long. How many metres in length would sixteen sections cover?

7. A man earns £9.50 per hour. How much does he earn in a day assuming that he works for 8.5 hours?

8. Find the cost of 6.5 kg of potatoes at £0.18 per kg.

9. What is 0.5 of 28.6?

10. Find 0.2 of 3.14

11. A sheet of paper measures 28.4 cm by 19.7 cm. Find its area.

12. A rectangular floor measures 6.5 m by 4.2 m. What is its area?

13. Find the total cost of three pairs of socks at £4.50 a pair and four shirts at £36.50 each.

14. Find the product of 3.6, 6.8 and 9.1.

15. Find the cost of 43.2 litres of petrol at 52.6 p per litre.

Straight decimal division

When the divisor has two or more digits Straight division should be used as the general method. This was described in Chapter 15 for whole number remainders but we can easily apply the method to division with decimals. As with Chapter 15 we will only deal with two-digit divisors The sutra is *On the flag*.

The first type of Straight decimal division is where the decimal point in the divisor lies between the two digits. When this is the case the decimal point in the dividend is carried straight down into the answer.

$38.34 \div 5.4$

$$5 . \overline{\underset{\underset{7.10}{3\ 0}}{|\ 3\ 8\ .\ 3\ 4}}$$

$$\overset{4}{}$$

The sum is set out with the decimal point of the answer directly below that of the dividend.
5 into 3 doesn't go.
5 into 38 = 7 rem. 3
$33 - (4 \times 7) = 5$, 5 into 5 = 1 rem. 0
$4 - (4 \times 1) = 0$, 5 into 0 = 0
The answer is 7.1

Exercise 21h

1. $38.34 \div 5.4$
2. $84.75 \div 7.5$
3. $15.4 \div 2.2$
4. $40.92 \div 9.3$
5. $39.78 \div 3.4$
6. $71.61 \div 3.3$
7. $46.42 \div 2.2$
8. $85.26 \div 4.2$
9. $84.42 \div 4.2$
10. $71.24 \div 5.2$
11. $275.4 \div 5.4$
12. $164.3 \div 5.3$
13. $9.086 \div 2.2$
14. $83.391 \div 3.3$
15. $22.748 \div 2.2$
16. $682.56 \div 7.2$
17. $8.8452 \div 4.2$
18. $0.56925 \div 3.3$

Moving the decimal point

When the decimal point in the divisor does not lie between the two digits the points in both the divisor and the dividend can be moved an equal number of places in the same direction until this condition is satisfied. This slight adjustment does not alter the division but does make it easier to place the decimal point of the answer in the correct position. The sutra for the adjustment is *Proportionately*.

A simple example to demonstrate this is in dividing 200 by 50. By dividing both numbers by 10 we can see that the division is equivalent to $20 \div 5$.

$927.3 \div 22$

$= 927.3 \div 22.0$

$= 92.73 \div 2.2$

22 is the same as 22.0. Since the decimal point in 22.0 must be moved one place to the left the point in 927.3 must also be moved one place to the left. The division may now be carried out as before.

```
              2
    2 . 9 2 . 7 3 0
        1  0 1 1
        4 2 . 1 5 0
```

Note that a nought is added at the end of the dividend to continue the division until completion. The sutra for this adding of noughts is *By completion and non-completion.* If noughts are not added when there is a remainder then the division is incomplete.

Exercise 21i

1. $281.6 \div 55$

2. $39480. \div 940$

3. $69.96 \div 11$

4. $878.9 \div 85$

5. $741 \div 65$

6. $339.9 \div 330$

7. $8.316 \div 54$

8. $168 \div 14$

9. $75.9 \div 33$

10. $829.5 \div 0.75$

11. $8.153 \div 0.031$

12. $0.204 \div 0.51$

13. $6.48 \div 0.045$

14. $216600 \div 950$

15. $91.84 \div 0.041$

16. $27.01 \div 74$

17. $308 \div 44$

18. $1.564 \div 0.0085$

Chapter 22 - Percentages

What is a percentage?

A percentage is a fraction whose unwritten denominator is 100. The symbol used to indicate this is %. The sutra employed is *Proportionately*.

For example, 41% means $\dfrac{41}{100}$

To convert a percentage into a vulgar fraction write it as the numerator, put 100 as the denominator and reduce to lowest terms by dividing both numbers by their HCF.

Convert 35% into a vulgar fraction in its lowest terms.

$$35\% = \frac{35}{100} = \frac{7}{20}$$

To convert a vulgar fraction into a percentage multiply by 100 and simplify.

Convert $\frac{3}{5}$ into a percentage.

$$\frac{3}{5} \times 100 = \frac{3}{1} \times 20 = 60\%$$

To convert a percentage into a decimal fraction put a decimal point before the tens digit.

Write 38.4% as a decimal fraction.

$$38.4\% = 0.384$$

Note: This is the same as dividing 38.4 by 100.

To convert a decimal fraction into a percentage multiply by 100.

Write 0.125 as a percentage. $\qquad$ 0.125 = 12.5%

Exercise 22a Copy and complete

	Percentage	Vulgar fraction	Decimal fraction
1.	75%		
2.		$\frac{2}{5}$	
3.			0.36
4.	48%		
5.			0.45
6.		$\frac{11}{20}$	
7.	24%		
8.		$\frac{3}{5}$	
9.			0.8
10.	78%		

Finding a percentage of a given quantity

To find a percentage of a quantity multiply the percentage, as a fraction, by the given quantity.

Find 32% of £20

$0.32 \times £20 = £6.40$

There is a choice between using the percentage as a vulgar fraction or as a decimal fraction. In this case, the decimal fraction is easier.

or $\frac{32}{100} \times 20 = \frac{32}{5} = £6.40$ Here is the calculation using a vulgar fraction. Cancelling down should be done first and since 20 goes into 20 and 100 the resulting division is $32 \div 5 = 6.4$.

195

Exercise 22b Find;

1. 5% of 40p	11. 75% of 84 cm	21. 6% of 250 m
2. 10% of 600 m	12. 63% of 900 mm	22. 20% of 12 km
3. 15% of 60 cm	13. 35% of £80	23. 25% of 18 mm
4. 32% of £25	14. 2% of 300 km	24. 50% of 19 ml
5. 75% of 16 in	15. 95% of 240p	25. 8% of £50
6. 20% of £5	16. 40% of £15	26. 1% of 4000 m
7. 25% of $420	17. 50% of 28 yds	27. 32% of 50 kg
8. 12% of £150	18. 80% of £45	28. 86% of 450p
9. 27% of 250 g	19. 85% of 8000 kg	29. 5% of 323 m
10. 36% of 75 ft	20. 4% of 200 litres	30. 16% of 125 g

Expressing one quantity as a percentage of another

The task here is to express one quantity as a fraction of another quantity and with the unwritten denominator equal to 100. The method is to place the first quantity as a numerator, the second quantity as denominator, multiply by 100 and simplify.

Find £65 as a percentage of £250

$$\frac{65}{250} \times 100 = \frac{65}{5} \times 2 = 13 \times 2 = 26\%$$

65 is placed as numerator, 250 as denominator and this fraction is multiplied by 100. The answer is 26%.

Exercise 22c Express the first quantity as a percentage of the second

1. 2p, 10p	6. 18 m, 60 m	11. 13 m, 10 m	16. 4 km, 50 km
2. 8 m, 25 m	7. 25 kg, 125 kg	12. 14p, 56p	17. 9 hrs, 24 hrs
3. 5 g, 20 g	8. 45 cm, 50 cm	13. 45 m, 180 m	18. 36 g, 120 g
4. £15, £50	9. 32p, 50p	14. £6, £60	19. 65 m, 130 m
5. 3 g, 75 g	10. 12 kg, 25 kg	15. 11 cm, 55 cm	20. 17p, 20p

21. 16 cm, 4 m   **24.** 240 g, 2 kg   **27.** 24 in, 10 ft   **30.** £2.50, £300

22. 40p, £2   **25.** 60 m, 3 km   **28.** 380 m, 2 km   **31.** 450 g, 3 kg

23. 4 cm, 1 m   **26.** 72p, £3.60   **29.** 5 ft, 10 yds   **32.** £3.50, £12.50

Exercise 22d Problems

1. If a man spend 75% of his income, what percentage does he save?

2. If 6% of the girls in a school cannot swim, what percentage are swimmers?

3. In a cupboard 85% of the books are novels; what percentage are other types of books?

4. A farmer sells 20% of his land and gives 15% away; what percentage is left?

5. Find 65% of 700 kg.

6. Find 3.5% of £1250.

7. Gunpowder is made up of: nitre 75%, sulphur 10%, charcoal 15%. How many kg of each are there in a tonne of gunpowder?

8. A shop assistant receives 5% commission on her sales. What is her commission in a week when she has sold £800 worth of goods?

9. A man spends 30% of his income in a year on his car. How much does he spend if his income is £47,500 a year?

10. The duty on an imported article is 35% of its value. What is the duty on an article valued at £70?

11. Express 40p as a percentage of £1.20.

12. Express 81p as a percentage of £1.50.

13. A boy gets 84 marks on a paper for which full marks are 150. What percentage of full marks does he get?

14. What percentage is 35 of 105?

15. Express £37 as a percentage of £1850.

16. A boy made 45 runs out of a total of 75 runs scored by a team. What percentage of the total did he score?

17. A girl gets 56 out of 80 for a test. Express her mark as a percentage.

18. A man's income is £75,000 a year. If he spends 80% of his income, how much does he save each year?

19. If the price of a shirt marked at £35.00 is reduced by 30%, how much will it cost?

20. A man borrows £250 from a bank which lends money at 18% per year. How much will he have to repay at the end of the year?

21. Find $12\frac{1}{2}$ % of 144 miles.

22. Find 35% of 6940 men.

23. A house is bought for £242,500. Twenty per cent of the money is paid at once, how much remains?

Percentage increase and decrease

The change in the size or value of a quantity is often expressed as a percentage. For example, a plant with a height of 60 cm may grow at a rate of 10% per month during the summer months. At the end of one month it would then be 66 cm tall. 10% is the monthly percentage increase in height. As another example consider a car whose value is £30,000 when new. If at the end of 1 year the car is worth £24,000 the decrease in value is £6000. This is 20% of the original value of the car and we say that the car has depreciated in value by 20% after one year.

A percentage increase or decrease is always in relation to an original size or value.

Exercise 22e

By what must a number be multiplied to increase it by,

1. 19%   **2.** 73%   **3.** 60%   **4.** 25%   **5.** 142%

By what must a number be multiplied to decrease it by,

6. 9%   **7.** 23%   **8.** 40%   **9.** 75%   **10.** 2%

11. Increase 300 by 12%   **12.** Decrease 500 by 25%

13. Decrease 90 by 10%   **14.** Increase 40 by 30%

15. A man earns £35,000 a year and receives a salary increase of 15%. What is his new salary?

16. A car is valued at £9,000. One year later it is valued at £7650. By how much per cent has its value decreased?

17. If the price of an article is increased by 8%, write down
(a) the ratio of the new price to the old price;
(b) the ratio of the new price to the change in price;
(c) what the old price must be multiplied to give the new price.

18. The population of a town at one census was 14,500; at the next census it had increased by 6 per cent; what was the population then?

19. A man invested £90,000 for one year; at the end of that year he had £94,500, find the percentage increase.

Chapter 23 - Averages

Finding the average

The average of a group of numbers or quantities is a single number in the middle of the group which is equally placed. For example the average of 4 and 8 is 6 because it is half way between 4 and 8.

The average for 4 and 8 is found by adding 4 and 8 together and dividing the answer by 2, that is,

$$\frac{4 + 8}{2} = \frac{12}{2} = 6$$

We can find the average by adding up the quantities in the group and dividing by the number of quantities. So, for example, the average of 1, 4 and 9 is found by adding 1, 4 and 9 together and dividing the answer by 3.

$$\frac{1 + 4 + 9}{3} = \frac{14}{2} = 7$$

The sutra for finding an average is *Individuality and Totality*. In terms of this sutra the average is an individual number or quantity found by getting the total of all the quantities and dividing by the number of individuals.

The formula is, Average $= \dfrac{\text{Total of the individuals}}{\text{Number of individuals}}$

Find the average weight of seven people with weights, 32 kg, 51 kg, 74 kg, 48 kg, 38 kg, 66 kg and 48 kg.

Average $= \dfrac{357}{7} = 51$ kg

$$
\begin{array}{r}
32 \\
51 \\
74 \\
48 \\
38 \\
66 \\
+\ 48 \\
\hline
357
\end{array}
\qquad
\begin{array}{r}
51 \\
7)\overline{357}
\end{array}
$$

Exercise 23a Find the average of the following, set out all working:

1. 6, 16

2. 3, 7, 11

3. 12, 26, 13

4. 12, 28, 30, 32

5. 29, 18, 10, 61, 45, 89

6. 32, 94, 44, 60, 88, 22, 24

7. 94, 17, 99, 22, 58

8. 56, 72, 55, 55, 77, 82, 23, 16

9. 84, 32, 70, 43, 93, 62

10. 19, 10, 26, 53

11. 62, 59, 67, 22, 42, 52, 44, 77, 43

12. 3.8, 1.3, 8.6, 3.7, 7.0, 8.6

13. 6.8, 3.1, 2.3, 6.2, 1.0, 2.2

14. 0.37, 0.33, 0.35, 0.84, 0.56, 0.13

15. 0.81, 0.68, 0.34, 0.65, 0.77

16. 82, 51, 38, 80, 20, 11

17. 435, 152, 763, 231, 884, 349

18. 92, 78, 96, 94, 90, 91, 89

19. 23, 45, 12, 62, 34

20. 965, 543, 323, 700

Exercise 23b In these problems set out the working as previously

1. Eight girls sat an exam and obtained the following results: 70%, 44%, 66%, 87%, 28%, 80%, 40% and 81%. Find their average mark.

2. A school play was performed on four successive evenings. The numbers in the audience on those four nights were 253, 247, 283 and 293. What was the average number in the audience?

3. The number of articulated lorries passing under a certain bridge across a motorway in each of five consecutive hours was 67, 87, 67, 84 and 90. Find the average number of lorries passing per hour.

4. In five cricket matches a batsman scored 11, 48, 97, 73 and 16 runs. What was his batting average for these matches?

5. A bowler took six wickets in a game and 57 runs were scored against him. What is his bowling average (runs per wicket)?

6. A football team scores 4, 3, 6, 0, 5, 2, 0, 0, 4, 2, 6, 4 goals in twelve matches. What is the average number of goals scored per match?

7. A girl aged 12 years has parents aged 41 and 52 years. Living in the same house are two of her grandparents who are 74 and 81 years old. What is the average age of those living in the house?

8. A man travels 90 miles in 2 hours and then another 50 miles in 2 hours. Find his average speed in miles per hour for the whole journey.

9. The heights of four girls in a class are 4ft 8in, 5ft, 1in, 4ft 11in and 5ft 4in. Find the average height of the girls.

10. A man earns £1350 for nine days' work, and then a further £990 for three days' work. Find the average amount earned per day.

11. A batsman's average at the end of the season was 24. If he had eleven completed innings, what was the total number of runs he scored?

12. The average age of a form of 19 boys is 10 years 7 months. Find the total of their ages.

13. If I buy a dozen books at an average price of £6.75, how much change will I receive from £100?

14. A boat's crew weigh 10 st 11 lb, 10 st 13 lb, 11 st 7 lb and 10 st 7 lb; find the average weight per man.

15. The population in England in 1841 was 14,995,132, and in 1851 it was 16,854,142. Find the average annual increase between the two dates.

16. A member of Parliament was elected with 30,000 votes in his constituency. The average number of votes in each parish within the constituency was 5000. How many parishes were there?

17. I have four uncles. I have been told that their average age is 44 and that three of them are aged 57, 38 and 32 years. What is the age of the fourth uncle?

18. A boy runs a hundred metres in five races. His times were 12.3 s, 12.6 s, 12.2 s, 12.0 s and 11.9 s. Find his average time for these races.

19. If six marks in an exam marked out of 100 were, 85, 85, 85, 85, 85 and 19, find the average mark. In this case is the average mark a fair representation of the results in the test?

20. A girl scored 45%, 68% and 72% in three exams. What would she have to score in the fourth exam in order to obtain an average of 63%?

Using a module to find the average

When all the numbers or quantities are fairly close to one another the calculation of the average may be made easier using a module. A module is a standard to which all the numbers may be related. The sutra is *By elimination and retention*.

To take a very simple example consider finding the average of 12 and 14. We can eliminate the ten, find the average of 2 and 4, that is 3, and then restore the ten making 13. In this case 10 is the module and 2 and 4 are the only numbers involved in the calculation of the average.

We can also find the average when the numbers are less than the module. For example, to find the average of 19 and 15 we could take 20 as the module. By eliminating 20 we have $\bar{1}$ and $\bar{5}$, the average for which is $\bar{3}$. On replacing the 20 the answer is $20 + \bar{3}$ or 17.

There is a choice of which number to use as a module and this depends upon the numbers in the group. Always choose the most convenient.

Find the average of 146, 134, 140, 124, 131, 123.

Using a module of 130,

$$\text{Average} = 130 + \frac{16 + 4 + 10 - 6 + 1 - 7}{6}$$

$$= 130 + \frac{18}{6} = 133$$

Exercise 23c Choose a convenient module to find the average, setting them out as shown in the example.

1. 99, 88, 91, 90

2. 60, 64, 63, 49, 55, 55, 52, 42

3. 10, 13, 26, 9, 7, 15, 14, 26

4. 86, 102, 90, 104, 80, 78

5. 74, 71, 84, 93, 74, 91, 83, 90, 69

6. 104, 80, 78, 94, 79, 90, 84

7. 790, 700, 840, 670, 820, 740

8. 80, 72, 83, 64, 63, 70, 84, 69, 81

9. 33, 33, 41, 59, 39, 40, 49

10. 6.5, 5.0, 5.9, 7.0, 5.8, 6.0, 7.2

11. 8.5, 8.4, 7.7, 8.2

12. 3.4, 4.1, 4.5, 5.9, 4.0, 4.5

13. 233, 220, 214, 207, 216

14. 0.55, 0.47, 0.74, 0.46, 0.58

15. 0.62, 0.77, 0.83, 0.70

16. 148, 146, 129, 124, 137, 124, 130

17. 61, 43, 42, 38, 44, 54, 46, 37, 58

18. 7.3, 6.0, 5.7, 5.0, 6.0, 4.6, 6.0, 7.4

19. 5500, 5600, 4500, 5700, 5900, 4600

20. 800, 890, 910, 890, 830, 830, 940

Exercise 23d

1. Eight girls obtained the following marks in an exam: 56%, 62%, 60%, 46%, 60%, 57%, 47%, 52%. What was the average mark?

2. Ten sports cars were road tested to find the time taken to reach 60 mph from a standing start. The times in seconds were, 3.6, 3.9, 5.3, 4.9, 2.9, 3.1, 4.6, 4.2, 3.6, 3.9. Find the average time taken.

3. A shop sells a particular newspaper everyday. The numbers sold on each of six days is shown in the table below.

MON	TUE	WED	THUR	FRI	SAT
124	121	127	113	111	106

   (a) On which day were the most sold?
   (b) On which day were the least sold?
   (c) What was the average number sold?

4. In a 100 m race the times in seconds of seven runners were 12.1, 13.2, 11.7, 13.9, 12.2, 14.2 and 14.4. Find the average time taken.

5. In a certain rowing team there are eight oarsmen. Their weights in pounds are shown in the table.

Position in boat	Bow	No.2	No.3	No.4	No.5	No.6	No.7	Stroke
Weight in lbs	162	165	175	186	181	180	175	176

   (a) Which crew member is the second lightest?
   (b) What is the average of their weights
   (c) How much heavier than the average is No.4?

204

Chapter 24 - Graphs

A Graph is a diagram representing relationships between variable quantities. Graphs usually have two axes or lines along which the quantities are measured.

Distance/Time Graphs

A distance/time graph is a diagram showing how something moves in relation to time. It has to do with speed distance and time. There are several units of measurement used to measure speed. Kilometres per hour (km/h), miles per hour (m.p.h.), metres per second (m/s), feet per second (ft/s) are all examples of units used to measure speed.

The speed of light is 186,000 miles per second. It takes about eight and a half minutes for light to get from the sun to here. The sun is about 93 million miles away. From the nearest star to here light takes four years! This is a very long way indeed for even at the speed of light it takes four years for the light from the closest star to reach us. The long and the short of this is that light is quite quick. It is very much faster than sound. If you stand a long way off, but still within earshot of a man working with a sledge hammer, you will see the hammer being brought down a short time before you can hear the sound. This is because light is faster than sound.

So light is the fastest thing in the physical world but it is not as fast as the mind. In thought one can move to the other side of the solar system and back in a split second. Again the mind is not as fast as the Self or pure consciousness. The Self is instantaneous.

> The Self is one. Unmoving, it moves faster than the mind. The senses
> lag but Self runs ahead. Unmoving, it outruns pursuit. Out of Self
> comes the breath that is the life of all things.
>
> [Isa Upanishad]

If a car covers a distance of 80 miles in 2 hours how many miles per hour does it go? It goes at a speed of 40 m.p.h because 80 : 2 :: 40 : 1.

The formula for finding speed is,

$$\text{speed} = \frac{\text{distance}}{\text{time}}$$

The following example is used to show how to draw a distance/time graph.

A cyclist leaves home at 10 00 am and travels 40 km in $2\frac{1}{2}$ hrs. He then rests for lunch taking half an hour. He then returns home and arrives there at 3 00 pm. Draw a distance - time graph showing his journey and use it to find his speed whilst returning.

A distance/time has a vertical axis and a horizontal axis. The horizonatal axis is used to denote time and the vertical axis is used to denote distance. We have to look at the distance involved in the problem, which in this case is 40 km, and measure out the vertical axis to the distance using a scale of, say, 2 cm for every 10 km. We look at the time he takes, which is 5 hours, and measure out the horizontal axis using a scale of, say, 2 cm for every hour. The choice of scale for the axes depends on the size of the piece of paper and the detail required in the graph.

The arrows on the ends of the axes indicate that they are increasing in that direction. When the axes have been marked off then it is necessary to label the axes. The quantity and its units are written next to each axis.

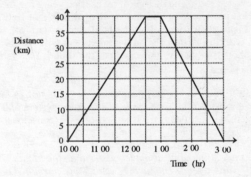

The graph shows that he stops moving at 12 30. As time passes he is neither increasing nor decreasing his distance from home and this is indicated with the horizontal section.

In which part of his journey is he travelling with the greatest speed? By looking at the two parts where is is moving we can see that the greater distance covered in each hour is on his return journey. The steeper the line the faster he is moving.

This is a distance/time graph. The lines drawn on the graph show his jounrey. We now need to use the graph to find his speed on the return journey. By looking at the graph we can see that he took 2 hrs to get home and during this time he travelled 40 km. Using the formula above we can find the speed.

$$\text{Speed} = \frac{\text{distance}}{\text{time}} = \frac{40}{2} = 20 \text{ km/h}$$

Exercise 24a

1.

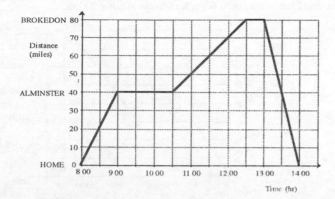

The graph represents a man's car journey from his home to a town called Alminster and to another town called Brokedon. He leaves home at 8 00 am and travels to Alminster which is 40 km away. Here he stops for a while to do some shopping and then continues on his way to Brokedon. After half an hour at Brokedon he returns home and arrives at 2 pm (14 00 hrs).

(a) How long did it take him to get from home to Alminster?

(b) What was his speed between home and Alminster? [Use speed = $\frac{\text{distance}}{\text{time}}$]

(c) For how long was he at Alminster?

(d) How long did it take him to get from Alminster to Brokedon?

(e) How far is it from Alminster to Brokedon?

(f) Find his speed for this part of the journey.

(g) How long did it take him to get from Brokedon to home?

(h) Find his speed for this part of the journey?

(i) What is the total distance which he travelled during that day?

(j) How far from home was he at 11 00 am?

2. Draw a distance time graph for a hiker on a day's walk. The hiker leaves camp at 9 00 am walks at 20 km in 4 hours and then sits down to rest for half an hour. He then walks for another 8 km which takes him 2 hours. After resting for one hour he feels somewhat lazy and so catches the bus home and this takes him half an hour.

(a) Use a vertical axis 14 cm long and marked 2 km for every centimetre.

(b) Draw a horizontal axis using 2 cm to represent each hour of his journey.

(c) Draw the graph of his journey including the rest periods and his return journey.

3. A cyclist makes a journey starting at 2 00 pm. In the first hour /he travels 15 km and from 4 30 pm to 6 pm he travels another 20 km.

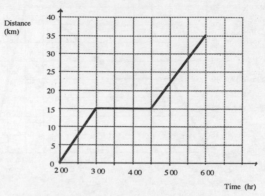

(a) What is his speed during the first hour?
(b) Describe what is happening between 3 00 pm and 4 30 pm.
(c) At what speed did he make the second part of his journey?
(d) How far from home was he at 6 00 pm?
(e) At what time was he 25 km from home?

4. A train leaves station A at 7 00 hr and reaches staion B at 8 30 hr. At 9 00 hr it leaves station B and goes to station C. At 12 30 it leaves station C and goes to station D. On the return journey it goes straight back to station A without stopping. The distance/time graph for this trip is shown below.

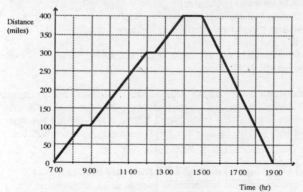

(a) For how long did it stop at station C?
(b) For how long did it stop at station D?
(c) Find the speed of the train for each part of its journey.
(d) How far from station A was the train at 16 00 hrs?

5. A train leaves London at 10 00 am bound for Birmingham 100 miles away. It travels at a speed of 80 mph. On reaching Birmingham it waits for 15 mins and then returns to London at the same speed as on its outward journey. Using a vertical axis with 1 cm or every 10 miles and a horizontal axis with 1 cm for every 15 minutes, draw a distance/time graph showing the journey of the train from London to Birmingham and back.

Frequency tables

A frequency table is a means of collecting pieces of similar information. For example, suppose we have a list of percentage marks obtained by 50 children in an exam.

45	76	83	32	44	89	96	36	21	56
90	43	65	23	21	78	96	14	75	84
36	25	76	78	85	91	66	58	59	54
40	28	77	59	54	63	50	69	81	83
82	94	73	72	76	78	59	68	63	61

To have some idea of the general trend of these marks we can group together the number of marks in certain ranges. This is done using a frequency table. There are two columns, one for the range and the other for the number of marks within that range. The number of marks within a range is called the frequency. When the number of marks within a particular range is needed scan through the table counting each mark. This process is an application of the sutra, *By elimination and retention*.

Range	Frequency
0 - 10	0
11 - 20	1
21 - 30	5
31 - 40	4
41 - 50	4
51 - 60	7
61 - 70	7
71 - 80	10
81 - 90	8
91 - 100	4
Check	50

Exercise 24b Make frequency tables using the groups suggested.

1. The following numbers are the heights in centimetres of a group of 50 children aged twelve.

146	146	151	159	153	140	132	154	151	138
155	140	142	138	152	162	145	151	139	152
148	152	145	162	149	155	165	146	132	152
156	156	134	142	156	151	149	136	155	160
135	163	156	147	138	149	153	161	158	152

Use groups 131 - 135 cm, 136 - 140 cm, 141 - 145 cm, 146 - 150 cm, 151 - 155 cm, 156 - 160 cm, 161 - 165 cm.

2. The list below shows the diameters, in millimetres, of oak tress on a small plantation formed fifteen years ago.

180	175	195	192	178	189	206	175	185	198
177	187	207	184	172	191	190	208	187	194
205	176	190	201	195	206	195	184	178	189
172	172	201	183	176	179	193	188	197	194
204	188	193	178	187	187	199	197	196	191
207	203	178	194	183	182	185	204	186	206

Use groups 171 - 175 mm, 176 - 180 mm, 181 - 185 mm, 186 - 190 mm, 191 - 195 mm, 196 - 200 mm, 201 - 205 mm, 206 - 210 mm.

3. The following numbers show the percentage marks obtained by a class of twenty pupils for three exams.

48	68	40	93	70	43	100	71	54	36
98	80	93	91	51	84	55	44	35	65
23	64	39	95	48	36	93	65	65	21
85	76	93	66	68	49	75	70	38	28
77	43	20	48	78	96	57	62	74	68
86	74	89	35	48	53	68	71	72	86

Use groups 0 - 10, 11 - 20, 21 - 30, 31 - 40, 41 - 50, 51 - 60, 61 - 70, 71 - 80, 81 - 90, 91 - 100

Bar charts

A bar chart is used to convey information which may be easier to appreciate in a diagram form rather than a list of numbers. Diagrams such as bar charts are easier because we live in a society in which visual images are very dominating.

The table below shows the number of new books published during a period of seven weeks.

Week commencing	June 30	July 7	July 14	July 21	July 28	August 4	August 11
Books	142	170	147	148	157	150	160

The bar chart below shows this information displayed

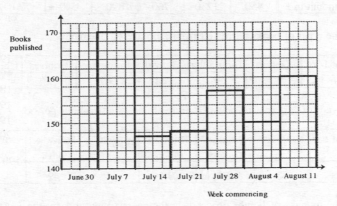

Exercise 24c

In numbers 1 - 7 make a bar chart to represent the given information. Remember to label each axes clearly.

1. Cars sold by a car dealer in eight successive months:

Month	Jan	Feb	Mar	Apr	May	June	July	Aug
Number sold	42	56	62	51	44	63	74	58

2. The average daily receipts of a green-grocer

Day	Mon	Tue	Wed	Thur	Fri	Sat
Receipts in £	623	420	435	526	542	865

3. The number of votes cast for each party in an election in a certain constituency, rounded off to the nearest thousand:

Party	Labour	Conservative	Liberal/ Democrats	Independent	National	Looney
Votes	9,000	8,000	12,000	4,000	1,000	2,000

4. The amount of money, rounded to the nearest £10, raised for charity by each form in a school.

Form	I	II	III	IV	V	VI
Amount in £	450	1230	760	890	540	770

5. The types of books borrowed from a library on one day

Type of book	Fiction	Biography	Travel	Reference	Hobbies	Children's
Number	85	36	44	62	38	75

6. Types of cars passing on a certain road during a two-hour period.

Type of car	Saloon	Hatchback (3 door)	Hatchback (5 door)	Sports	Four-wheel drive	Estate
Number	35	64	38	4	42	25

7. The tonnage of bombs dropped, to the nearest thousand, by the R.A.F. on Germany and the Luftwaffe on Great Britain for the half-years from July 1940 to June 1943 was as follows:

	1940	1941		1942		1943
R.A.F. tons	5,000	10,000	13,000	16,000	21,000	54,000
Luftwaffe tons	36,000	20,000	2,000	2,000	1,000	2,000

Use two bars within each half-year, one for the R.A.F. and the other for the Luftwaffe.

For numbers **8 - 10** make a bar chart from each of the frequency tables made in Exercise 24b.

Chapter 25 - Calculations Using Vinculums

Vinculums are minus or negative numbers. The word *vinculum* (pronounced *winkulum*) is a Latin word meaning *chain* or *bond*. The idea is that a number is bonded to the next base of ten above by a deficiency. For example, 8 is bonded to 10 by the deficiency 2, 39 is bonded to 40 by the deficiency 1.

Vinculums are used to make large digits smaller. For example, $39 = 4\bar{1}$. This means that since 39 is made up of 3 tens and 9 units it is the same as 4 tens and minus 1 unit, or $4\bar{1}$. The 9 of 39 has been replaced by a $\bar{1}$. To change a digit into a vinculum number, to *vinculate*, subtract that number from 10 and increase the next digit to the left by 1. For example, $58 = 6\bar{2}$, that is 8 from $10 = 2$ and $5 + 1 = 6$. The sutra employed here is *Transpose and adjust*.

Exercise 25a Change each units digit into a vinculum.

1. 39	**5.** 58	**9.** 27	**13.** 99	**17.** 476
2. 49	**6.** 78	**10.** 38	**14.** 468	**18.** 488
3. 29	**7.** 59	**11.** 79	**15.** 528	**19.** 899
4. 19	**8.** 48	**12.** 98	**16.** 136	**20.** 398

To devinculate a number, subtract it from 10 and reduce the digit to the left by 1. For example, $3\bar{4} = 26$, that is 4 from $10 = 6$ and $3 - 1 = 2$.

Exercise 25b Devinculate:

1. $4\bar{1}$	**5.** $2\bar{1}$	**9.** $9\bar{1}$	**13.** $91\bar{1}$	**17.** $38\bar{2}$
2. $3\bar{2}$	**6.** $7\bar{3}$	**10.** $8\bar{4}$	**14.** $19\bar{3}$	**18.** $10\bar{1}$
3. $7\bar{4}$	**7.** $6\bar{3}$	**11.** $23\bar{2}$	**15.** $54\bar{2}$	**19.** $20\bar{4}$
4. $5\bar{1}$	**8.** $2\bar{4}$	**12.** $64\bar{4}$	**16.** $24\bar{1}$	**20.** $800\bar{4}$

Multiplcation

29×3	$3\bar{1}$	The 9 of 29 is vinculated giving $3\bar{1}$.
	$\underline{\times\ 3}$	$3 \times \bar{1} = \bar{3}$ and $3 \times 3 = 9$ which gives $9\bar{3}$. We can
	$9\bar{3}$	then devinculate by taking 1 off 9 and subtracting
	$\overline{87}$	the 3 from 10, leaving 87 as the answer.

With such a simple example there does not appear to be much advantage other than the fact that it is easier to multiply 3 by 1 than 3 by 9. Nevertheless, simple practice now will be of great benefit later.

Here is another example but this time involving the carrying of a vinculum digit.

47×6

$$
\begin{array}{r}
5\bar{3} \\
\times\ 6 \\
\hline
29\bar{8} \\
\hline
282
\end{array}
$$

47 is replaced by $5\bar{3}$.

$6 \times \bar{3} = \bar{1}8$, put down 8 and mentally carry $\bar{1}$.

$6 \times 5 = 30$ and add the $\bar{1}$ makes 29. We then have $29\bar{8}$ and on devinculating this becomes 282.

Exercise 25c Set out each sum with a vinculum digit in place of the units digit.

1. 29×2	9. 28×3	17. 429×7	25. 78×7
2. 39×3	10. 48×4	18. 618×4	26. 86×4
3. 69×2	11. 68×3	19. 128×3	27. 427×5
4. 19×4	12. 37×2	20. 617×3	28. 328×8
5. 49×3	13. 18×4	21. 48×7	29. 518×6
6. 79×8	14. 58×3	22. 67×4	30. 447×9
7. 89×5	15. 239×5	23. 57×6	31. 228×8
8. 99×6	16. 437×3	24. 46×3	32. 427×5

More than one figure in a number can be vinculated. For example, 188 is 12 less than 200 and so $188 = 2\bar{1}\bar{2}$. 12 is, in fact, the complement of 88 and as such can be found using the *All from nine and the last from ten* sutra.

Exercise 25d Vinculate all digits except the first.

1. 287	6. 2768	11. 28677	16. 38765
2. 376	7. 5999	12. 39987	17. 38997
3. 489	8. 3768	13. 48679	18. 18007
4. 598	9. 2907	14. 19999	19. 36789
5. 699	10. 3709	15. 38898	20. 26667

Numbers can be devinculated in the same way but reducing the digit to the left by 1. For example, $2\overline{3}2\overline{1} = 1678$, again using *All from nine and the last from ten.*

Exercise 25e Devinculate:

1. $5\overline{1}\,\overline{1}$	6. $6\overline{1}3$	11. $6\overline{3}\,\overline{1}\,\overline{2}$	16. $500\overline{3}$
2. $6\overline{3}\,\overline{2}$	7. $50\overline{1}$	12. $5\overline{2}\,\overline{2}\,\overline{3}$	17. $6\overline{4}0\overline{6}$
3. $4\overline{2}\,\overline{1}$	8. $4\overline{3}\,\overline{2}$	13. $7\overline{5}6\overline{8}$	18. $3\overline{2}\,\overline{1}\,\overline{1}\,\overline{2}$
4. $7\overline{4}\,\overline{2}$	9. $57\overline{8}$	14. $9\overline{5}\overline{4}\,\overline{1}$	19. $8\overline{6}\,5\overline{7}\,\overline{2}$
5. $8\overline{2}\overline{4}$	10. $3\overline{3}\,\overline{3}$	15. $76\overline{8}9$	20. $1\overline{9}\,\overline{1}\,\overline{1}\,\overline{1}$

Further multiplcation using vinculums

3879×4	$\begin{array}{r} 4\overline{1}\,2\overline{1} \\ \times\quad 4 \\ \hline 16\overline{4}8\overline{4} \\ 15516 \end{array}$	3879 is replaced by $4\overline{1}\,2\overline{1}$ $4\overline{1}\,2\overline{1} \times 4 = 16\overline{4}8\overline{4}$ On devinculating this becomes 15516.

Exercise 25f Use vinculums:

1. 288×3	6. 1998×2	11. 27688×3	16. 37699×8
2. 389×4	7. 2879×3	12. 38899×6	17. 36899×7
3. 499×5	8. 2776×4	13. 28799×8	18. 299989×8
4. 687×3	9. 4998×2	14. 49879×9	19. 597899×9
5. 276×6	10. 8799×5	15. 47688×5	20. 3879697×7

Rules for multiplying vinculums

When the signs are the same the answer is positive,
When the signs are different the answer is negative

$3 \times 2 = 6$	$3 \times \overline{2} = \overline{6}$
$\overline{3} \times \overline{2} = 6$	$\overline{3} \times 2 = \overline{6}$

Exercise 25g Use the above rules to find,

1. $6 \times \bar{4}$	6. $4 \times \bar{3}$	11. $\bar{7} \times \bar{8}$	16. $\bar{9} \times \bar{2}$
2. $7 \times \bar{2}$	7. $\bar{6} \times \bar{2}$	12. $\bar{3} \times 9$	17. $\bar{1}\bar{1} \times \bar{6}$
3. $\bar{8} \times 3$	8. 7×8	13. $9 \times \bar{4}$	18. $\bar{7} \times 4$
4. $\bar{6} \times 2$	9. $\bar{7} \times 8$	14. $\bar{5} \times \bar{5}$	19. $9 \times \bar{5}$
5. $9 \times \bar{3}$	10. $7 \times \bar{8}$	15. $7 \times \bar{3}$	20. $\bar{1}\bar{2} \times \bar{3}$

Adding and subtracting vinculums

If a number has no sign preceding it it is understood to be positive. Zero is neither positive nor negative.

When the signs are the same then the number is added to the previous number. When the signs are different then the number is subtracted from the previous number. These rules are applied to the following examples.

In the fourth example on the left, $7 - \bar{2} = 9$, we look at the signs, – on top of the 2 and – preceeding this. Since these are the samethen we are to add 2 to the previous number 7, making 9.

$7 + 2 = 9$	$\bar{7} + 2 = \bar{5}$
$7 - 2 = 5$	$\bar{7} - 2 = \bar{9}$
$7 + \bar{2} = 5$	$\bar{7} + \bar{2} = \bar{9}$
$7 - \bar{2} = 9$	$\bar{7} - \bar{2} = \bar{5}$

Exercise 25h Use the above rules to find,

1. $5 + \bar{1}$	9. $3 - \bar{2}$	17. $2 - \bar{3}$	25. $\bar{2} + \bar{7}$	33. $\bar{8} - 4 + 7$
2. $5 - \bar{1}$	10. $6 - \bar{3}$	18. $\bar{3} - \bar{2}$	26. $\bar{2} - \bar{5}$	34. $\bar{1} + \bar{1} + \bar{1}$
3. $6 - \bar{2}$	11. $\bar{2} + \bar{4}$	19. $\bar{3} + 4$	27. $4 + \bar{7}$	35. $4 - \bar{2} + \bar{4}$
4. $7 + \bar{3}$	12. $\bar{3} - 1$	20. $\bar{3} + \bar{1}$	28. $\bar{3} - \bar{9}$	36. $\bar{2} - \bar{2} + \bar{4}$
5. $8 - \bar{4}$	13. $\bar{4} + 1$	21. $0 + \bar{1}$	29. $\bar{3} - \bar{3}$	37. $\bar{9} - 4 - \bar{1}\bar{4}$
6. $\bar{3} + 0$	14. $\bar{2} - \bar{2}$	22. $1 + \bar{1}$	30. $2 - \bar{4}$	38. $7 + \bar{9} - \bar{2}$
7. $1 + \bar{2}$	15. $\bar{3} - \bar{4}$	23. $\bar{3} + 3$	31. $3 + 4 - 1$	39. $4 + \bar{1} - 7$
8. $\bar{3} - 2$	16. $\bar{1} + 5$	24. $\bar{4} - \bar{4}$	32. $2 - 5 + 6$	40. $\bar{3} + 5 - \bar{2}$

Vertically and crosswise multiplication with vinculums

39×28 The 9 in 39 is vinculated to give $4\bar{1}$ and 28 is transposed into $3\bar{2}$.

$$
\begin{array}{r}
4\bar{1} \\
\times\ 3\bar{2} \\
\hline
11\bar{1}2 \\
1092
\end{array}
$$

$\bar{1} \times \bar{2} = 2$

$\bar{2} \times 4 + \bar{1} \times 3 = \bar{8} + \bar{3} = \bar{1}\bar{1}$

$3 \times 4 + \bar{1} = 11$

The answer is then $11\bar{1}2$ and on devinculating this becomes 1092.

Exercise 25i   Use vinculums in the units column:

1. 29×38	**6.** 19×48	**11.** 46×19	**16.** 38×38
2. 18×28	**7.** 59×18	**12.** 37×47	**17.** 26×69
3. 17×29	**8.** 28×38	**13.** 59×9	**18.** 57×29
4. 28×49	**9.** 37×69	**14.** 49×39	**19.** 9×9
5. 27×59	**10.** 28×79	**15.** 79×26	**20.** 59×59

Chapter 26 - Geometry 3 - Angles

Types of angle

There are several different types of angles and all are based on the division of a sphere or a circle.

A solid angle is the division of a sphere from its centre and bounded by planes or curves which meet at the centre. The internal model of the dodecahedron in Chapter 9 consists of twelve equal solid angles.

A plane angle is the divided part of a circle where the two lines making the angle meet at the centre. When the two lines are straight it is called a rectilinear angle. This chapter will be dealing with some aspects of rectilinear angles.

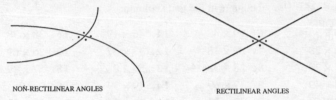

NON-RECTILINEAR ANGLES   RECTILINEAR ANGLES

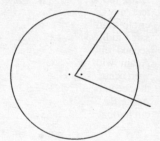

When a circle is divided by two lines which meet at the centre two angles are formed.

If the two lines are in the same line then both the angles will be straight-line angles, otherwise one angle will be smaller than the other.

The unit for angles

For rectilinear angles the unit used is the degree and one degree is the three-hundred and sixtieth part of a circle. Each degree is sub-divided into sixty minutes of arc. Each minute of arc is sub-divided into sixty seconds of arc. So there are 3600 seconds of arc in one degree. This finest unit for measuring angles is used in navigation and astronomy where the radius of the circle is very large.

The degree is a an ancient and convenient measure for angles. It is so ancient that nobody really knows where it originated. 360 is certainly a very convenient number to use because it can be sub-divided into so many numbers. How many factors of 360 are there?

$$360 = 2 \times 180 = 3 \times 120 = 4 \times 90 = 5 \times 72 = 6 \times 60 = 8 \times 45$$
$$= 9 \times 40 = 10 \times 36 = 12 \times 30 = 15 \times 24 = 18 \times 20$$

To draw an angle equal to 60°

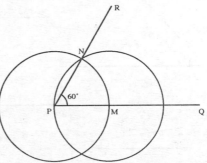

Draw the line PQ. With any suitable radius and centre P draw a circle cutting PQ at M. With centre M and the same radius draw another circle. Let this circle cut the first circle at N. Draw a line PR, from P through N.

Angle QPR is one sixth of a whole circle, that is, 60°.

To draw an angle of 30°

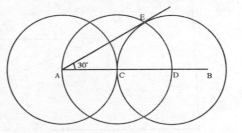

Draw the line AB. With centre A and any suitable radius draw a circle cutting AB at C. With the same radius and centre C draw a second circle cutting AB at D. Again with the same radius but with centre D draw a circle cutting the second circle at E. Join AE.
Angle BAE is one twelfth part of a circle, that is, 30°.

Measuring angles

A protractor is an instrument for measuring or drawing angles. It consists of either a half or a full circle with degrees marked round the edge. The larger the protractor the more accurate it is likely to be. The best protractors to use are full circles with half-degrees clearly marked.

To measure an angle place the centre of the protractor at the point about which the angle is to be measured. Turn the protractor round until the zero line lies over one of the lines of the angle. Read off the position of the other line of the angle. Most protractors have angles marked clockwise and anti-clockwise and so some practice is necessary to master the instrument.

Exercise 26a Use a protractor to measure these angles. Give your answer correct to the nearest whole degree.

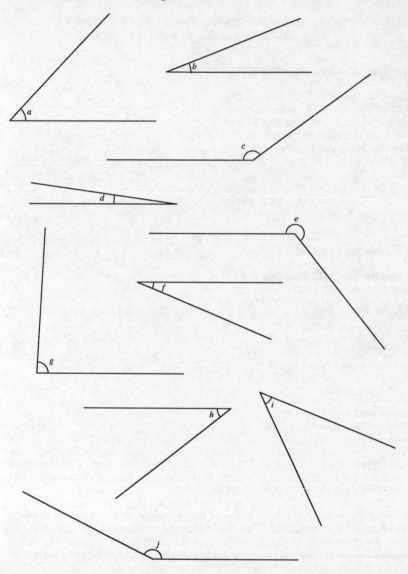

Exercise 26b Using a protractor carefully construct the following angles.

1. 20°	**4.** 54°	**7.** 100°	**10.** 15°	**13.** 48°
2. 32°	**5.** 50°	**8.** 145°	**11.** 172°	**14.** 45°
3. 78°	**6.** 93°	**9.** 131°	**12.** 103°	**15.** 120°

Types of angle

There are three types of rectilinear angle; namely, acute, obtuse and reflex.

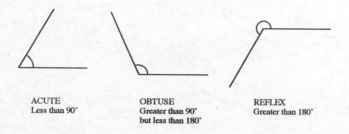

ACUTE
Less than 90°

OBTUSE
Greater than 90°
but less than 180°

REFLEX
Greater than 180°

Exercise 26c Give the name of each type of angle in Exercise 26a

Angles about a point

Since the circle is divided into 360° it follows that lines meeting at a point make angles which together make 360°.

Angles about a point add up to 360°.

From this it follows that if we know all the angles about a point except one then we can subtract the known angles from 360° to find the unknown angle.

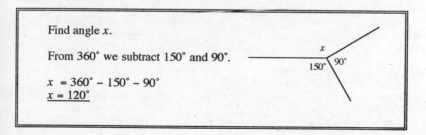

Find angle x.

From 360° we subtract 150° and 90°.

$x = 360° - 150° - 90°$
$\underline{x = 120°}$

Exercise 26d Calculate the missing angles

1.

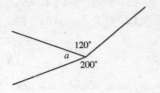

120°
a
200°

6.

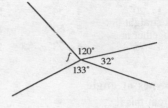

f 120°
32°
133°

2.

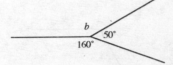

b
50°
160°

7.

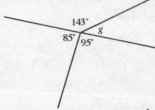

143°
g
85° 95°

3.

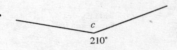

c
210°

8.

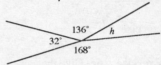

136° *h*
32°
168°

4.

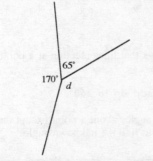

65°
170°
d

9.

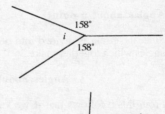

158°
i
158°

10.

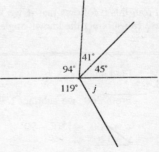

41°
94° 45°
119° *j*

5.

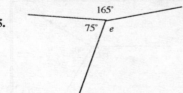

165°
75° *e*

Angles on a straight line

A straight line angle is half a circle and therefore measures 180°. Angles meeting together at a point on a straight line make 180°.

Angles on a straight line add up to 180°.

From this it follows that we can again find an unknown angle by subtraction.

Find angle x

$x = 180° - 152°$
$\underline{x = 28°}$

152°

x

Exercise 26e Find the missing angles

1.

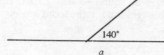

140°

a

4.

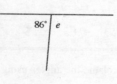

35°

d

2.

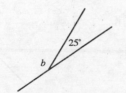

25°

b

5.

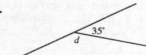

86° e

3.

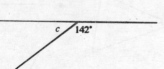

c 142°

6.

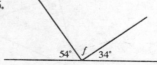

54° f 34°

223

7.

48° g 15°

9.

97° i 38°

8.

20° 132° h

10.

30° 60° 70°
j

Naming angles

For purposes of clarity, in geometry, angles are frequently named using three capital letters. The three letters give three points; the first two labelling one line and the second and third labelling the other line. Since both lines meet at a single point, the middle letter is used to denote the point where those lines meet.

∠ABC, denotes the angle formed at the point B by the two lines AB and CB. The outer two letters may also be placed the other way round so that ∠ABC is the same as ∠CBA. The ∠ symbol is used as an abbreviation for the word *angle*.

C

A   B

Name the angles using three-letter notation.

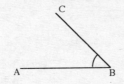

a = ∠PQR, b = ∠QPR, c = ∠PRQ, d = ∠SRT, e = ∠RST, f = ∠RTS

Exercise 26f Name the angles using three letter notation.

1.

2.
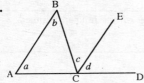

3.
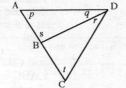

4.
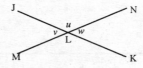

5.
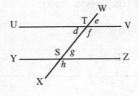

6.
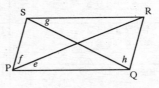

Chapter 27 - Practice and Revision 3

Exercise 27a

1.	75647 768 + 1205	**15.**	Express $\frac{16}{24}$ in lowest terms.
2.	574832 −349186	**16.**	Find $\frac{5}{6}$ of one hour in minutes.
3.	Add together £34.89, £25.50 and £16.78.	**17.**	$\frac{3}{7} + \frac{2}{5}$
4.	Subtract £108.67 from £500	**18.**	$\frac{3}{4} \times \frac{2}{3}$
5.	Multiply £56.85 by six.	**19.**	$10219 \div 89$
6.	Divide £29.52 by 8	**20.**	Find the HCF of 36 and 64.
7.	456 × 42	**21.**	Find the LCM of 12 and 16.
8.	1006 ×1012	**22.**	Reduce the ratio 16:24 to its simplest form.
9.	988 ×997	**23.**	$4\frac{3}{5} - 2\frac{1}{4}$
10.	Divide 4567 by 34 leaving a whole number remainder.	**24.**	$3\frac{3}{8} + 5\frac{5}{6}$
11.	$0.46 + 3.2 + 0.98$	**25.**	Simplify $2a + 4a + 6a - 7a$
12.	$3.651 - 1.816$	**26.**	Simplify $5x - 6y + 3x + 9y$
13.	0.2×1.3	**27.**	Multiply out $3(5a - 2b)$
14.	Write down the next two numbers in the sequence, 0, 12, 22, 30, 36, ___, ___	**28.**	Solve $4x + 11 = 31$

Exercise 27b

1.	How many weeks are there in 56 days?	**14.**	What is 0.45 as a vulgar fraction in its lowest terms?
2.	How many 250 g bars of fudge can be made from a 3 kg block?	**15.**	What is $\frac{3}{4}$ as a decimal fraction?
3.	Alice receives £2.50 pocket money each week. If she saves half of this amount for 10 weeks, how much will she have saved?	**16.**	Express 36 as the product of two numbers as many times as possible.
4.	From a 3 m length of string how many parcels can be tied up each of which uses 70 cm of string?	**17.**	A hockey pitch is 82 m long and 58 m wide. What is its area?
5.	Write down the next two prime numbers after 31.	**18.**	A train travels 300 miles in 5 hours. What is its speed?
6.	Pads of paper are sold at 84 p each. How much saving is there in buying five pads for £3.75?	**19.**	Find $\frac{3}{8}$ of 4.8 m
7.	Write down three fractions equivalent to $\frac{2}{5}$	**20.**	Find 25% of £6.00
8.	Find the total cost of a dining table at £785 and six chairs at £190 each.	**21.**	Solve the equation, $4x - 13 = 39$
9.	Anne bought three times as many apples as pears and she bought 20 pieces of fruit altogether. How many apples did she buy?	**22.**	Given that $x = 3$, $y = 2$ and $t = 4$, find the value of, (a) $x^2 - ty$ (b) $3t^2 + y^2$
10.	Subtract 3.06 from 20	**23.**	$2\frac{4}{5} - \frac{1}{2}$
11.	Multiply 60.3 by 0.7	**24.**	$2\frac{1}{2} \div 5$
12.	$5.08 + 7.3 - 4.83$	**25.**	$6\frac{3}{4} \div \frac{9}{10}$
13.	Write $\frac{21}{8}$ as a mixed number.	**26.**	Express $5\frac{3}{8}$ as an improper fraction.

Exercise 27c

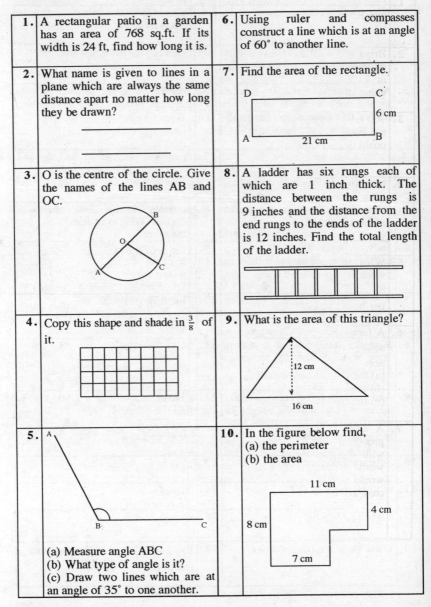

1. A rectangular patio in a garden has an area of 768 sq.ft. If its width is 24 ft, find how long it is.

2. What name is given to lines in a plane which are always the same distance apart no matter how long they be drawn?

3. O is the centre of the circle. Give the names of the lines AB and OC.

4. Copy this shape and shade in $\frac{3}{8}$ of it.

5.
(a) Measure angle ABC
(b) What type of angle is it?
(c) Draw two lines which are at an angle of 35° to one another.

6. Using ruler and compasses construct a line which is at an angle of 60° to another line.

7. Find the area of the rectangle.

6 cm
21 cm

8. A ladder has six rungs each of which are 1 inch thick. The distance between the rungs is 9 inches and the distance from the end rungs to the ends of the ladder is 12 inches. Find the total length of the ladder.

9. What is the area of this triangle?

12 cm
16 cm

10. In the figure below find,
(a) the perimeter
(b) the area

11 cm
4 cm
8 cm
7 cm

Exercise 27d

1.	Find the difference between 350 g and 1.5 kg.	**8.**	How many tiles, each a square of side 15 centimetres are required to cover a floor 2.4 m by 3 m?
2.	Brian and Charles started a game of chess at 5 45 pm and finished at 7 20 pm. How long did the game last?	**9.**	How many slabs of concrete, each measuring 70 cm by 50 cm are needed to cover a path 2.5 m wide and 10.5 m long?
3.	760 ml of milk were poured into a 5 litre bucket. How much more could the bucket hold?	**10.**	A man invests £480 for one year at an interest rate of 8%. How much does he have altogether at th end of that year?
4.	Mrs Bulgypurse spends £134.99 on a dress, £78.99 on a pair of shoes and £34.42 on lunch. How much money does she have left given that she started with £300?	**11.**	The daily return fare to Victoria is £3.20. How much do I save in buying a monthly season ticket for £60.80 given that in one month there are 24 working days?
5.	What is the total pay for one week of five days if a man works $8\frac{1}{2}$ hrs a day and earns £12.50 per hour?	**12.**	6 kg of tea at £1.75 per kg are mixed with 4 kg of tea at £2.35 per kg. What should be charged for 1 kg of the mixture?
6.	A farmer owns 12,200 acres and sells $\frac{3}{8}$ of his land at £5000 per acre. Find, (a) the area of land he sells, (b) the area of land he keeps, (c) the amount he receives.	**13.**	Mary timed herself to walk 60 m and found that it took her 40 seconds. Find her speed in km/hr. *[To change m/s into km/hr divide the speed by 1000 and multiply it by 60 × 60]*
7.	A story is typed onto a word processor and takes up 36 pages with 40 lines per page and 15 words per line. How many pages would it take up at 36 lines per page and 12 words per line?	**14.**	Five boys raised £62, £74, £33.50, £46.34 and £83.66 for a charity by a sponsored swim. (a) What was the average amount raised? (b)How much more would each boy have to raise to bring the total up to £300?

Exercise 27e

1. $\frac{2}{3} + \frac{2}{9}$ 7. $3\frac{1}{6} - 1\frac{5}{6}$ 13. $\frac{1}{2} \times \frac{2}{9}$ 19. $\frac{2}{3} \div \frac{3}{5}$

2. $\frac{1}{2} + \frac{7}{8}$ 8. $\frac{2}{3} - \frac{1}{8}$ 14. $\frac{3}{4} \times \frac{5}{9}$ 20. $\frac{1}{4} \div \frac{2}{5}$

3. $\frac{7}{12} + \frac{7}{8}$ 9. $\frac{3}{4} - \frac{1}{16}$ 15. $\frac{2}{3} \times \frac{15}{22}$ 21. $\frac{11}{12} \div \frac{1}{18}$

4. $3\frac{1}{8} + 2\frac{3}{16}$ 10. $4\frac{2}{3} - 1\frac{1}{2}$ 16. $3\frac{3}{4} \times 6\frac{2}{5}$ 22. $\frac{7}{12} \div 2\frac{5}{8}$

5. $2\frac{3}{8} + 5\frac{4}{5}$ 11. $11\frac{7}{8} - 1\frac{5}{12}$ 17. $2\frac{3}{4} \times \frac{8}{11}$ 23. $4\frac{1}{5} \div 1\frac{1}{3}$

6. $6\frac{2}{7} + 3\frac{9}{14}$ 12. $3\frac{1}{6} - 2\frac{5}{6}$ 18. $3\frac{2}{5} \times 1\frac{1}{9}$ 24. $8\frac{1}{8} \div 1\frac{6}{7}$

25.	The sum of two numbers is $9\frac{1}{2}$. If one of the numbers is $1\frac{3}{5}$, find the other.	32.	Find the cost of $2\frac{3}{4}$ yards of ribbon at 36p per yard.
26.	A girl gave $\frac{1}{4}$ of her money to a friend and spent $\frac{1}{3}$ on clothes. What fraction did she have left?	33.	A length of timber, 12.5 m long, is cut shorter and is now $\frac{9}{10}$ of its original length. How long is it now?
27.	Take $\frac{3}{4}$ from $5\frac{5}{8}$ and then subtract $2\frac{7}{8}$ from the result.	34.	Divide $3\frac{2}{9}$ by $2\frac{1}{3}$ and add to the result of $\frac{2}{7}$ of $8\frac{3}{4}$
28.	What fraction of 1 m is 20 cm?	35.	Find $\frac{2}{5}$ of £128.00
29.	Express 150 g as a fraction of 750 g and bring to lowest terms.	36.	Find the value of $\frac{1}{2}$ of $\frac{3}{4}$ of 10 kg.
30.	There are 256 children in a primary school of whom $\frac{9}{16}$ are girls. What fraction are boys and how many boys are there?	37.	Sam has £72.00. David has $\frac{7}{18}$ as much as Sam and John has $\frac{2}{5}$ as much as David. How much does John have?
31.	Write down the following fractions in order of size starting with the smallest and subtract the smallest from the largest. $\frac{1}{3} \quad \frac{1}{5} \quad \frac{1}{9} \quad \frac{1}{7}$	38.	If $\frac{4}{5}$ of the air is nitrogen and $\frac{4}{25}$ is oxygen, what fraction is made of other gases?

Appendix - Tables of Weights and Measures

British Measures

Avoirdupois Weight*

16	drams	make	1 ounce (1 oz)
16	ounces	....	1 pound (1 lb)
14	pounds	....	1 stone (1 st)
2	stones	....	1 quarter (1 qr)
or 28	pounds		
4	quarters	....	1 hundredweight (1 cwt)
or 112	pounds		
20	hundredweights	....	1 ton

* The name *Avoirdupois* is traditionally used for British measures of weight and comes from old french, *aveir de peis*, meaning *goods of weight*.

Linear Measure

12	inches (in)	make	1 foot (ft)
3	feet	....	1 yard (yd)
22	yards	....	1 chain
10	chains	....	1 furlong
8	furlongs	....	1 mile
or 1760	yards		

Also, 100	links	make	1 chain
$5\frac{1}{2}$	yards	....	1 pole, rod or perch
40	poles	....	1 furlong
4	inches	....	1 hand
6	feet	....	1 fathom
600	feet	....	1 cable
about 6080	feet	....	1 nautical mile
1	knot	....	1 nautical mile per hour

Square Measure

144	sq. inches	make	1 sq. foot	4840	sq. yards	make	1 acre
9	sq. feet	....	1 sq. yard	$30\frac{1}{4}$	sq. yards	....	1 sq. pole
484	sq. yards	....	1 sq. chain	40	sq. poles	....	1 rood
10	sq. chains	....	1 acre	4	roods	....	1 acre
640	acres	....	1 sq. mile				

Cubic Measure

1728 cubic inches make 1 cubic foot
27 cubic feet .... 1 cubic yard

Liquid Measure

4 gills   make 1 pint (pt.)
2 pints   .... 1 quart (qt.)
4 quarts .... 1 gallon
36 gallons .... 1 barrel

Dry or Corn Measure

4 gills   make 1 pint
2 pints   .... 1 quart
4 quarts .... 1 gallon
2 gallons .... 1 peck
4 pecks   .... 1 bushel
8 bushels .... 1 quarter
4 quarters .... 1 ton (cargo)

Metric Measures

The base units for the metric system are the gram, litre and metre. Each of these are given prefixes for subdivisions and multiples. Latin words for ten hundred and a thousand form the prefixes for the sub-divisions, such as *centi*litre, *centi*gram and *centi*metre. Greek words for 10, 100 and 1000 form the prefixes for the multiples, such as *deca* litre, *deca*gram and *deca*metre.

	Prefix	Relation to unit
Latin	milli	$\frac{1}{1000}$
	centi	$\frac{1}{100}$
	deci	$\frac{1}{10}$
Greek	deca	10
	hecto	100
	kilo	1000

Measures of Weight

10	milligrams (mg.)	make	1	centigram (cg.)
10	centigrams	....	1	decigram (dg.)
10	decigrams	....	1	GRAM (g.)
10	grams	....	1	decagram (dag.)
10	decagrams	....	1	hectogram (hg.)
10	hectograms	....	1	kilogram (kg.)
100	kilograms	....	1	quintal (q.)
1000	kilograms	....	1	tonne (t.)

Measures of Length

10	millimetres (mg.)	make	1	centimetre (cm.)
10	centimetres	....	1	decimetre (dm.)
10	decimetres	....	1	METRE (m.)
10	metres	....	1	decametre (dam.)
10	decametres	....	1	hectometre (hm.)
10	hectometres	....	1	kilometre (km.)

Measures of Area

100	sq. millimetres (mm^2)	make	1	sq. centimetre (cm^2)
100	sq. centimetres	....	1	sq. decimetre (dm^2)
100	sq. decimetres	....	1	sq. metre (m^2)
100	sq. metres	....	1	sq. decametre (dam^2) = 1 are
100	sq. decametres	....	1	sq. hectometre (hm^2) = 1 hectare
100	sq. hectometres	....	1	sq. kilometre (km^2)

Measures of Volume

1000	cubic millimetres (mm^3.)	make	1	cubic centimetre (cm^3.)
1000	cubic centimetres	....	1	cubic decimetre (dm^3.)
1000	cubic decimetres	....	1	cubic metre (m^3.)

233

Measures of Capacity

10	millilitres (ml.)	make	1 centilitre (cl.)
10	centilitres	....	1 decilitre (dl.)
10	decilitres	....	1 LITRE (l.)
10	litres	....	1 decalitre (dal.)
10	decalitres	....	1 hectolitre (hl.)
10	hectolitres	....	1 kilolitre (kl.)

Measures of Angles, Number and Time

Measures of Angles

60	seconds of arc (60")	make	1 minute (1')
60	minutes of arc	....	1 degree
90	degrees	....	1 right angle

Measures of Number

12	units	make	1 dozen	24	sheets of paper	make	1 quire
20	units	....	1 score	20	quires	....	1 ream
12	dozen	....	1 gross	10	reams	....	1 bale

Measures of Time

60	seconds	make	1 minute
60	minutes	....	1 hour
24	hours	....	1 day
7	days	....	1 week
28, 29, 30 or 31	days	....	1 calender month
12	months	....	1 year
365	days	....	1 common year
366	days	....	1 leap year
100	years	....	1 century
1000	years	....	1 millenium

Answers

Chapter 1 Multiplying by *All from 9 and the last from 10*

Exercise 1a   Page 2

1. 13	**7.** 36	**13.** 097	**19.** 8889	**25.** 4996600
2. 06	**8.** 72	**14.** 8660	**20.** 61270	**26.** 876020
3. 64	**9.** 56	**15.** 6436	**21.** 72537	**27.** 546399
4. 58	**10.** 46	**16.** 1996	**22.** 645400	**28.** 635280
5. 12	**11.** 126	**17.** 69540	**23.** 29397	**29.** 7241593
6. 25	**12.** 574	**18.** 1362	**24.** 00008	**30.** 3333333

Exercise 1b   Page 3

1. 25	**15.** 101	**29.** 32	**42.** 98	**55.** 145	**68.** 4 r 6
2. 37	**16.** 82	**30.** 341	**43.** 58	**56.** 796	**69.** 3 r 3
3. 65	**17.** 85	**31.** 101	**44.** 38	**57.** 897	**70.** 2 r 2
4. 54	**18.** 355	**32.** 152	**45.** 138	**58.** 196	**71.** 2 r 3
5. 37	**19.** 84	**33.** 103	**46.** 117	**59.** 594	**72.** 2 r 5
6. 48	**20.** 87	**34.** 205	**47.** 177	**60.** 996	**73.** 87
7. 39	**21.** 208	**35.** 465	**48.** 57	**61.** 2 r 2	**74.** 23°F
8. 16	**22.** 355	**36.** 841	**49.** 87	**62.** 3 r 3	**75.** £149.85
9. 69	**23.** 270	**37.** 134	**50.** 297	**63.** 5 r 5	**76.** 232 miles
10. 194	**24.** 340	**38.** 507	**51.** 195	**64.** 1 r 1	**77.** £11.94
11. 62	**25.** 680	**39.** 413	**52.** 95	**65.** 2 r 2	**78.** £4.95
12. 71	**26.** 54	**40.** 504	**53.** 245	**66.** 3 r 7	**79.** £1180
13. 36	**27.** 49	**41.** 78	**54.** 295	**67.** 2 r 2	**80.** 11.70 m
14. 45	**28.** 202				

Exercise 1c   Page 5

1. 45	**3.** 81	**5.** 54	**7.** 63
2. 56	**4.** 48	**6.** 49	**8.** 64

Exercise 1d   Page 6

1. 9216	**8.** 3663	**15.** 111104	**21.** 931198	**27.** 78626405
2. 8740	**9.** 984064	**16.** 650076	**22.** 12335064	**28.** 865266
3. 7372	**10.** 773115	**17.** 397602	**23.** 98690868	**29.** 989028
4. 8272	**11.** 454176	**18.** 880684	**24.** 10097980	**30.** 94564815
5. 8463	**12.** 109890	**19.** 692818	**25.** 99980001	**31.** 99750100
6. 6566	**13.** 979104	**20.** 980100	**26.** 98760244	**32.** 93163395
7. 8352	**14.** 350814			

Exercise 1e Page 7

1. 225	**5.** 180	**9.** 196	**13.** 256	**17.** 144
2. 224	**6.** 187	**10.** 270	**14.** 228	**18.** 169
3. 182	**7.** 168	**11.** 154	**15.** 210	**19.** 306
4. 143	**8.** 208	**12.** 195	**16.** 121	**20.** 266

Exercise 1f Page 7

1. 10712	**8.** 12546	**15.** 15965	**22.** 1016063	**29.** 15620
2. 11988	**9.** 11130	**16.** 12584	**23.** 1519545	**30.** 1071268
3. 11663	**10.** 14976	**17.** 1011030	**24.** 1426284	**31.** 1071330
4. 11872	**11.** 12430	**18.** 1048176	**25.** 11449	**32.** 1236468
5. 11766	**12.** 11984	**19.** 1023130	**26.** 15080	
6. 19897	**13.** 11639	**20.** 1019084	**27.** 1342331	
7. 11970	**14.** 13843	**21.** 1016039	**28.** 240	

Exercise 1g Page 8

1. 9408	**7.** 882672	**13.** 1034000	**19.** 980099	**25.** 1002001
2. 8272	**8.** 272	**14.** 1879752	**20.** 12960	**26.** 1919061618
3. 13534	**9.** 11336	**15.** 458370	**21.** 121756	**27.** 9369206307
4. 252	**10.** 27	**16.** 761175	**22.** 20196	**28.** 177009165
5. 96566	**11.** 11881	**17.** 1253715	**23.** 98730372	**29.** 4545045450
6. 13020	**12.** 1228638	**18.** 20099	**24.** 1579640	**30.** 176588250

Exercise 1h Page 9

1a 04	**g** 00020	**6.** £94.05	**12.** 12190	**c** 998001
b 103	**h** 89100	**7.** 11550	**13.** 6958 m^2	**d** 99980001
c 2935	**2.** 6664	**8.** 46785960	**14.** 109212754	**e** 121
d 220	**3.** 977120	**9.** £123.05	**15.** 843200	**f** 12321
e 4019	**4.** 6305	**10.** 95002964	**16a** 81	**g** 1234321
f 65479	**5.** 12064	**11.** £1119784	**b** 9801	**h** 123454321

Exercise 1i Page 10

1. 38	**7.** 27	**13.** 556	**19.** 897	**25.** 368
2. 29	**8.** 9	**14.** 867	**20.** 96	**26.** 5688
3. 56	**9.** 78	**15.** 6538	**21.** 379	**27.** 57286
4. 19	**10.** 86	**16.** 7089	**22.** 278	**28.** 1977
5. 68	**11.** 338	**17.** 8938	**23.** 469	**29.** 4966
6. 47	**12.** 119	**18.** 199	**24.** 589	**30.** 169986

| 31. 5658 | 33. 6889 | 35. 4103 | 37. 863457 | 39. 656409 |
| 32. 4877 | 34. 7795 | 36. 77724 | 38. 88497 | 40. 1997564 |

Exercise 1j   Page 11

1. 10152	8. 9797	15. 6901	22. 1229064	29. 153
2. 9785	9. 10304	16. 8112	23. 988848	30. 88
3. 9936	10. 9672	17. 1001992	24. 985760	31. 77
4. 10395	11. 10368	18. 999975	25. 135	32. 130
5. 9737	12. 9999	19. 997997	26. 162	
6. 9360	13. 14504	20. 989944	27. 108	
7. 10780	14. 7752	21. 1108664	28. 99	

Exercise 1k   Page 11

1. 9702	10. 8245	19. 6790	28. 988011	37. 880008
2. 9504	11. 4018	20. 8550	29. 986013	38. 851001
3. 9506	12. 7008	21. 7560	30. 888112	39. 745008
4. 9408	13. 7708	22. 7830	31. 982032	40. 828002
5. 9215	14. 5888	23. 7600	32. 982045	41. 943260
6. 8330	15. 7826	24. 7470	33. 983052	42. 752458
7. 7938	16. 8910	25. 6440	34. 982056	43. 788640
8. 8232	17. 7920	26. 998001	35. 980075	44. 905924
9. 8342	18. 6860	27. 992007	36. 477044	45. 404782

Exercise 1l   Page 12

1. 121	7. 224	13. 10403	19. 12705	25. 1219065
2. 132	8. 216	14. 10404	20. 13832	26. 101270492
3. 120	9. 272	15. 10506	21. 1123242	27. 113243963
4. 130	10. 221	16. 15450	22. 1238705	28. 121290615
5. 144	11. 10201	17. 19380	23. 1527084	29. 11532545966
6. 180	12. 10302	18. 13728	24. 1465926	30. 1234328405926

Exercise 1m   Page 12

1. 84	7. 144	13. 10152	19. 9844	25. 1001880
2. 96	8. 112	14. 9523	20. 14308	26. 1007935
3. 153	9. 171	15. 9568	21. 999996	27. 1014946
4. 91	10. 104	16. 9975	22. 1019956	28. 1007935
5. 66	11. 9701	17. 9776	23. 1029901	29. 1236522
6. 117	12. 9660	18. 6901	24. 987972	30. 960624

Chapter Two Multiplication by Vertically and crosswise

Exercise 2a Page 14

1. 483	6. 273	11. 364	16. 735	21. 529	26. 5628
2. 208	7. 420	12. 476	17. 848	22. 1456	27. 6825
3. 247	8. 312	13. 2091	18. 576	23. 1216	28. 110
4. 378	9. 836	14. 675	19. 1003	24. 1638	29. 374
5. 512	10. 770	15. 546	20. 630	25. 3763	30. 286

Exercise 2b Page 14

1. 1472	3. 4452	5. £848	7. £30.72	9. 1785
2. 1104	4. 1176	6. 288	8. £952	10. 744

Exercise 2c Page 16

1. 14883	7. 91663	13. 35370	19. 7950	25. 23751
2. 23328	8. 150750	14. 165200	20. 25272	26. 119079
3. 44958	9. 221229	15. 189440	21. 66144	27. 184266
4. 105369	10. 263110	16. 10608	22. 26999	28. 378228
5. 57717	11. 128544	17. 20208	23. 226772	29. 93240
6. 33957	12. 85869	18. 13090	24. 95469	30. 19485

Exercise 2d Page 17

1. 29160	3. 62620	5. 9288	7. £1124.50	9. £109,200
2. 65280	4. £4081.75	6. 7056	8. £21.60	

Exercise 2e Page 19

1. 1,359,773	7. 1,096,173	13. 3,579,910	19. 1,457,090	25. 602,112
2. 1,446,864	8. 13,228,650	14. 30,622,300	20. 10,827,672	26. 815,057
3. 3,616,800	9. 2,496,429	15. 47,523,840	21. 65,059,452	27. 297,383
4. 5,299,852	10. 12,707,100	16. 54,183,558	22. 6,614,299	28. 172,128
5. 15,550,326	11. 12,048,000	17. 5,455,514	23. 2,192,372	29. 175,360
6. 2,258,472	12. 8,478,699	18. 30,066,330	24. 1,657,628	30. 443,700

Exercise 2f Page 19

1. 126,942,373	5. 23,354,633	9. 7,128,772,913,241
2. 161,763,264	6. 25,894,848	10. 724,941,088,920,621
3. 1,656,197,378	7. 21,652,669,611	11. 20,924,052,310,000
4. 358,504,377,922	8. 5,371,883,049,403	12. 111,132

13. 300,846	16. 8,453,561	19. 234,567,531
14. 4911933	17. 9,159,258	20. 5,876,322,331
15. 63,853,224	18. 26,785	

Exercise 2g Page 20

1. 352	6. 858	11. 2,541	16. 7,110,983
2. 594	7. 1,078	12. 5,852	17. 6,041,651
3. 682	8. 715	13. 38,962	18. 698,029,981
4. 176	9. 506	14. 475,321	19. 990,290,972
5. 781	10. 847	15. 2,545,950	20. 589,890,508,130

Exercise 2h Page 21

1. 276	6. 1044	11. 3,744	16. 64,104
2. 168	7. 828	12. 4,956	17. 104,292
3. 384	8. 1140	13. 50,412	18. 840,516
4. 492	9. 552	14. 53,424	19. 3,043,848,600
5. 624	10. 888	15. 18,516	20. 119,999,999,988

Exercise 2i Page 22

1. 27,300	9. 2,144,000	17. 158,400,000	25. 16,020,400,000
2. 224,000	10. 864,000	18. 183,600,000	26. 29,056,000,000
3. 46,200	11. 86,800	19. 90,100,000	27. 6,825,000
4. 7,560	12. 805,000	20. 21,000,000	28. 131,300,000
5. 11,250,000	13. 260,100	21. 20,000,000	29. 4,892,400,000
6. 207,900	14. 67,500	22. 6,076,000	30. 27,060,000,000
7. 499,800	15. 40,700,000	23. 2,368,000,000	
8. 38,820,000	16. 3,600,000	24. 970,200,000	

Chapter Three - Division

Exercise 3a Page 23

1. 1 r 2	9. 0 r 4	17. 6 r 2	25. 10 r 6	33. 2 r 3
2. 1 r 2	10. 2 r 1	18. 4 r 1	26. 8 r 3	34. 2 r 3
3. 1 r 1	11. 4 r 3	19. 1 r 5	27. 6 r 2	35. 3 r 1
4. 0 r 1	12. 4 r 1	20. 3 r 1	28. 11 r 5	36. 4 r 12
5. 0 r 1	13. 8 r 1	21. 2 r 7	29. 8 r 6	37. 2 r 5
6. 0 r 1	14. 1 r 4	22. 4 r 2	30. 23 r 0	38. 7 r 8
7. 0 r 2	15. 2 r 1	23. 12 r 3	31. 0 r 10	39. 2 r 2
8. 0 r 0	16. 3 r 4	24. 5 r 3	32. 1 r 21	40. 0 r 1

Exercise 3b Page 24

1. 269	**5.** 183	**9.** 216 r 1	**13.** 68 r 3	**17.** 800 r 1
2. 144	**6.** 154 r 3	**10.** 135 r 2	**14.** 201 r 2	**18.** 906 r 2
3. 62 r 4	**7.** 493 r 1	**11.** 271 r 1	**15.** 124 r 1	**19.** 388 r 2
4. 185 r 2	**8.** 223 r 1	**12.** 365 r 1	**16.** 1710 r 3	**20.** 629

Exercise 3c Page 24

1. 1167	**3.** 428	**5.** 7500 acres	**7.** 28	**9.** 149
2. 442	**4.** £2413	**6.** £10.67	**8.** 287	**10.** 1479 r 4

Exercise 3d Page 25

1. $\frac{1}{3}$	**5.** $\frac{5}{24}$	**9.** $\frac{8}{12}$	**13.** $\frac{1}{4}$	**17.** $\frac{4}{7}$
2. $\frac{5}{9}$	**6.** $\frac{3}{2}$	**10.** $\frac{9}{10}$	**14.** $\frac{6}{7}$	**18.** $\frac{3}{8}$
3. $\frac{12}{13}$	**7.** $\frac{4}{6}$	**11.** $\frac{2}{3}$	**15.** $\frac{3}{4}$	**19.** $\frac{3}{7}$
4. $\frac{3}{4}$	**8.** $\frac{5}{4}$	**12.** $\frac{1}{5}$	**16.** $\frac{7}{9}$	**20.** $\frac{10}{5}$

Exercise 3e Page 25

1. $2 \div 1$	**5.** $3 \div 2$	**9.** $2 \div 1$	**13.** $9 \div 2$	**17.** $7 \div 5$
2. $3 \div 1$	**6.** $4 \div 3$	**10.** $2 \div 1$	**14.** $9 \div 7$	**18.** $2 \div 1$
3. $5 \div 1$	**7.** $4 \div 3$	**11.** $3 \div 2$	**15.** $7 \div 5$	**19.** $25 \div 3$
4. $4 \div 3$	**8.** $5 \div 2$	**12.** $8 \div 5$	**16.** $19 \div 11$	**20.** $8 \div 5$

Exercise 3f Page 26

1. 2.5	**5.** 133.75	**9.** 155.275	**13.** 13.44	**17.** 0.8024
2. 2.5	**6.** 16417.5	**10.** 0.625	**14.** 867.25	**18.** 141.825
3. 2.4	**7.** 0.268	**11.** 4.5	**15.** 11798.375	**19.** 127.875
4. 11.5	**8.** 6.912	**12.** 54.375	**16.** 11.5715	**20.** 0.37685

Exercise 3g Page 27

DIVISION	WITH REMAINDERS	VULGAR FRACTION	DECIMAL FRACTION
$1 \div 2$ or 2 into 1	0 rem 1	$\frac{1}{2}$	0.5
$1 \div 3$ or 3 into 1	0 rem 1	$\frac{1}{3}$	0.333...
$2 \div 5$ or 5 into 2	**0 r 2**	$\frac{2}{5}$	0.4
$1 \div 10$ or 10 into 1	**0 r 1**	$\frac{1}{10}$	**0.1**
$3 \div 2$ or **2 into 3**	1 r 1	$\frac{3}{2}$	**1.5**

$13 \div 2$ or **2 into 13**	**6 r 1**	$\frac{13}{2}$	**6.5**
$1 \div 4$ or 4 into 1	**0 r 1**	$\frac{1}{4}$	0.25
$5 \div 4$ or **4 into 5**	**1 r 1**	$\frac{5}{4}$	**1.25**
$9 \div 4$ or **4 into 9**	**2 r 1**	$\frac{9}{4}$	**2.25**
$3 \div 10$ or **10 into 3**	**0 r 3**	$\frac{3}{10}$	**0.3**
$5 \div 15$ or **15 into 5**	**0 r 5**	$\frac{5}{15}$	**0.333...**
$1 \div 7$ or **7 into 1**	**0 r 1**	$\frac{1}{7}$	0.142857...

Exercise 3h Page 28

1. 2/6	**5.** 1/6	**9.** 4/4	**13.** 4/6	**17.** 266/7
2. 3/7	**6.** 2/6	**10.** 3/6	**14.** 3/4	**18.** 444/4
3. 12/5	**7.** 2/3	**11.** 2/7	**15.** 11/1	**19.** 258/8
4. 12/6	**8.** 2/6	**12.** 6/7	**16.** 155/6	**20.** 2/0

Exercise 3i Page 29

1. 1/33	**4.** 1/28	**7.** 1/332	**10.** 1/4196	**13.** 1/336	**16.** 1/446
2. 1/35	**5.** 1/61	**8.** 1/368	**11.** 1/4132	**14.** 1/662	**17.** 1/28
3. 1/49	**6.** 1/56	**9.** 1/3157	**12.** 1/422	**15.** 1/305	**18.** 1/261

Exercise 3j Page 31

1. 11/42	**4.** 112/53	**7.** 12/53	**10.** 11/243	**13.** 12/582	**16.** 114/801
2. 12/66	**5.** 123/54	**8.** 12/74	**11.** 12/599	**14.** 113/568	**17.** 11/3243
3. 12/79	**6.** 113/66	**9.** 11/322	**12.** 12/735	**15.** 114/797	**18.** 12/5367

Exercise 3k Page 32

1. 268/1	**5.** 397/0	**9.** 153/7	**13.** 1388/7	**17.** 516/3
2. 151/2	**6.** 98/6	**10.** 165/1	**14.** 303/0	**18.** 4123/4
3. 384/7	**7.** 497/4	**11.** 55/4	**15.** 314/2	**19.** 8564/1
4. 3479/2	**8.** 1379/4	**12.** 378/6	**16.** 2742/2	**20.** 219/6

Exercise 3l Page 32

1. 4	**5.** 0	**9.** 2	**13.** 43	**17.** 3	**21.** 6	**25.** 3
2. 3	**6.** 5	**10.** 7	**14.** 52	**18.** 13	**22.** 6	**26.** 0
3. 5	**7.** 1	**11.** 12	**15.** 47	**19.** 25	**23.** 1	**27.** 0
4. 4	**8.** 3	**12.** 13	**16.** 10	**20.** 13	**24.** 4	**28.** 3

Exercise 3m Page 33

1. 12/0	8. 32/5	15. 1435/4	21. 2121/0	27. 1211/0
2. 13/1	9. 11/5	16. 114/1	22. 3012/2	28. 33324/0
3. 14/5	10. 24/0	17. 123/3	23. 3100/7	29. 43412/7
4. 24/3	11. 42/3	18. 2123/1	24. 4114/1	30. 30313/3
5. 14/1	12. 21/4	19. 1101/5	25. 5111/6	31. 11111/1
6. 11/1	13. 113/2	20. 2110/8	26. 2113/0	32. 2222/0
7. 22/5	14. 224/4			

Exercise 3n Page 34

1. 22/16	5. 11/57	9. 141/32	13. 11/645	17. 22/233
2. 11/04	6. 102/63	10. 101/22	14. 23/015	18. 12/000
3. 21/11	7. 161/31	11. 11/111	15. 21/125	19. 10/351
4. 13/30	8. 243/14	12. 21/220	16. 31/036	20. 211/00

Exercise 3o Page 35

1. 1468/8	5. 137/5	9. 7296/4	13. 258/83	17. 3007/21
2. 2215/0	6. 136/45	10. 123/66	14. 12/145	18. 89072/2
3. 8865/3	7. 11786/4	11. 150/21	15. 21/121	19. 3335/52
4. 1304/1	8. 230/12	12. 28901/1	16. 213/912	20. 1213/12

Chapter 4   Subtraction by *All from nine and the last from ten*

Exercise 4a Page 37

1. 1334	5. 1459	9. 3835	13. 8877	17. 45712
2. 3865	6. 779	10. 2667	14. 38989	18. 28788
3. 1128	7. 1899	11. 18443	15. 3013	19. 3889
4. 3369	8. 2889	12. 18884	16. 34889	20. 58999

Exercise 4b Page 38

1. 2812	5. 5697	9. 4657	13. 18135	17. 23943
2. 1691	6. 3900	10. 3694	14. 17110	18. 14123
3. 1895	7. 472	11. 17934	15. 33910	19. 58851
4. 1850	8. 7910	12. 46891	16. 59901	20. 48891

Exercise 4c Page 39

1. 4467	3. 5156	5. 3168	7. 2168	9. 339
2. 1132	4. 6606	6. 6255	8. 1286	10. 119

11. 3189	16. 4214	21. 34089	25. 22458	29. 31459
12. 1849	17. 21022	22. 40784	26. 42889	30. 346
13. 2209	18. 33813	23. 40086	27. 41087	31. 30078
14. 5214	19. 20185	24. 33875	28. 41085	32. 63878
15. 4005	20. 3409			

Exercise 4d Page 40

1. 41542	5. 488843	9. 23457	13. 350534	17. 208646
2. 36883	6. 419754	10. 757346	14. 453998	18. 270336
3. 61782	7. 203086	11. 117802	15. 136712	19. 315907
4. 192860	8. 34148	12. 631939	16. 186049	20. 528216

Exercise 4e Page 41

1. £274	4. £29500	7. 193	10. 2784	13. 2129
2. 33234	5. 38 cm	8. £1288	11. 379	14. 129
3. 5561	6. 244	9. 636	12. £185	15. £12.58

Exercise 4f Page 42

1. 299995	5. 377774	9. 488775	13. 978893	17. 4885864
2. 199992	6. 4899875	10. 599887	14. 3666664	18. 3788299
3. 188889	7. 2899984	11. 5787976	15. 966566	19. 7776769
4. 488886	8. 5878795	12. 4999889	16. 3658799	20. 9909882

Chapter Five - Prime and Composite Numbers

Exercise 5a Page 43

1. 1×12
   2×6
   3×4
2. 1×6
   2×3
3. 1×8
   2×4
4. 1×14
   2×7
5. 1×20
   2×10
   4×5

6. 1×15
   3×5
7. 1×16
   2×8
   4×4
8. 1×19
9. 1×7
10. 1×30
    2×15
    3×10
    5×6

11. 1×32
    2×16
    4×8
12. 1×36
    2×18
    3×12
    4×9
    6×6
13. 1×40
    2×20
    4×10
    5×8

14. 1×56
    2×28
    4×14
    7×8
15. 1×18
    2×9
    3×6
16. 1×28
    2×14
    4×7
17. 1×64
    2×32
    4×16
    8×8

18. 1×100
    2×50
    4×25
    5×20
    10×10
19. 1×50
    2×25
    5×10
20. 1×112
    2×56
    4×28
    7×16
    8×14

Exercise 5b Page 44

1. 6	**5.** 12	**9.** 1	**13.** 8	**17.** 8
2. 10	**6.** 6	**10.** 2	**14.** 10	**18.** 22
3. 3	**7.** 5	**11.** 4	**15.** 5	**19.** 15
4. 2	**8.** 5	**12.** 7	**16.** 8	**20.** 12

Exercise 5c Page 44

1. 2	**5.** 4	**9.** 3	**13.** 3	**17.** 1
2. 3	**6.** 3	**10.** 5	**14.** 6	**18.** 16
3. 2	**7.** 4	**11.** 5	**15.** 10	**19.** 7
4. 4	**8.** 3	**12.** 12	**16.** 5	**20.** 9

Exercise 5d Page 45

1. 10 **11** 12 **13** 14 15 16 **17** 18 **19** 20

2. 37

3. 41, 43, 47, 53, 59

4. 22, 24, 25, 26, 27, 28, 30, 32, 33, 34, 35, 36, 38, 39

5. $1 \times 2 \times 3 = 6$ $1 \times 2 \times 3 \times 5 = 30$ $1 \times 2 \times 3 \times 5 \times 7 = 210$

6.

Number, n	n × n	Add n	Add 17	Is it prime?
1	1	2	19	Yes
2	4	6	23	Yes
3	9	12	29	Yes
4	16	20	37	Yes
5	25	30	47	Yes
6	36	42	59	Yes
7	49	56	73	Yes
8	64	72	89	Yes
9	81	90	107	Yes
20	400	420	437	No

Exercise 5e Page 46

1. $8 = 2 \times 2 \times 2$	**8.** $22 = 2 \times 11$	**15.** $35 = 5 \times 7$
2. $10 = 2 \times 5$	**9.** $24 = 2 \times 2 \times 2 \times 3$	**16.** $40 = 2 \times 2 \times 2 \times 5$
3. $16 = 2 \times 2 \times 2 \times 2$	**10.** $9 = 3 \times 3$	**17.** $36 = 2 \times 2 \times 3 \times 3$
4. $20 = 2 \times 2 \times 5$	**11.** $30 = 2 \times 3 \times 5$	**18.** $42 = 2 \times 3 \times 7$
5. $6 = 2 \times 3$	**12.** $21 = 3 \times 7$	**19.** $64 = 2 \times 2 \times 2 \times 2 \times 2 \times 2$
6. $18 = 2 \times 3 \times 3$	**13.** $27 = 3 \times 3 \times 3$	**20.** $81 = 3 \times 3 \times 3 \times 3$
7. $15 = 3 \times 5$	**14.** $14 = 2 \times 7$	

Exercise 5f Page 46

1. 12	**5.** 35	**9.** 15	**13.** 50	**17.** 60
2. 6	**6.** 24	**10.** 15	**14.** 60	**18.** 24
3. 8	**7.** 20	**11.** 60	**15.** 16	**19.** 20
4. 40	**8.** 30	**12.** 30	**16.** 12	**20.** 60

Exercise 5g Page 47

1. 24	**5.** 56	**9.** 84	**13.** 18	**17.** 75
2. 12	**6.** 20	**10.** 28	**14.** 150	**18.** 54
3. 60	**7.** 30	**11.** 24	**15.** 120	**19.** 72
4. 30	**8.** 60	**12.** 60	**16.** 45	**20.** 168

Exercise 5h Page 48

1. 12	**5.** 168	**9.** 24	**13.** 30	**17.** 120
2. 120	**6.** 16	**10.** 30	**14.** 180	**18.** 210
3. 60	**7.** 10	**11.** 72	**15.** 72	**19.** 280
4. 84	**8.** 30	**12.** 72	**16.** 180	**20.** 150

Exercise 5i Page 48

	2	3	4	5	6	7	8	9	10
2	·	×	·	×	·	×	·	×	·
3	×	·	×	×	·	×	×	·	×
4	·	×	·	×	·	×	·	×	·
5	×	×	×		×	×	×	×	·
6	·	·	·	×	·	×	·	·	·
7	×	×	×	×	×		×	×	×
8	·	×	·	×	·	×	·	×	·
9	×	·	×	×	·	×	·	·	×
10	·	×	·	×	·	×	·	×	·

Exercise 5j Page 50

1. 1, 2, 3, 4, 6, 8, 12, 16, 24, 48	**6.** 8
2. 63, 66, 69, 72, 75, 78	**7.** $48 = 2 \times 2 \times 2 \times 2 \times 3$
3. 6, 12, 18, 24	**8.** 36
4. 1, 2, 3, 6	**9.** 105
5. They each total nine.	**10.** Eg. 4 and 9
	11. Eg. 60

12. 2520
13. 12
14. 15, Sunday
15. 120 in
16. £2.25
17. 16 years

Chapter Six - Fractions

Exercise 6a Page 48

1. £3
2. 24 p
3. 16 m
4. 25 cm

5. 60 miles
6. 75 feet
7. 8 pints
8. 56 hours

9. 31 days
10. 43 km
11. 19 g
12. 28 litres

13. 5.5 tons
14. 1.5 seconds
15. 2.5 mm
16. 49 minutes

17. 132 acres
18. 3216 years
19. 740 sq.ft
20. $67.50

Exercise 6b Page 52

1. £0.80
2. 3 kg
3. 4 m
4. 4 ft

5. 6 g
6. £3.00
7. 6 sec
8. 15 mm

9. $4
10. 33 litres
11. 12 min
12. £20

13. 9 kg
14. 25 m
15. 20 days
16. 42 cm

17. 27 in
18. 18 hrs
19. £1.40
20. 140 miles

Exercise 6c Page 53

1. $\frac{1}{3}$
2. $\frac{1}{2}$
3. $\frac{1}{2}$
4. $\frac{1}{2}$
5. $\frac{1}{5}$

6. $\frac{3}{4}$
7. $\frac{3}{4}$
8. $\frac{2}{3}$
9. $\frac{3}{4}$
10. $\frac{3}{4}$

11. $\frac{2}{3}$
12. $\frac{3}{4}$
13. $\frac{3}{4}$
14. $\frac{1}{3}$
15. $\frac{2}{5}$

16. $\frac{2}{3}$
17. $\frac{1}{2}$
18. $\frac{2}{5}$
19. $\frac{2}{3}$
20. $\frac{5}{8}$

21. $\frac{8}{15}$
22. $\frac{6}{7}$
23. $\frac{3}{5}$
24. $\frac{1}{3}$
25. $\frac{1}{3}$

Exercise 6d Page 53

1. 3
2. 20
3. 14
4. 25
5. 16

6. 6
7. 16
8. 8
9. 15
10. 21

11. 15
12. 2
13. 18
14. 12
15. 15

16. 3
17. 20
18. 36
19. 8
20. 21

21. 70
22. 16
23. 5
24. 3
25. 44

26. 5
27. 5
28. 3
29. 5
30. 8

31. 120
32. 250

Exercise 6e Page 54

1. 3
2. $1\frac{1}{2}$
3. 2
4. $2\frac{1}{4}$
5. $5\frac{1}{2}$

6. $2\frac{3}{5}$
7. 3
8. $9\frac{1}{2}$
9. 5
10. $4\frac{5}{6}$

11. 6
12. $5\frac{5}{7}$
13. 6
14. $7\frac{4}{5}$
15. $5\frac{5}{11}$

16. $8\frac{5}{6}$
17. 4
18. $8\frac{4}{7}$
19. $4\frac{2}{9}$
20. $3\frac{3}{10}$

21. $7\frac{5}{11}$
22. $4\frac{11}{12}$
23. $7\frac{3}{4}$
24. $8\frac{5}{9}$
25. $12\frac{4}{5}$

248

Exercise 6f Page 54

1. $\frac{5}{4}$ 6. $\frac{49}{8}$ 11. $\frac{35}{3}$ 16. $\frac{50}{9}$ 21. $\frac{64}{9}$

2. $\frac{21}{5}$ 7. $\frac{27}{8}$ 12. $\frac{77}{6}$ 17. $\frac{62}{7}$ 22. $\frac{34}{7}$

3. $\frac{18}{5}$ 8. $\frac{21}{10}$ 13. $\frac{79}{8}$ 18. $\frac{127}{10}$ 23. $\frac{59}{10}$

4. $\frac{19}{4}$ 9. $\frac{31}{9}$ 14. $\frac{74}{9}$ 19. $\frac{125}{11}$ 24. $\frac{109}{12}$

5. $\frac{21}{4}$ 10. $\frac{57}{10}$ 15. $\frac{85}{8}$ 20. $\frac{33}{5}$ 25. $\frac{43}{5}$

Exercise 6g Page 55

1. $\frac{3}{8}$ 8. $\frac{6}{25}$ 15. $\frac{1}{6}$ 22. $\frac{15}{28}$ 29. $\frac{1}{7}$

2. $\frac{10}{21}$ 9. $\frac{3}{4}$ 16. $\frac{4}{7}$ 23. $\frac{4}{44}$ 30. $\frac{3}{16}$

3. $\frac{2}{15}$ 10. $\frac{3}{35}$ 17. $\frac{7}{18}$ 24. $\frac{1}{15}$ 31. $\frac{3}{20}$

4. $\frac{7}{16}$ 11. $\frac{5}{24}$ 18. $\frac{2}{3}$ 25. $\frac{2}{9}$ 32. $\frac{1}{3}$

5. $\frac{3}{7}$ 12. $\frac{14}{27}$ 19. $\frac{5}{48}$ 26. $\frac{2}{31}$

6. $\frac{4}{63}$ 13. $\frac{3}{20}$ 20. $\frac{1}{2}$ 27. $\frac{22}{45}$

7. $\frac{6}{35}$ 14. $\frac{6}{7}$ 21. $\frac{1}{9}$ 28. 1

Exercise 6h Page 57

1. $\frac{2}{3}$ 7. $\frac{7}{8}$ 13. 30   19. 30   25. 7

2. 2   8. 2   14. $1\frac{4}{9}$ 20. $12\frac{1}{2}$ 26. 15

3. $\frac{3}{4}$ 9. $16\frac{1}{3}$ 15. $7\frac{1}{2}$ 21. $1\frac{1}{2}$ 27. $\frac{3}{5}$

4. $11\frac{1}{5}$ 10. $\frac{17}{21}$ 16. 9   22. 2   28. $6\frac{1}{3}$

5. $\frac{1}{2}$ 11. 14   17. 10   23. $13\frac{1}{2}$ 29. 23

6. $\frac{1}{2}$ 12. 4   18. 3   24. 14   30. 9

Exercise 6i Page 58

1. 10   6. 18   11. $\frac{3}{92}$ 16. $2\frac{1}{3}$ 21. 21

2. 21   7. 16   12. $1\frac{1}{2}$ 17. 49   22. 15

3. 45   8. $\frac{3}{4}$ 13. $\frac{2}{5}$ 18. $\frac{2}{3}$

4. 99   9. $1\frac{1}{5}$ 14. 1   19. 14

5. 30   10. 28   15. 39   20. 20

Exercise 6j Page 59

1. $10\frac{1}{2}$ 6. $6\frac{2}{3}$ 11. 6   16. 6   21. $2\frac{1}{2}$
2. $2\frac{1}{2}$ 7. $\frac{9}{10}$ 12. $2\frac{2}{3}$ 17. $1\frac{3}{7}$ 22. 12
3. $5\frac{1}{3}$ 8. $4\frac{5}{6}$ 13. 12   18. $3\frac{1}{3}$ 23. $\frac{1}{2}$
4. 6   9. $1\frac{4}{5}$ 14. 6   19. 12   24. 10
5. $2\frac{8}{11}$ 10. 4   15. $5\frac{3}{5}$ 20. $\frac{3}{13}$ 25. 8

Exercise 6k Page 59

1. 13   5. £1.60   9. 15   13. $\frac{11}{20}$ 17. 320 sq.ft.
2. $\frac{3}{13}$ 6. 3 m   10. $2\frac{1}{4}$ 14. 2   18. 40 miles
3. $\frac{1}{4}$ 7. 16   11. $2\frac{1}{2}$ 15. 124 cm   19. $\frac{1}{5}$
4. £375   8. $1\frac{1}{8}$ m   12. $30\frac{7}{8}$ tons   16. 35 litres   20. 63

Chapter Seven - Algebra

Exercise 7a Page 61

1. 2   2. 3   3. 4   4. 4   5. 3   6. 2   7. 4   8. 5

Exercise 7b Page 62

1. 11   4. 56   7. 18   10. 33   13. 6
2. 4   5. 10   8. 3   11. 34   14. -9
3. 5   6. 10   9. 0   12. 27   15. 4

Exercise 7c Page 62

1. 7   5. 12   9. 4   13. 0   17. 8   21. 120
2. 7   6. 9   10. 9   14. 9   18. 1   22. 0
3. 6   7. 9   11. 8   15. 7   19. 1   23. 17
4. 20   8. 3   12. 8   16. 7   20. 8   24. 15

Exercise 7d Page 63

1. 26   4. 5   7. 22   10. 9   13. 0
2. 13   5. 29   8. 12   11. 3   14. 36
3. 26   6. 0   9. 24   12. 35   15. 220

Exercise 7e Page 63

1. $12p$	7. $3w$	13. $4g + 3m$	19. $2m + 16n$	25. $9k + q$
2. $13q$	8. $9m$	14. $13y$	20. $x + 5y$	26. $16m - 3y$
3. $11y$	9. $5h$	15. $11h - 15n$	21. $18y + 8q$	27. $3h + 14k$
4. $13d$	10. $7x - 7$	16. $2h + 8m$	22. $2k + 15$	28. $6m + 3a$
5. $6a$	11. $7x + 6y$	17. $9y + 10z - 8w$	23. $15g + 6h$	29. $k + 15w$
6. $10q$	12. c	18. $12 + 5h$	24. $2n + 10w$	30. $6w$

Exercise 7f Page 64

1. $7x + 6y$	7. $18y + 8q$	13. $10w + 13y$	19. $9w + q$	25. $16m - 3y$
2. $10m + 14k$	8. $17x + m$	14. $2m + 16n$	20. $15h$	26. $3a + 14b$
3. $6a + 12k$	9. $6a + 2b + 6c$	15. $x + 5y$	21. $4g + 13m$	27. $13y$
4. $15 + 11y$	10. $12a + 13g$	16. c	22. $n + 10w$	28. $6m + 3a$
5. $3p + 7m$	11. $7a + 6b$	17. $2k + 15$	23. $9k + q$	29. $5q - 3$
6. $16x + 6c$	12. $9g + 2h$	18. $15g + 6h$	24. $2x + 15m$	30. $12 + 5h$

Exercise 7g Page 65

1. 3	6. 3	11. 7	16. 5	21. 6	26. 3
2. 3	7. 4	12. 6	17. 5	22. 9	27. 11
3. 3	8. 1	13. 8	18. 8	23. 8	28. 2
4. 5	9. 3	14. 8	19. 8	24. 3	29. 1
5. 2	10. 0	15. 8	20. 10	25. 10	30. 2

Exercise 7h Page 66

1. 4	6. 20	11. 16	16. 0	21. $6\frac{2}{5}$	26. 8
2. 3	7. 5	12. 5	17. 1	22. 9	27. 4
3. 2	8. 9	13. 1	18. 3	23. 106	28. $\frac{1}{3}$
4. 2	9. 8	14. 1	19. $\frac{1}{2}$	24. 60	29. 0
5. 3	10. 5	15. 8	20. 0	25. 7	30. 8

Exercise 7i Page 67

1. 5	6. 87	11. 4	16. 38	21. 72	26. 120
2. 8	7. 95	12. 34	17. 50	22. 36	27. 14
3. 6	8. 87	13. 6	18. 23	23. 12	28. 5
4. 122	9. 261	14. 64	19. 290	24. 131	29. 100
5. 87	10. 86	15. 14	20. 38	25. 49	30. 184

Exercise 7j Page 68

1. 9	**10.** 6	**19.** 12	**28.** 24	**37.** 5
2. 7	**11.** 21	**20.** 21	**29.** 32	**38.** 5
3. 9	**12.** 1	**21.** 10	**30.** 3	**39.** 2
4. 6	**13.** 1	**22.** 12	**31.** 2	**40.** 1
5. 3	**14.** 49	**23.** 10	**32.** 13	**41.** 5
6. 8	**15.** 1	**24.** 21	**33.** 8	**42.** 7
7. 11	**16.** 15	**25.** 4	**34.** 3	**43.** 5
8. 1	**17.** 6	**26.** 27	**35.** 2	**44.** 12
9. 9	**18.** 10	**27.** 32	**36.** 5	**45.** 25

Exercise 7k Page 69

1. $12ac$	**5.** $12abc$	**9.** $21bcd$	**13.** $3mnpq$	**17.** $72abx$
2. $24abc$	**6.** $24xy$	**10.** $32abc$	**14.** $12ab$	**18.** $12pq$
3. $20rst$	**7.** $6xyz$	**11.** $35x$	**15.** $56abc$	**19.** $15abc$
4. $24ab$	**8.** $48abc$	**12.** $6b$	**16.** $40xyz$	**20.** $54mnpq$

Exercise 7l Page 70

1. $4 \times 5 = 20$	**6.** $\frac{1}{3} \times 12 = 4$	**11.** $\frac{3}{4} \times 8 = 6$	**16.** $42 + 12 = 54$
2. $6 \times 7 = 42$	**7.** $5 \times 2 = 10$	**12.** $\frac{2}{5} \times 15 = 6$	**17.** $56 - 21 = 35$
3. $10 \times 8 = 80$	**8.** $4 \times 5 = 20$	**13.** $15 + 5 = 20$	**18.** $40 - 30 = 10$
4. $44 \times 10 = 40$	**9.** $5 \times 11 = 55$	**14.** $8 + 32 = 40$	**19.** $15 - 6 = 9$
5. $\frac{1}{2} \times 8 = 4$	**10.** $7 \times 5 = 35$	**15.** $6 + 36 = 42$	**20.** $28 - 20 = 8$

Exercise 7m Page 71

1. $3c + 3d$	**11.** $gh - gk$	**21.** $16 + 8e$	**31.** $2ab + 8a$
2. $7e + 7f$	**12.** $mn + mp$	**22.** $9 - 3f$	**32.** $12k - 3km$
3. $9g + 9h$	**13.** $ab + 4a$	**23.** $12 - 2g$	**33.** $3cd - 15c$
4. $4k + 4m$	**14.** $cd - 6c$	**24.** $6d - 18$	**34.** $10n - 2np$
5. $6n - 6p$	**15.** $2e + ef$	**25.** $5 - 5h$	**35.** $4ef + 4e$
6. $2q - 2r$	**16.** $5g - gh$	**26.** $6a + 15$	**36.** $6q^2 + 12$
7. $\frac{1}{2}t - \frac{1}{2}v$	**17.** $2a + 8$	**27.** $6b - 4$	**37.** $5gh - 5g$
8. $\frac{2}{3}x - \frac{2}{3}y$	**18.** $4b - 8$	**28.** $8c - 12$	**38.** $3t^2 - 9t$
9. $ab + ac$	**19.** $5c - 15$	**29.** $15d + 5$	**39.** $21hk + 15hn$
10. $de - df$	**20.** $7d + 21$	**30.** $18 + 12h$	**40.** $15gh - 5g$

Exercise 7n Page 71

1. $6x + 1$
2. $18 + 10x$
3. $3x + 7$
4. $14x - 18$
5. $17 + 4x$

6. $6x - 15$
7. $5x + 23$
8. $17x - 23$
9. $5x + 5$
10. $3 + 3x$

11. $-3x - 8$
12. $-15 - 4x$
13. $6c - 2$
14. $x - 8$
15. $7 - 8x$

16. $6a - 6$
17. $2 - 12x$
18. $38 - 10w$
19. $-3y - 12$
20. $2 - 15z$

21. $25x + 12$
22. $27 - 6c$
23. $14m - 20$
24. $3 - 6x$
25. $6x - 4$

26. $13 - 8g$
27. $-2 + x$
28. $4f + 12$
29. $-3 + 4s$
30. $5x - 2$

Exercise 7p Page 72

1. 2^3
2. 1^5
3. 5^3
4. 3^4
5. 6^5
6. 7^2

7. 3^5
8. 8^3
9. 7^4
10. 4^5
11. $a^3 b^2$
12. $ab^2 c^2$

13. ad^4
14. x^5
15. $xy^2 z$
16. $c^3 d^2$
17. ef^4
18. ab^3

19. $tu^2 v^2$
20. $g^3 h^2$
21. $x^2 y^3$
22. $ab^2 c^3$
23. $p^5 q$
24. abc^4

25. $x^3 y^3$
26. $a^2 bc^2$
27. $m^3 n^3$
28. $p^2 q$
29. $a^3 b^2$
30. $r^2 s^2 t^2$

Exercise 7q Page 73

1. y^5
2. m^5
3. k^6
4. c^6
5. b^9

6. m^{73}
7. b^9
8. n^4
9. h^{10}
10. r^9

11. h^4
12. n^5
13. p^8
14. y^4
15. w^3

16. 3^5
17. 2^9
18. k^6
19. x^2
20. x^3

21. a^5
22. m^{12}
23. k^8
24. n^8
25. b^{12}

26. h^{18}
27. x^{50}
28. y^{90}
29. d^{300}
30. a^{33}

Exercise 7r Page 74

1. $4m^7$
2. $15w^5$
3. $4c^7$
4. $6k^5$
5. $20p^9$

6. $18y^5$
7. $4m^5$
8. $3n^7$
9. $15g^8$
10. $3a^3$

11. $15x^3$
12. $6q^4$
13. $8c^2$
14. $56h^7$
15. $54n^{15}$

16. $72m^{15}$
17. $48q^5$
18. $5b^6$
19. $4v^2$
20. $42d^{12}$

21. $25v^3$
22. $30y^7$
23. $35w^6$
24. $8p^{15}$
25. $9q^9$

26. s^5
27. $8m^5$
28. $4r^4$
29. $6n^9$
30. $60a^{19}$

Chapter Eight - Practice and Revision

Exercise 8a Page 75

1. 86
2. 76
3. 82

4. 616
5. 1223
6. 647

7. 975
8. 100513
9. 4750

10. 9923
11. 17562
12. 7333

13. 101,659
14. £97.84

Exercise 8b Page 75

1. 42	4. 4446	7. 199955	10. £43.46	13. 1469
2. 25	5. 4176	8. 3545428	11. 356	14. 2556
3. 56	6. 4315	9. 467	12. 491	

Exercise 8c Page 75

1 339	3. 738	5. 17717	7. 45387.
2. 432	4. 1844	6. 10280	8. 5366226

Exercise 8d Page 76

1. 72	5. 6208	9. 168	13. 1,119,784	17. 10,192
2. 8835	6. 990,016	10. 10,918	14. 100,790,078	18. 1,049,841
3. 9506	7. 872,615	11. 17,716	15. 88	19. 12,328
4. 8428	8. 99,450,106	12. 1,015,026	16. 10,864	20. 100,019,985

Exercise 8e Page 76

1. 483	5. 5655	9. 1560	13. 896 miles
2. 3312	6. 26,983	10. 8736	14. 1820
3. 4356	7. 208,975	11. £46.80	
4. 3780	8. 7,059,124	12. 8760	

Exercise 8f Page 76

1. 1203	5. 15,646	9. 45	13. 50
2. 1073	6. 22/5	10. 6	14. 3
3. 24,414	7. 96,398/2	11. £27	15. 13
4. 59	8. 3062	12. £3.50	16. £50,000

Exercise 8g Page 77

1. 13/6	4. 236/7	7. 13/7	10. 2/495	13. 24/96
2. 12/5	5. 255/6	8. 1/433	11. 2/446	14. 135/87
3. 134/4	6. 2/25	9. 11/55	12. 14/65	15. 22/664

Exercise 8h Page 77

1. 14/4	3. 25/2	5. 1021/6	7. 1211/0	9. 13/0
2. 24/5	4. 22/5	6. 2130/9	8. 20131/7	10. 21/22

Exercise 8i Page 77

1. product	3. every	5. divide	7. composite	9. lowest, divide 11. one, one
2. factors	4. multiple	6. divisible	8. primes	10. highest common factor

Exercise 8j Page 78

1. 9
2. 48
3. 31

4. composite
5. $1 \times 24, 2 \times 12$
   $3 \times 8, 4 \times 6$

6. $2 \times 2 \times 2 \times 3$
7. 4
8. 96

9. 3
10. No

11. 1
12. Yes

Exercise 8k Page 79

1. $\frac{4}{5}$
2. $\frac{3}{4}$

3. $\frac{29}{6}$
4. $4\frac{2}{5}$

5. 12
6. 7

7. £23.50
8. 8

9. 50
10. $4\frac{4}{9}$

Exercise 8l Page 79

1. $\frac{6}{35}$
2. $\frac{1}{6}$
3. $\frac{1}{2}$
4. $\frac{3}{5}$

5. $\frac{1}{12}$
6. $\frac{1}{3}$
7. $\frac{3}{20}$
8. $\frac{2}{9}$

9. 24
10. 24
11. 65
12. $\frac{5}{8}$

13. $2\frac{2}{3}$
14. $\frac{3}{5}$
15. $\frac{1}{12}$
16. 4

17. $1\frac{5}{6}$
18. $\frac{1}{32}$
19. 2
20. $\frac{5}{18}$

Exercise 8m Page 79

1. 13
2. 8
3. 21
4. 63
5. 11
6. 69

7. 7
8. 10
9. 9
10. 16
11. 11
12. 7

13. 0
14. 6
15. 1
16. 0
17. 1
18. 40

19. 18
20. 10
21. 16
22. 3a
23. 4b
24. c

25. 4a
26. 3x
27. 11p
28. 6w
29. 8n
30. 7h

31. 5y – 7
32. 7a + 6b
33. 0
34. 3g + 3h
35. 13x + y
36. 11y – 17z

Exercise 8n Page 80

1. 3
2. 4
3. 15
4. 5

5. 4
6. 15
7. 20
8. 10

9. 0
10. 2
11. 3
12. 8

13. 25
14. 37
15. 44
16. 30

17. 11
18. 22
19. 11
20. 2

21. 2
22. 3
23. 131
24. 1

Exercise 8o Page 80

1. 2c + 2d
2. 5e + 5f
3. 8g + 8h
4. 4a – 4b

5. ab + ac
6. ab – 4a
7. 18 + 9x
8. 12 – 4y

9. 30 – 5g
10. 4ab + 16a
11. 8k – 2km
12. 5cd – 20c

13. 8x + 10
14. 12x + 56
15. 6x + 14
16. 14x – 13

17. 7c – 5
18. 3x – 15

Exercise 8p Page 80

1. f^4	4. ab^2c^2	7. a^5	10. b^4	13. $2y^7$	15. $12x^3$
2. b^3	5. d^2b^3	8. n^5	11. x^6	14. $10w^5$	16. $18q^4$
3. p^4	6. r^3s^2	9. d^4	12. m^{12}		

Exercise 8q Page 81

1. 48	9. 985036	17. £13.10	24. $\frac{2}{5}$	32. £543.13
2. 115	10. 1097	18. $34x$ pence	25. $\frac{1}{6}$	33. $x + 2$
3. 12	11. 2415	19. 16	26. 86,400	34. £36.30
4. 23	12. £10.11	20. £2.60	27. 6 23 pm	35. £12.70
5. £23.70	13. 6875	, 21. One hundred and ninety-three thousand and fifty	28. 864	36. 180
6. 6	14. £2.66		29. 456	37. £31,500
7. 729	15. 1568	22. 5337	30. 17	38. £17.08
8. 134/78	16. $\frac{3}{5}$	23. 22/11	31. 9	39. 133/7237

Chapter Ten - Digital roots

Exercise 10a Page 100

1. 5	4. 1	7. 2	10. 9	13. 1	15. 9	17. 1	19. 3
2. 2	5. 5	8. 8	11. 6	14. 2	16. 3	18. 8	20. 8
3. 8	6. 9	9. 2	12. 9				

Exercise 10b Page 101

1. 3	6. 2	11. 4	16. 6	21. 1	26. 7	31. 9	36. 1
2. 6	7. 8	12. 6	17. 4	22. 4	27. 5	32. 4	37. 7
3. 7	8. 2	13. 9	18. 6	23. 8	28. 6	33. 9	38. 3
4. 2	9. 8	14. 5	19. 8	24. 8	29. 1	34. 9	39. 9
5. 5	10. 2	15. 9	20. 3	25. 7	30. 6	35. 3	40. 3

Exercise 10c Page 102 The answers are given followed by their digital roots

1. 1110, 3	6. 76110, 6	11. 1574444, 2	16. 540429, 6
2. 535, 4	7. 29998, 1	12. 814197, 3	17. 218012, 5
3. 6530, 5	8. 38394, 9	13. 513780, 6	18. 462948, 6
4. 7982, 8	9. 186543, 9	14. 614176, 7	19. 45645, 6
5. 5275, 1	10. 1788, 6	15. 1076, 5	20. 35710, 7

Exercise 10d Page 103 The answers are given followed by their digital roots

1. 41542, 7	6. 419754, 3	11. 117802, 1	16. 186049, 1
2. 36883, 1	7. 203086, 1	12. 631939, 4	17. 208646, 8
3. 61782, 6	8. 34148, 2	13. 350534, 2	18. 270336, 3
4. 192860, 8	9. 23457, 3	14. 453998, 2	19. 315907, 7
5. 488843, 8	10. 757346, 5	15. 136712, 2	20. 528216, 6

Exercise 10e Page 104 The answers are given followed by their digital roots

1. 529, 7	6. 5628, 3	11. 95469, 6	16. 93240, 9
2. 1456, 7	7. 6825, 3	12. 23751, 9	17. 19485, 9
3. 1216, 1	8. 66144, 3	13. 119079, 9	18. 5000856, 6
4. 1638, 9	9. 26999, 8	14. 184266, 9	19. 3602178, 9
5. 3763, 1	10. 226772, 8	15. 378228, 3	20. 8478699, 6

Exercise 10f Page 105 The answers are given followed by the digital root of the dividend

1. 290/1, 7	5. 175/2, 9	9. 216/1, 1	13. 68, 4	17. 997, 3
2. 134, 5	6. 152/3, 7	10. 137, 3	14. 229/1, 4	18. 9016/2, 6
3. 59/2, 5	7. 463/1, 9	11. 267, 3	15. 231/3, 9	19. 3987/1, 1
4. 189, 9	8. 203/1, 3	12. 96/5, 8	16. 1634/3, 1	20. 9606/6, 3

Capter Eleven - Divisibility

Exercise 11a Page 106

	Number	Divisible by 10?	Divisible by 2?	Divisible by 5?
1.	4225	×	×	√
2.	340	√	√	√
3.	67	×	×	×
4.	34509	×	×	×
5.	65475	×	×	√
6.	34532	×	√	×
7.	56090	√	√	√
8.	656500	√	√	√
9.	212345	×	×	√
10.	600040	√	√	√

Exercise 11b Page 107

A	B	C
04	4	
08	8	
12	4	
16	8	
20	4	
24	8	
28	12	4
32	8	
36	12	4
40	8	
44	12	4
48	16	8
52	12	4

A	B	C
56	16	8
60	12	4
64	16	8
68	20	4
72	16	8
76	20	4
80	16	8
84	20	4
88	24	8
92	20	4
96	24	8
100	0	0

Exercise 11c Page 108 The ultimate and twice the penultimate is given followed the answer to the question, *yes* or *no*.

1. 18 No	**6.** 13 No	**11.** 22 No	**16.** 20 Yes
2. 13 No	**7.** 12 Yes	**12.** 0 Yes	**17.** 16 Yes
3. 8 Yes	**8.** 24 Yes	**13.** 4 Yes	**18.** 20 Yes
4. 11 No	**9.** 18 No	**14.** 10 No	**19.** 20 Yes
5. 10 No	**10.** 12 Yes	**15.** 22 No	**20.** 22 Yes

Exercise 11d Page 108 The ultimate, twice the penultimate and four times the pen-penultimate is given followed by the answer to the question.

1. 24 Yes	**6.** 50 No	**11.** 15 No	**16.** 0 Yes
2. 16 Yes	**7.** 40 Yes	**12.** 38 No	**17.** 26 No
3. 39 No	**8.** 26 No	**13.** 10 No	**18.** 54 No
4. 30 No	**9.** 32 Yes	**14.** 24 Yes	**19.** 48 Yes
5. 22 No	**10.** 14 No	**15.** 16 Yes	**20.** 32 Yes

Exercise 11e Page 109 The digital root is given followed by the answer, *yes* or *no*.

1. 9 Yes	**6.** 9 Yes	**11.** 2 No	**16.** 9 Yes
2. 1 No	**7.** 1 No	**12.** 9 Yes	**17.** 6 No
3. 3 No	**8.** 9 Yes	**13.** 3 No	**18.** 4 No
4. 9 Yes	**9.** 9 Yes	**14.** 1 No	**19.** 9 Yes
5. 9 Yes	**10.** 9 Yes	**15.** 9 Yes	**20.** 7 No

Exercise 11f Page 110 The amswers give the result of casting out three's or the digital root and whether or not the number is divisible by 3.

1. 0 Yes	**6.** 1 No	**11.** 4 No	**16.** 4 No
2. 0 Yes	**7.** 0 Yes	**12.** 0 Yes	**17.** 0 Yes
3. 1 No	**8.** 4 No	**13.** 0 Yes	**18.** 5 No
4. 0 Yes	**9.** 0 Yes	**14.** 0 Yes	**19.** 0 Yes
5. 7 No	**10.** 0 Yes	**15.** 8 No	**20.** 1 No

Exercise 11g Page 111

1. 546378, 768574, 214636
2. 365748, 1212369, 3245463
3. 812, 13780, 46376, 25308
4. 53425, 576800, 32530
5. 19344, 85752, 25167128
6. 432, 873, 7857, 30708
7. 63450, 5400, 9586000

Exercise 11h Page 111

1. 498, 5634, 342222
2. 288, 7992
3. 7860, 9870, 12300, 4638765
4. 4284, 187632, 32054526
5. 560, 2400, 785400, 879880
6. None
7. 780, 4650, 92700

Chapter Twelve - Adding and Subtracting Fractions

Exercise 12a Page 112

1. $\frac{1}{2}$	5. $\frac{2}{7}$	9. $\frac{2}{5}$	13. $1\frac{1}{4}$	17. $\frac{1}{3}$
2. $\frac{2}{3}$	6. 1	10. $\frac{2}{9}$	14. $1\frac{1}{3}$	18. $\frac{3}{5}$
3. $\frac{8}{9}$	7. $\frac{4}{7}$	11. $\frac{2}{3}$	15. $\frac{3}{4}$	19. $\frac{6}{7}$
4. $\frac{2}{5}$	8. $\frac{6}{7}$	12. $\frac{4}{5}$	16. $\frac{7}{9}$	20. $\frac{1}{4}$

Exercise 12b Page 113

1. $\frac{3}{4}$	5. $\frac{4}{9}$	9. $\frac{8}{9}$	13. $\frac{29}{30}$	17. $\frac{7}{12}$
2. $\frac{1}{2}$	6. $\frac{5}{6}$	10. $\frac{3}{5}$	14. $\frac{17}{18}$	18. $1\frac{1}{40}$
3. $\frac{5}{8}$	7. $\frac{7}{16}$	11. $\frac{11}{12}$	15. $\frac{17}{32}$	19. 1
4. $\frac{7}{10}$	8. $\frac{17}{20}$	12. $\frac{23}{24}$	16. $\frac{37}{42}$	20. $\frac{7}{10}$

Exercise 12c Page 114

1. $\frac{11}{12}$	5. $\frac{25}{28}$	9. $\frac{13}{14}$	13. $\frac{7}{10}$	17. $1\frac{5}{24}$	21. $\frac{19}{24}$
2. $\frac{5}{6}$	6. $\frac{29}{36}$	10. $1\frac{1}{6}$	14. $\frac{8}{15}$	18. $\frac{23}{132}$	22. $1\frac{4}{33}$
3. $\frac{7}{12}$	7. $\frac{9}{20}$	11. $1\frac{5}{12}$	15. $\frac{16}{21}$	19. $\frac{13}{18}$	23. $\frac{43}{63}$
4. $\frac{23}{30}$	8. $\frac{13}{20}$	12. $1\frac{1}{10}$	16. $1\frac{11}{20}$	20. $\frac{17}{20}$	24. $\frac{31}{99}$

Exercise 12d Page 115

1. $\frac{5}{12}$ 5. $\frac{19}{21}$ 9. $\frac{11}{12}$ 13. $\frac{11}{24}$ 17. $1\frac{1}{18}$ 21. $\frac{5}{36}$

2. $\frac{11}{12}$ 6. $\frac{11}{36}$ 10. $\frac{27}{40}$ 14. $\frac{19}{36}$ 18. $\frac{19}{24}$ 22. $\frac{23}{120}$

3. $\frac{13}{18}$ 7. $\frac{47}{72}$ 11. $\frac{7}{24}$ 15. $1\frac{7}{12}$ 19. $\frac{11}{20}$ 23. $\frac{5}{6}$

4. $\frac{14}{15}$ 8. $\frac{7}{60}$ 12. $\frac{11}{20}$ 16. $1\frac{5}{24}$ 20. $\frac{43}{80}$ 24. $\frac{13}{84}$

Exercise 12e Page 116

1. $\frac{1}{4}$ 5. $\frac{1}{5}$ 9. $\frac{1}{6}$ 13. $\frac{1}{5}$ 17. $\frac{3}{8}$

2. $\frac{2}{5}$ 6. $\frac{1}{2}$ 10. $\frac{2}{7}$ 14. $\frac{2}{3}$ 18. $\frac{3}{5}$

3. $\frac{1}{3}$ 7. $\frac{1}{2}$ 11. $\frac{1}{11}$ 15. $\frac{7}{10}$ 19. $\frac{1}{2}$

4. $\frac{2}{3}$ 8. $\frac{1}{2}$ 12. $\frac{1}{5}$ 16. $\frac{3}{4}$ 20. $\frac{4}{15}$

Exercise 12f Page 116

1. $\frac{1}{4}$ 5. $\frac{11}{15}$ 9. $\frac{21}{50}$ 13. $\frac{5}{8}$ 17. $\frac{7}{24}$

2. $\frac{1}{6}$ 6. $\frac{5}{9}$ 10. $\frac{2}{5}$ 14. $\frac{2}{11}$ 18. $\frac{4}{25}$

3. $\frac{3}{8}$ 7. $\frac{11}{18}$ 11. $\frac{17}{32}$ 15. $\frac{19}{42}$ 19. $\frac{23}{36}$

4. $\frac{1}{9}$ 8. $\frac{3}{8}$ 12. $\frac{4}{15}$ 16. $\frac{33}{80}$ 20. $\frac{35}{64}$

Exercise 12g Page 117

1. $\frac{5}{12}$ 5. $\frac{1}{14}$ 9. $\frac{3}{10}$ 13. $\frac{7}{24}$ 17. $\frac{1}{18}$ 21. $\frac{2}{35}$

2. $\frac{1}{10}$ 6. $\frac{2}{15}$ 10. $\frac{2}{15}$ 14. $\frac{1}{6}$ 18. $\frac{9}{77}$ 22. $\frac{7}{20}$

3. $\frac{1}{12}$ 7. $\frac{5}{18}$ 11. $\frac{5}{12}$ 15. $\frac{19}{30}$ 19. $\frac{7}{72}$ 23. $\frac{7}{15}$

4. $\frac{1}{6}$ 8. $\frac{13}{24}$ 12. $\frac{1}{10}$ 16. $\frac{16}{35}$ 20. $\frac{5}{14}$ 24. $\frac{11}{72}$

Exercise 12h Page 118

1. $\frac{1}{12}$ 5. $\frac{9}{20}$ 9. $\frac{8}{15}$ 13. $\frac{1}{20}$ 17. $\frac{11}{15}$ 21. $\frac{1}{24}$

2. $\frac{1}{12}$ 6. $\frac{13}{24}$ 10. $\frac{3}{20}$ 14. $\frac{7}{24}$ 18. $\frac{1}{12}$ 22. $\frac{31}{56}$

3. $\frac{7}{12}$ 7. $\frac{1}{18}$ 11. $\frac{17}{30}$ 15. $\frac{11}{36}$ 19. $\frac{1}{24}$ 23. $\frac{5}{36}$

4. $\frac{1}{24}$ 8. $\frac{5}{18}$ 12. $\frac{11}{24}$ 16. $\frac{7}{18}$ 20. $\frac{11}{18}$ 24. $\frac{17}{60}$

Exercise 12i Page 119

1. $\frac{7}{8}$ 4. $\frac{3}{5}$ 7. $1\frac{7}{30}$ 10. $\frac{26}{45}$ 13. $\frac{13}{24}$ 16. $1\frac{1}{20}$

2. $\frac{3}{10}$ 5. $\frac{1}{2}$ 8. $\frac{17}{96}$ 11. $1\frac{5}{24}$ 14. $\frac{13}{30}$

3. $1\frac{1}{2}$ 6. $\frac{3}{16}$ 9. $\frac{3}{8}$ 12. $\frac{47}{72}$ 15. $\frac{19}{88}$

Exercise 12j Page 119

1. 3   5. $3\frac{5}{6}$ 9. $3\frac{1}{16}$ 13. 7   17. $1\frac{1}{16}$

2. $2\frac{4}{5}$ 6. $8\frac{11}{12}$ 10. $14\frac{2}{3}$ 14. $6\frac{3}{16}$ 18. $1\frac{7}{12}$

3. $6\frac{1}{4}$ 7. $11\frac{1}{3}$ 11. $4\frac{1}{16}$ 15. $3\frac{5}{12}$ 19. $1\frac{1}{10}$

4. 1   8. $13\frac{5}{16}$ 12. $7\frac{7}{24}$ 16. $6\frac{1}{16}$ 20. $7\frac{11}{12}$

Exercise 12k Page 120

1. $5\frac{7}{20}$ 4. $5\frac{7}{20}$ miles   7. $1\frac{7}{15}$ km   10. $\frac{5}{6}$

2. $11\frac{1}{2}$ 5. $10\frac{3}{20}$ 8. $18\frac{9}{10}$ m   11. $12\frac{11}{40}$ kg

3. $8\frac{1}{5}$ metres.   6. $5\frac{19}{24}$ inches   9. $\frac{9}{40}$ 12. $6\frac{3}{20}$

Chapter Thirteen - Decimal Fractions

Exercise 13a Page 122

		TH	H	T	U	.	t	h	th	t.th
	134.062		1	3	4	.	0	6	2	
1.	2.6				2	.	6			
2.	32.1			3	2	.	1			
3.	4556.03	4	5	5	6	.	0	3		
4.	0.09				0	.	0	9		
5.	7101.3	7	1	0	1	.	3			
6.	4.0017				4	.	0	0	1	7
7.	8732.046	8	7	3	2	.	0	4	6	
8.	129.0013		1	2	9	.	0	0	1	3
9.	670.005		6	7	0	.	0	0	5	
10.	0.0092				0	.	0	0	9	2

Exercise 13b Page 123

1. 6.17	7. 92.77	13. 53.18	19. 26.22	25. 5.85
2. 10.61	8. 98.95	14. 4.25	20. 23.765	26. 38.2351
3. 65.2	9. 30.81	15. 8.74	21. 22.825	27. 0.12366
4. 107.9	10. 42.124	16. 14.72	22. 5.37	28. 57.03
5. 11.58	11. 3.33	17. 4.73	23. 41.75	29. 92.095
6. 10.95	12. 33	18. 24.05	24. 58.5	30. 37.22

Exercise 13c Page 123

1. £1.43	6. £725.87	11. £7.52	16. £9.70
2. £8.79	7. £114.73	12. £22.89	17. £201.50
3. £397.43	8. £27.86	13. £8.87	18. £275.34
4. £1.25	9. £41.75	14. £6.22	19. £22.98
5. £43.55	10. £12.67	15. £3.01	20. £6.94

Exercise 13d Page124

1. 130.84	6. 19.450	11. 619.209	16. 15.585
2. 6.328	7. 95.256	12. 161.47	17. 140.576
3. 44.056	8. 2.0538	13. 443.59	18. 54.2485
4. 6.15	9. 58.28	14. 302.69	19. 117.465
5. 55.47	10. 100	15. 68.273	20. 18.5855

Exercise 13e Page125

1. 6.3	6. 3.28	11. 5.673	16. 15.8
2. 1.91	7. 3.88	12. 38.7	17. 25.83
3. 14.72	8. 3.53	13. 6.33	18. 46.13
4. 13.8	9. 25.55	14. 33.95	19. 1.575
5. 372.8	10. 6.63	15. 2.06	20. 0.63

Exercise 13f Page 126

1. $\frac{1}{5}$	8. $2\frac{1}{100}$	15. $\frac{41}{200}$	22. $\frac{3}{50}$
2. $1\frac{1}{4}$	9. $1\frac{4}{5}$	16. $\frac{29}{10000}$	23. $\frac{9}{25}$
3. $1\frac{3}{10}$	10. $1\frac{7}{10}$	17. $\frac{41}{10000}$	24. $\frac{18}{25}$
4. $\frac{7}{1000}$	11. $15\frac{1}{2}$	18. $\frac{17}{100}$	25. $2\frac{1}{8}$
5. $\frac{1}{10000}$	12. $8\frac{3}{50}$	19. $\frac{71}{1000}$	26. $\frac{3}{20}$
6. $6\frac{2}{5}$	13. $\frac{73}{100}$	20. $\frac{7}{20}$	27. $\frac{1}{40}$
7. $\frac{7}{10}$	14. $\frac{81}{1000}$	21. $\frac{63}{100}$	28. $3\frac{17}{20}$

Exercise 13g Page 127

1. 0.1	**7.** 0.1	**13.** 0.013	**19.** 3.82
2. 0.3	**8.** 0.11	**14.** 0.055	**20.** 6.44
3. 0.9	**9.** 0.2	**15.** 0.542	**21.** 7.08
4. 0.01	**10.** 0.67	**16.** 1.2	**22.** 6.1
5. 0.05	**11.** 0.001	**17.** 2.6	**23.** 0.61
6. 0.09	**12.** 0.009	**18.** 2.45	**24.** 0.061

Exercise 13h Page 127

1. 0.8	**7.** 0.3	**13.** 0.26	**19.** 4.64
2. 0.12	**8.** 0.22	**14.** 0.9	**20.** 6.6
3. 0.3	**9.** 0.12	**15.** 0.168	**21.** 7.03
4. 0.64	**10.** 0.04	**16.** 0.15	**22.** 0.644
5. 0.4	**11.** 0.8	**17.** 0.004	**23.** 0.42
6. 0.4	**12.** 0.36	**18.** 2.9	**24.** 0.048

Chapter Fourteen - Perimeters and Areas

Exercise 14a Page 128   **Exercise 14b** Page 129

1. 22 m	**6.** 12.4 in	**1.** 94 ft	**6.** 24.6 mm
2. 24 m	**7.** 22 in	**2.** 19.2 yds	**7.** 16 cm
3. 32 m	**8.** 38 in	**3.** 48 mm	**8.** 38.4 in
4. 20 yds	**9.** 11 cm	**4.** 228 cm	**9.** 12.5 in
5. 130 mm	**10.** 13.6 cm	**5.** 20 cm	**10.** 20 cm

Exercise 14c Page 131

1. 32 in	**6.** 19 ft	**11.** 14
2. 152 ft	**7.** 42 yds	**12.** 484 yds
3. 41 m	**8.** £56.80	**13.** 92 cm, 76 cm, 62 cm
4. 3 cm	**9.** 300 s or 5 min	**14.** 113 m 70 cm
5. 19.2 cm	**10.** 256 ft	**15.** 38.7 km

Exercise 143d Page 133

1. $30 \, m^2$	**6.** 9.6 sq in
2. $32 \, cm^2$	**7.** 18 sq in
3. $64 \, m^2$	**8.** 84 sq in
4. 24 sq yds	**9.** $6 \, cm^2$
5. $1050 \, mm^2$	**10.** $11.2 \, cm^2$

Exercise 14e Page 134

1. $12 \, \text{m}^2$
2. $8 \, \text{m}^2$
3. $432 \, \text{cm}^2$
4. 1302 sq in
5. 1750 sq ft
6. 11 cm
7. $12\,000 \, \text{m}^2$
8. 128 tiles

9. 1210 sq yds
10. 43 560 sq ft
11. £58 800
12. (a) 9600 sq yds (b) 400 yds
13. $18.75 \, \text{m}^2$
14. $36 \, \text{m}^2$
15. $21.6 \, \text{m}^2$
16. $8.01 \, \text{m}^2$

17. 50 m
18. 55 cm, $3025 \, \text{cm}^2$
19. 7 hectares
20. 10 acres
21. 2560 acres
22. 896

Exercise 14f Page 136

1. $13 \, \text{cm}^2$
2. $36 \, \text{m}^2$
3. $24 \, \text{in}^2$
4. $1320 \, \text{cm}^2$
5. Whoops!

6. $192 \, \text{in}^2$
7. $1128 \, \text{cm}^2$
8. $17 \, \text{in}^2$
9. $55 \, \text{m}^2$
10. $90 \, \text{in}^2$

11. $104 \, \text{in}^2$
12. $124 \, \text{cm}^2$
13. $27 \, \text{cm}^2$
14. $640 \, \text{in}^2$
15.

Exercise 14g Page 139

1. $40 \, \text{cm}^2$
2. $14 \, \text{cm}^2$
3. $14 \, \text{cm}^2$

4. $25 \, \text{in}^2$
5. $12 \, \text{in}^2$
6. $60 \, \text{cm}^2$

7. $21 \, \text{mm}^2$
8. $45 \, \text{cm}^2$
9. $30 \, \text{in}^2$

10. $13.5 \, \text{m}^2$
11. $38.5 \, \text{cm}^2$
12. $14 \, \text{in}^2$

13. $70 \, \text{mm}^2$
14. $240 \, \text{cm}^2$

Chapter Fifteen - Straight Division

Exercise 15a Page 141

1. 27/11
2. 10/8
3. 6/5
4. 51/7
5. 10/3
6. 32/13
7. 12/1
8. 20/3

9. 36/0
10. 14/15
11. 42/6
12. 21/6
13. 20/14
14. 11/16
15. 72/2
16. 3/26

17. 33/12
18. 10/1
19. 13/12
20. 20/9
21. 21/0
22. 11/0
23. 21/0
24. 11/0

25. 11/0
26. 22/0
27. 33/0
28. 12/3
29. 10/12
30. 30/0
31. 7/17
32. 10/39

Exercise 15b Page 142

1. 223/1
2. 153/15
3. 30/2
4. 134/18

5. 136/3
6. 151/1
7. 145/0
8. 57/28

9. 55/10
10. 116/37
11. 230/5
12. 452/4

13. 32/18
14. 112/24
15. 132/44
16. 112/25

17. 101/18	**21.** 40/44	**25.** 31/2	**29.** 150/14
18. 112/40	**22.** 40/30	**26.** 23/24	**30.** 306/9
19. 158/47	**23.** 43/14	**27.** 120/27	**31.** 30/48
20. 132/18	**24.** 31/17	**28.** 241/1	**32.** 124/18

Exercise 15c Page 142

1. 4263/7	**5.** 2123/4	**9.** 1235/2	**13.** 1176/54	**17.** 1215/16
2. 2816/9	**6.** 2532/11	**10.** 3546/8	**14.** 1451/20	**18.** 1136/33
3. 2443/9	**7.** 1573/4	**11.** 1118/12	**15.** 1322/13	**19.** 1191/37
4. 2246/5	**8.** 2183/20	**12.** 1375/45	**16.** 1242/2	**20.** 1222/31

Exercise 15d Page 142

1. 2113 acres	**5.** 12	**9.** 54	**13.** 15, 22	**17.** £11,151
2. 15	**6.** 230	**10.** 14	**14.** 10	**18.** 103 m
3. 666	**7.** 21	**11.** 21	**15.** 322, 18 cm	**19.** 72 acres
4. 204	**8.** 18	**12.** 46	**16.** £22.50	**20.** 1127

Exercise 15e Page 144

1. 7 r 1 6 r 3 5 r 5 4 r 7	**5.** 5 r 3 4 r 8 3 r 13 2 r 18	**9.** 6 r 5 5 r 12 4 r 19 3 r 26	**13.** 9 r 5 8 r 11 7 r 17 6 r 23	**17.** 10 r 2 9 r 10 8 r 18 7 r 26
2. 5 r 2 4 r 5 3 r 8 2 r 11	**6.** 5 r 3 4 r 7 3 r 11 2 r 15	**10.** 9 r 7 8 r 16 7 r 25 6 r 34	**14.** 7 r 1 6 r 7 5 r 13 4 r 19	**18.** 7 r 8 6 r 17 5 r 26 4 r 35
3. 10 r 1 9 r 3 8 r 5 7 r 7	**7.** 6 r 3 5 r 9 4 r 15 3 r 21	**11.** 5 r 5 4 r 13 3 r 21 2 r 29	**15.** 9 r 0 8 r 9 7 r 18 6 r 27	**19.** 9 r 5 8 r 12 7 r 19 6 r 26
4. 6 r 1 5 r 4 4 r 7 3 r 10	**8.** 8 r 3 7 r 7 6 r 11 5 r 15	**12.** 9 r 0 8 r 4 7 r 8 6 r 12	**16.** 8 r 1 7 r 9 6 r 17 5 r 25	**20.** 9 r 2 8 r 10 7 r 18 6 r 26

Exercise 15f Page 145

1. 142/4	**7.** 253/1	**13.** 164/2	**19.** 126/34	**25.** 19/10	**31.** 64/8
2. 189/5	**8.** 468/8	**14.** 121/1	**20.** 164/10	**26.** 43/12	**32.** 237/65
3. 170/22	**9.** 229/3	**15.** 447/2	**21.** 18/0	**27.** 54/0	
4. 357/3	**10.** 243/1	**16.** 287/17	**22.** 105/41	**28.** 16/6	
5. 238/4	**11.** 249/1	**17.** 267/7	**23.** 61/5	**29.** 86/0	
6. 229/27	**12.** 140/14	**18.** 355/8	**24.** 58/20	**30.** 230/3	

Exercise 15g Page 146

1. 2598	**5.** 67	**9.** 23	**13.** 8930 tons	**17.** 28
2. 38557/15	**6.** 34	**10.** 138 min	**14.** 1 year	**18.** 220 g
3. 1905	**7.** 400	**11.** 68 days	**15.** 3258	**19.** 2800
4. 63	**8.** 308	**12.** 126	**16.** 4235	**20.** £3437

Chapter 16 - Practice and Revision 2

Exercise 16a Page 147

1. a) 1 b) 3	**7.** 1501	**14.** 9310	**21.** 78426/6	**28.** 12
2. c) 4 d) 7	**8.** 263397	**15.** 995006	**22.** 123/56	**29.** 121/401
2. 183	**9.** 4440025	**16.** 1007010	**23.** 235/87	**30.** 16/10
3. 9249	**10.** 19599	**17.** 11742	**24.** 113/555	**31.** 164/0
4. 69681477	**11.** 1035	**18.** 882	**25.** 12/476	**32.** 135/27
5. 90.44	**12.** 616	**19.** 957	**26.** 122/4	**33.** 18144/17
6. 521	**13.** 145248	**20.** 5708/5	**27.** 1212/3	

Exercise 16b Page 148

1. 6574, 453232, 7700   **5.** 1000, 79152   **9.** 348, 1428, 904632876
2. 546, 222, 1011, 81453 **6.** 7112048571   **10.** 315, 68775, 8088962430
3. 724, 768548   **7.** 2500, 450, 5060
4. 5675, 987600, 87567435 **8.** 876, 4584, 342612

Exercise 16c Page 148

1. $\frac{1}{2}$	**5.** $6\frac{1}{3}$	**9.** $4\frac{1}{8}$	**13.** $9\frac{43}{72}$	**17.** $4\frac{23}{48}$
2. $1\frac{4}{15}$	**6.** $4\frac{2}{3}$	**10.** $5\frac{5}{6}$	**14.** $3\frac{5}{21}$	**18.** $1\frac{7}{12}$
3. $6\frac{1}{3}$	**7.** $3\frac{7}{8}$	**11.** $3\frac{8}{15}$	**15.** $2\frac{7}{90}$	**19.** $4\frac{19}{30}$
4. $3\frac{3}{5}$	**8.** $6\frac{11}{16}$	**12.** $3\frac{9}{40}$	**16.** $3\frac{19}{24}$	**20.** $13\frac{7}{60}$

Exercise 16d Page 148

1. $2\frac{1}{2}$	**5.** $1\frac{1}{20}$	**9.** $\frac{3}{17}$	**13.** $3\frac{1}{3}$	**17.** $4\frac{3}{8}$
2. 10	**6.** $1\frac{7}{25}$	**10.** $12\frac{2}{3}$	**14.** $3\frac{3}{20}$	**18.** 51
3. $\frac{7}{12}$	**7.** 2	**11.** $\frac{5}{21}$	**15.** 18	**19.** $14\frac{7}{10}$
4. $\frac{3}{8}$	**8.** $10\frac{1}{3}$	**12.** 9	**16.** 2	**20.** $46\frac{1}{2}$

Exercise 16e Page 149

1 . 3.8	**5** . 89.66	**9** . 145.86	**13** . 50.8	**17** . 5.33
2 . 1.86	**6** . 5.6	**10** . 0.4549	**14** . 156.87	**18** . 3.99
3 . 77.52	**7** . 5.27	**11** . 12.421	**15** . 63.66	**19** . 8.17
4 . 7.7	**8** . 122.39	**12** . 90.01	**16** . 0.7596	**20** . 2.266

Exercise 16f Page 149

1 . $\frac{3}{10}$	**3** . $\frac{1}{2}$	**5** . $\frac{1}{1000}$	**7** . $\frac{17}{25}$	**9** . $\frac{1}{20}$
2 . $\frac{17}{20}$	**4** . $\frac{9}{20}$	**6** . $\frac{1}{50}$	**8** . $\frac{3}{4}$	**10** . $\frac{1}{250}$

11 . 0.3	**15** . 0.13	**19** . 0.237	**23** . 0.8	**27** . 0.35
12 . 0.7	**16** . 0.81	**20** . 0.0002	**24** . 0.44	**28** . 0.58
13 . 0.4	**17** . 0.001	**21** . 0.6	**25** . 0.4	**29** . 0.19
14 . 0.03	**18** . 0.011	**22** . 0.28	**26** . 0.8	**30** . 0.12

Exercise 16g Page 149

1 . 6.8	**5** . 364.35	**9** . 367.42	**13** . £57.35	**15** . 206 m
2 . 17.5	**6** . 4.25	**10** . $x = 13$	£12.65	2380 m^2
3 . 4.2	**7** . 92.095	**11** . $a + 2b$	**14** . 1.79 m	**16** . $\frac{1}{6}$
4 . 16.7	**8** . 37.22	**12** . 84		

Exercise 16h Page 150

1 . 28 cm   **2** . 110 cm   **3** . 36 in   **4** . 216 mm   **5** . 72 cm   **6** . 24 in   **7** . 36 cm

Exercise 16i Page 150

1 . 49 cm^2 **2** . 736 cm^2 **3** . 51 in^2 **4** . 1520 mm^2 **5** . 256 cm^2 **6** . 24 in^2 **7** . 54 cm^2

Exercise 16j Page 151

1 . 684	**6** . 2661	**10** . 81366	**15** . 2532/11	**17** . 7
2 . 60	**7** . 16, 22	**11** . $\frac{1}{5}$	**16** . Five million, four hundred	**18** . Yes
3 . 11.25	**8** . (a) 722	**12** . $\frac{9}{25}$	and seven thousand and	**19** . 6
4 . 365	(b) 1444	**13** . 0.55	sixty-eight	**20** . £65.05
5 . 2700	**9** . 0.0251 m^2	**14** . 0.168		

Exercise 16k Page 151

1. $2 \times 2 \times 3 \times 3 \times 5$
2. 720
3. £1.80
4. 20,000 cm^2
5. 4 min 20 sec
6. 39.75 kg, 90.25 kg

7. 20
8. £19.20
9. 15p
10. £10
11. 6
12. 60.5p per litre

13. £18.54
14. 55 cm
    3025 cm^2
15. 32
    8 cm

16. 8.6 m
17. 2 h 46 m 40 s
18. 1
19. 2.16 km

Chapter 17 - Working Base Multiplication

Exercise 17a Page 153

1. 462
2. 528
3. 992
4. 1763
5. 1056
6. 2652

7. 1024
8. 41412
9. 165633
10. 95472
11. 1848
12. 506

13. 1804
14. 41406
15. 93328
16. 47268
17. 166439
18. 259588

19. 9027020
20. 4018008
21. 1023
22. 3782
23. 2756
24. 94550

25. 168096
26. 256536
27. 4028033
28. 25065036
29. 9357888
30. 4282938

Exercise 17b Page 154

1. 2703
2. 3135
3. 3127
4. 2915
5. 550
6. 4221

7. 2068
8. 616
9. 367235
10. 258048
11. 43680
12. 44485

13. 168678
14. 54775
15. 110622
16. 107841
17. 280125
18. 380664

19. 278720
20. 4268264
21. 4236777
22. 9648848
23. 10553560
24. 2633670534668

Exercise 17c Page 155

1. 342
2. 306
3. 812
4. 2303
5. 2304
6. 3306

7. 729
8. 1482
9. 157608
10. 85255
11. 304
12. 783

13. 1406
14. 3422
15. 2352
16. 89102
17. 38220
18. 354021

19. 482330
20. 155618
21. 696
22. 1332
23. 2160
24. 667

25. 79299
26. 238620
27. 33908
28. 306688
29. 15972010
30. 63048678

Exercise 17d Page 156

1. 2303
2. 2304
3. 2205

4. 2208
5. 1812
6. 1599

7. 1519
8. 576
9. 1196

10. 672
11. 2808
12. 2912

13. 2916
14. 2704
15. 3016

16. 1444	22. 2915	28. 2475	34. 2392	40. 2035
17. 1517	23. 3135	29. 2451	35. 2794	41. 2565
18. 1443	24. 3111	30. 2279	36. 3479	42. 3249
19. 1408	25. 3721	31. 2773	37. 3264	43. 3525
20. 1512	26. 2499	32. 2436	38. 2867	44. 3936
21. 2601	27. 2491	33. 2376	39. 1978	45. 1173

Exercise 17e Page 156

1. 2808	7. 258055	13. 2303	19. 202455	25. 257033
2. 2703	8. 24708	14. 2112	20. 229272	26. 41004
3. 3132	9. 64008	15. 1927	21. 65021	27. 24941200
4. 702	10. 14036	16. 259072	22. 66040	28. 6260003
5. 2208	11. 3016	17. 290156	23. 61005	29. 2566005296
6. 506	12. 2915	18. 230144	24. 25630369	30. 57120

Exercise 17f Page 157

1. 2856	6. 246512	11. 3074	16. 41208
2. 2862	7. 257550	12. 1978	17. 60756
3. 2254	8. 38407	13. 756	18. 3974022
4. 754	9. 483	14. 241560	19. 2500550028
5. 253512	10. 59774	15. 257544	20. 55304

Exercise 17g Page 158

1. 2808	7. 258055	13. 2303	19. 202455	25. 257033
2. 2703	8. 247008	14. 2112	20. 229272	26. 41004
3. 3132	9. 64008	15. 1927	21. 65021	27. 23971200
4. 783	10. 14036	16. 259072	22. 66040	28. 6260003
5. 2208	11. 648	17. 147684	23. 61005	29. 2566405296
6. 506	12. 1824	18. 230144	24. 25630369	30. 57120

Chapter 18 - Ratio and Proportion

Exercise 18a Page 159

1. 2:3	7. 4:1	13. 7:1	19. 2:3	25. 4:5	31. 2:3
2. 4:5	8. 4:5	14. 7:13	20. 4:3	26. 4:1	32. 1:3
3. 2:3	9. 1:6	15. 3:2	21. 5:6	27. 20:1	
4. 2:3	10. 25:22	16. 8:7	22. 2:1	28. 2:11	
5. 4:3	11. 8:25	17. 1:4	23. 1:11	29. 5:16	
6. 5:6	12. 1:10	18. 3:4	24. 4:9	30. 1:2	

Exercise 18b Page 160

1. 3 : 1
2. 12 : 1
3. (a) 2 : 3
   (b) 150
   (c) $\frac{3}{5}$
4. (a) 90 miles
   (b) 60 miles

   (c) 2 : 3
5. (a) 24 cm
   (b) 32 cm
   (c) 3 : 4
   (d) 36 cm^2
   (e) 64 cm^2
   (f) 9 : 16

6. (a) 18 hrs
   (b) 1 : 3
   (c) 3 : 1
7. 18 ounces
8. £25
9. Laura 12, Lisa 24
10. 60 children

Exercise 18c Page 161

1. 6
2. 12
3. 6
4. 15
5. 3
6. 5

7. 3
8. 4
9. 2
10. 16
11. 20
12. 4

13. 14
14. $\bar{1}$
15. 5
16. 1
17. 1
18. 12

19. 12
20. 18
21. 60
22. 9
23. 42
24. 1

25. 50
26. 100
27. 1
28. $\bar{6}$
29. $\bar{2}$
30. $2\frac{1}{2}$

Exercise 18d Page 162

1. 6
2. 12
3. 14
4. 25
5. 21
6. 10

7. 18
8. 3
9. 4
10. 5
11. 2
12. 5

13. 15
14. 20
15. 3
16. 48
17. 4
18. 7

19. 7
20. 6
21. 5
22. 3
23. 12
24. 7

25. 2
26. 9
27. 10
28. 50
29. 36
30. 3.6

Exercise 18e Page 163

1. 32
2. 2
3. 15
4. $1\frac{1}{5}$
5. $4\frac{1}{2}$
6. $2\frac{6}{7}$

7. $2\frac{2}{9}$
8. $3\frac{3}{5}$
9. 21
10. 63
11. 60
12. 4

13. $\frac{1}{4}$
14. $10\frac{1}{2}$
15. $\frac{1}{5}$
16. $\frac{2}{5}$
17. $\frac{3}{5}$
18. $\frac{1}{3}$

19. $\frac{11}{15}$
20. $1\frac{1}{2}$
21. $3\frac{1}{3}$
22. $1\frac{3}{10}$
23. 3
24. $\frac{6}{7}$

25. $\frac{3}{5}$
26. $1\frac{1}{5}$
27. 10
28. 50
29. 36
30. 3.6

Exercise 18f Page 164

1. (a) £120
   (b) 3 : 5
   (c) 3 : 5
   (d) same
2. (a) £0.90
   (b) 20 : 1

3. 2 kg
4. £1.92
5. 37.5 m²
6. 600 g
7. 24 pints

8. £144
9. 40 km
10. 35 minutes
11. £30
12. 15

13. 12.5 kg
14. 150 km
15. £630
16. £16
17. £2500

Exercise 18g Page 166

1. 30 km/h
2. 10 days
3. 16 minutes
4. 7 weeks
5. 30 boxes

6. $3\frac{1}{2}$ hrs
7. 9 days
8. 20 minutes
9. 40 days
10. 45 bunches

11. 27 rows
12. 4 pumps
13. 48 days
14. 60 hrs
15. 40 days

16. 18 people
17. 360 revolutions
18. 20 yrs

Chapter 20 - Order of Operations

Exercise 20a Page 180

1. 36
2. 84
3. 300
4. 70
5. 108

6. 64
7. 300
8. 70
9. 150
10. 150

11. 180
12. 144
13. 96
14. 189
15. 198

16. 252
17. 264
18. 224
19. 700
20. 360

21. 168
22. 150
23. 336
24. 600
25. 300

26. 64
27. 180
28. 324
29. 630
30. 432

Exercise 20b Page 181

1. 42
2. 10
3. 8
4. 27
5. 24

6. 49
7. 32
8. 28
9. 44
10. 24

11. 106
12. 32
13. 15
14. 36
15. 42

16. 4
17. 20
18. 36
19. 350
20. 25

21. 12
22. 28
23. 8
24. 2

Exercise 20c Page 182

1. 59
2. 42
3. 41
4. 301
5. 96

6. 36
7. 10
8. 56
9. 22
10. 123

11. 36
12. 28
13. 748
14. 6477
15. 400

16. 68
17. 0
18. 380
19. 150
20. 400

21. 0.5
22. 2.02
23. 2
24. 65.5
25. 3.6

26. 24.2
27. 45.1
28. 47.4
29. 98.8
30. 3.7

Exercise 20d Page 183

1. $3d$	6. $8k$	11. $2a$	16. $-ab$	21. $20m$	26. $-10c^2$
2. 0	7. $7n$	12. $7b$	17. $12y$	22. $-11cd$	27. $-b^3$
3. f	8. $2m$	13. $4c$	18. $-6b$	23. 0	28. $8x^2y$
4. $6g$	9. $7p$	14. 0	19. $6pq$	24. $7p$	29. $54ab$
5. 0	10. $10r$	15. $8a$	20. $-54c$	25. $-10x$	30. $-3yz$

Exercise 20e Page 184

1. 22	6. 26	11. 30	16. 2	21. 2	26. 0
2. 2	7. 32	12. 30	17. 57	22. 20	27. 27
3. 12	8. 20	13. 64	18. 43	23. 40	28. 15
4. 3	9. 0	14. 8	19. 28	24. 6	29. 2925
5. 19	10. 53	15. 21	20. 16	25. 75	30. 180

Exercise 20f Page 185

1. 25	6. 63	11. 1	16. 2	21. 22	26. 1
2. 18	7. 4	12. 10	17. 22	22. 1	27. 9
3. 42	8. 10	13. 14	18. 18	23. 13	28. 64
4. 2	9. 9	14. 2	19. 53	24. 6	29. 20
5. 5	10. 6	15. 63	20. 27	25. 0	30. -40

Chapter 21 Multiplication and Division of Decimals

Exercise 21a Page 186

	×10	×100	×1000		×10	×100	×1000
1.	46.37	463.7	4637	11.	129.5	1295	12950
2.	86.43	864.3	8643	12.	0.376	3.76	37.6
3.	860.05	8600.5	86005	13.	43.234	432.34	4323.4
4.	5	50	500	14.	561.82	5618.2	56182
5.	146.2	1462	14620	15.	45658	456580	4565800
6.	1234.443	12344.43	123444.3	16.	3227.5	32275	322750
7.	74	740	7400	17.	0.0944	0.944	9.44
8.	1326.4	13264	132640	18.	0.2601	2.601	26.01
9.	08.723	087.23	0872.3	19.	0.0045	0.045	0.45
10.	276	2760	27600	20.	30.20765	302.0765	3020.765

Exercise 21b Page 187

	÷10	÷100	÷1000			÷10	÷100	÷1000
1.	200	20	2		11.	0.455	0.0455	0.00455
2.	50	5	0.5		12.	1.76	0.176	0.0176
3.	7	0.7	0.07		13.	86.89	8.689	0.8689
4.	56.7	5.67	0.567		14.	5.3	0.53	0.053
5.	8.3	0.83	0.083		15.	0.01	0.001	0.0001
6.	876.5	87.65	8.765		16.	0.045	0.00045	0.000045
7.	0.7	0.07	0.007		17.	345.0	34.50	3.450
8.	6.73	0.673	0.0673		18.	6570.0	657.00	65.700
9.	6.8003	0.68003	0.068003		19.	0.005	0.0005	0.00005
10.	0.23	0.023	0.0023		20.	0.6001	0.06001	0.006001

Exercise 21c Page 188

1.	46	8.	163.12	15.	0.02	22.	0.18	29.	0.1104
2.	1820	9.	3972	16.	0.1684	23.	0.912	30.	1.6
3.	51.2	10.	3240	17.	4.692	24.	1.2	31.	1.36
4.	820	11.	0.23	18.	0.71	25.	17	32.	2400
5.	3690	12.	0.462	19.	0.182	26.	90		
6.	8600	13.	0.22	20.	13.696	27.	421		
7.	2750	14.	0.212	21.	9	28.	1.3		

Exercise 21d Page 188

1.	29.2	8.	2712.8	15.	8.1	22.	0.087	29.	32.859
2.	1.05	9.	792.3	16.	76.04	23.	1292.014	30.	0.37
3.	336.7	10.	242.494	17.	141.9	24.	0.358	31.	22.435
4.	186.12	11.	4.6	18.	1.2130	25.	0.437	32.	124.02
5.	19.08	12.	2.3	19.	27.64	26.	72.96		
6.	11.2	13.	1.23	20.	0.95	27.	0.0524		
7.	11.34	14.	1.72	21.	305684.84	28.	0.0068		

Exercise 21e Page 189

1.	2.5	4.	11.5	7.	0.268	10.	0.625	13.	13.44
2.	2.5	5.	133.75	8.	6.912	11.	4.5	14.	867.25
3.	2.4	6.	16417.5	9.	155.275	12.	54.375	15.	11798.375

Exercise 21f Page 190

1. 4.32	8. 1.44	15. 0.09	22. 683.73	29. 0.2041
2. 40.32	9. 13.68	16. 4.9323	23. 214.2	30. 5.2955
3. 9.79	10. 57.4	17. 6.003	24. 74.76	31. 5.2955
4. 22.36	11. 0.1	18. 21.0021	25. 83.98	32. 5.2955
5. 2.6	12. 0.7	19. 32.886	26. 15.75	
6. 0.51	13. 0.53	20. 4.3148	27. 9.24	
7. 3.15	14. 0.64	21. 574.56	28. 0.0504	

Exercise 21g Page 191

1. £3.25	4. £17.408	7. £80.75	10. 0.628	13. £159.50
2. £51.66	5. 1.316	8. £1.17	11. 559.48 cm²	14. 222.768
3. 323 miles	6. 35.2	9. 14.3	12. 27.3 m²	15. £22.7232

Exercise 21h Page 192

1. 7.1	4. 4.4	7. 21.1	10. 13.7	13. 4.13	16. 94.8
2. 11.3	5. 11.7	8. 20.3	11. 51.0	14. 25.27	17. 2.106
3. 7.0	6. 21.7	9. 20.1	12. 31.0	15. 10.34	18. 0.1725

Exercise 21i Page 193

1. 5.12	4. 10.34	7. 0.154	10. 1106.0	13. 144.0	16. 0.365
2. 42.0	5. 11.4	8. 12.0	11. 263.0	14. 228.0	17. 7.0
3. 6.36	6. 1.03	9. 2.3	12. 0.4	15. 2240.0	18. 184.0

Chapter 22   Percentages

Exercise 22a Page 195

	Percentage	Vulgar Fraction	Decimal Fraction			Percentage	Vulgar Fraction	Decimal Fraction
1.	75%	$\frac{3}{4}$	0.75		6.	55%	$\frac{11}{20}$	0.55
2.	40%	$\frac{2}{5}$	0.4		7.	24%	$\frac{6}{25}$	0.24
3.	36%	$\frac{9}{25}$	0.36		8.	60%	$\frac{3}{5}$	0.6
4.	48%	$\frac{12}{25}$	0.48		9.	80%	$\frac{4}{5}$	0.8
5.	45%	$\frac{9}{20}$	0.45		10.	78%	$\frac{39}{50}$	0.78

Exercise 22b Page 196

1. 2p	**7.** $105	**13.** £28	**19.** 6800 kg	**25.** £4
2. 60 m	**8.** £18	**14.** 6 km	**20.** 8 litres	**26.** 40 m
3. 9 cm	**9.** 67.5 g	**15.** 228p	**21.** 15 m	**27.** 16 kg
4. £8	**10.** 27 ft	**16.** £6	**22.** 2.4 km	**28.** 387p
5. 12 in	**11.** 63 cm	**17.** 14 yds	**23.** 4.5 mm	**29.** 16.4 m
6. £1	**12.** 567 mm	**18.** £36	**24.** 9.5 ml	**30.** 20 g

Exercise 22c Page 196

1. 20%	**7.** 20%	**13.** 25%	**19.** 50%	**25.** 2%	**31.** 15%
2. 32%	**8.** 90%	**14.** 10%	**20.** 85%	**26.** 20%	**32.** 28%
3. 25%	**9.** 64%	**15.** 20%	**21.** 4%	**27.** 20%	
4. 30%	**10.** 48%	**16.** 8%	**22.** 20%	**28.** 19%	
5. 4%	**11.** 130%	**17.** 37.5%	**23.** 4%	**29.** 16.666...%	
6. 30%	**12.** 25%	**18.** 30%	**24.** 12%	**30.** 0.8333...%	

Exercise 22d Page 197

1. 25%	**7.** a)Nitre 750 kg	**11.** 33.3...%	**17.** 70%
2. 94%	b) Sulphur 100 kg	**12.** 54%	**18.** £15,000
3. 15%	c) Charcoal 150 kg	**13.** 56%	**19.** £24.50
4. 65%	**8.** £40	**14.** 33.3...%	**20.** £295 or £45
5. 455 kg	**9.** £14,250	**15.** 2%	
6. 43.25	**10.** £24.50	**16.** 60%	

Exercise 22e Page 198

1. 1.19	**5.** 2.42	**9.** 0.25	**13.** 81	**17.** a) 108 : 100
2. 1.73	**6.** 0.91	**10.** 0.98	**14.** 28	b) 108 : 8
3. 1.60	**7.** 0.77	**11.** 336	**15.** £40,250	c) 1.08
4. 1.25	**8.** 0.6	**12.** 375	**16.** 15%	**18.** 15,370
				19. 5%

Chapter 23 Averages

Exercise 23a Page 201

1. 11	**5.** 42	**9.** 64	**13.** 3.6	**17.** 469
2. 7	**6.** 52	**10.** 27	**14.** 0.43	**18.** 90
3. 17	**7.** 58	**11.** 52	**15.** 0.65	**19.** 35.2
4. 25.5	**8.** 54.5	**12.** 5.5	**16.** 47	**20.** 632.75

Exercise 23b Page 201

1. 62%	**6.** 3	**11.** 264	**16.** 6
2. 269	**7.** 52	**12.** 201 yrs 1 m	**17.** 49 yrs
3. 79	**8.** 35 mph	**13.** £19	**18.** 12.2 s
4. 49	**9.** 5 ft 0 in	**14.** 10 st 13 lbs	**19.** 74%, No
5. 9.5	**10.** £195	**15.** 185,901 per yr	**20.** 67%

Exercise 23c Page 203

1. 92	**5.** 81	**9.** 42	**13.** 218	**17.** 47
2. 55	**6.** 87	**10.** 6.2	**14.** 0.56	**18.** 6.0
3. 15	**7.** 760	**11.** 8.2	**15.** 0.73	**19.** 5300
4. 90	**8.** 74	**12.** 4.4	**16.** 134	**20.** 870

Exercise 23d Page 204

1. 55%	**3.** a) Wednesday	**4.** 13.1 s	**5.** a) No 2
2. 4.0 s	b) Saturday		b) 175 lbs
	c) 117		c) 11 lbs

Chapter 24 Graphs

Exercise 24a Page 207

1.a) 1 hr	**c)** $1\frac{1}{2}$ hrs	**e)** 40 km	**g)** 1 hr	**i)** 160 km
b) 40 km/h	**d)** 2 hrs	**f)** 20 km/h	**h)** 80 km/h	**j)** 50 km

2.

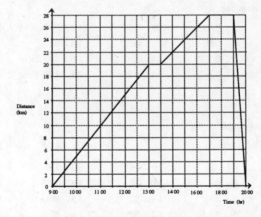

3. a) 15 km/h **b)** He is not moving. **c)** $23\frac{1}{3}$ km/h **d)** 35 km **e)** 5 15 pm

4. a) 30 min **b)** 1 hr **c)** $66\frac{2}{3}$ mph for A-B, B-C and C-D **d)** 300 miles

D-A 100 mph

5.

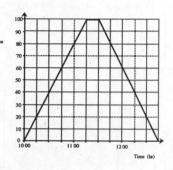

Exercise 24b Page 210

1.

Height	Frequency
131-135	4
136-140	7
141-145	4
146-150	8
151-155	15
156-160	7
161-165	5

2.

Diameter	Frequency
171-175	5
176-180	9
181-185	7
186-190	11
191-195	11
196-200	5
201-205	6
206-210	6

3.

Marks	Frequency
0-10	0
11-20	1
21-30	3
31-40	7
41-50	8
51-60	5
61-70	12
71-80	10
81-90	5
91-100	9

Exercise 24c Page 211

1.

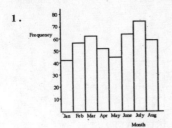

5.

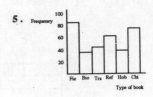

2.

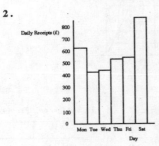

6.

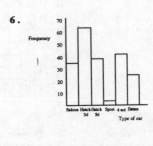

3.

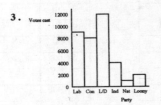

7.

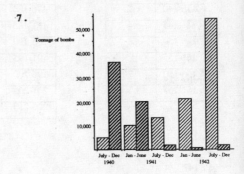

4.

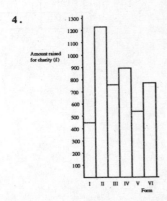

8.

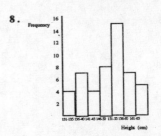

278

9.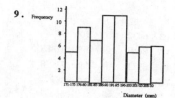

10.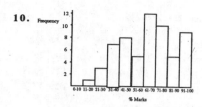

Chapter 25 Calculations using vinculums

Exercise 25a Page 213

1. 4$\bar{1}$	5. 6$\bar{2}$	9. 3$\bar{3}$	13. 10$\bar{1}$	17. 48$\bar{4}$
2. 5$\bar{1}$	6. 8$\bar{2}$	10. 4$\bar{2}$	14. 47$\bar{2}$	18. 49$\bar{2}$
3. 3$\bar{1}$	7. 6$\bar{1}$	11. 8$\bar{1}$	15. 53$\bar{2}$	19. 90$\bar{1}$
4. 2$\bar{1}$	8. 5$\bar{2}$	12. 10$\bar{2}$	16. 14$\bar{4}$	20. 40$\bar{2}$

Exercise 25b Page 213

1. 39	5. 19	9. 89	13. 909	17. 378
2. 28	6. 67	10. 76	14. 187	18. 99
3. 66	7. 57	11. 228	15. 538	19. 196
4. 49	8. 16	12. 636	16. 239	20. 7996

Exercise 25c Page 214

1. 58	7. 445	13. 72	19. 384	25. 546	31. 1824
2. 117	8. 594	14. 174	20. 1851	26. 344	32. 2135
3. 138	9. 84	15. 1195	21. 336	27. 2135	
4. 76	10. 192	16. 1311	22. 268	28. 2624	
5. 147	11. 204	17. 3003	23. 342	29. 3108	
6. 632	12. 74	18. 2472	24. 138	30. 4023	

Exercise 25d Page 214

1. 3$\bar{1}$3	5. 70$\bar{1}$	9. 30$\bar{9}$3	13. 5$\bar{1}$3$\bar{2}\,\bar{1}$	17. 4$\bar{1}$00$\bar{3}$
2. 4$\bar{2}\,\bar{4}$	6. 3$\bar{2}$3$\bar{2}$	10. 4$\bar{2}$9$\bar{1}$	14. 2000$\bar{1}$	18. 2$\bar{1}\,\bar{9}$9$\bar{3}$
3. 5$\bar{1}\,\bar{1}$	7. 600$\bar{1}$	11. 3$\bar{1}$3$\bar{2}$3	15. 4$\bar{1}$10$\bar{2}$	19. 43$\bar{2}\,\bar{1}\,\bar{1}$
4. 60$\bar{2}$	8. 4$\bar{2}$3$\bar{2}$	12. 400$\bar{1}$3	16. 4$\bar{1}\,\bar{2}\,\bar{3}\,\bar{5}$	20. 33$\bar{3}\,\bar{3}\,\bar{3}$

Exercise 25e Page 215

1. 489	5. 776	9. 422	13. 6432	17. 5594
2. 568	6. 587	10. 267	14. 8459	18. 27888
3. 379	7. 499	11. 5688	15. 6311	19. 73428
4. 658	8. 368	12. 4777	16. 4997	20. 889

Exercise 25f Page 215

1. 864	5. 1656	9. 9996	13. 230392	17. 258293
2. 1556	6. 3996	10. 43995	14. 448911	18. 2399912
3. 2495	7. 8637	11. 83064	15. 238440	19. 5381091
4. 2061	8. 11104	12. 233394	16. 301592	20. 27157879

Exercise 25g Page 216

1. $\bar{2}\bar{4}$	5. $\bar{2}\bar{7}$	9. $\bar{5}\bar{6}$	13. $\bar{2}\bar{4}$	17. 66
2. $\bar{1}\bar{4}$	6. $\bar{1}\bar{2}$	10. $\bar{5}\bar{6}$	14. 25	18. $\bar{2}\bar{8}$
3. $\bar{2}\bar{4}$	7. 12	11. 56	15. $\bar{2}\bar{1}$	19. $\bar{4}\bar{5}$
4. $\bar{1}\bar{2}$	8. 56	12. $\bar{2}\bar{7}$	16. 18	20. 36

Exercise 25h Page 216

1. 4	6. $\bar{3}$	11. $\bar{6}$	16. $\bar{6}$	21. $\bar{1}$	26. 3	31. 6	36. $\bar{4}$
2. 6	7. $\bar{1}$	12. $\bar{4}$	17. 5	22. 0	27. $\bar{3}$	32. 3	37. 1
3. 8	8. $\bar{5}$	13. $\bar{3}$	18. $\bar{1}$	23. 0	28. 6	33. $\bar{5}$	38. 0
4. 4	9. 5	14. 0	19. 1	24. 0	29. 0	34. $\bar{3}$	39. $\bar{4}$
5. 12	10. 9	15. 1	20. $\bar{4}$	25. $\bar{9}$	30. 6	35. 2	40. 4

Exercise 25i Page 217

1. 1102	5. 1593	9. 2553	13. 531	17. 1794
2. 504	6. 912	10. 2212	14. 1911	18. 1653
3. 493	7. 1062	11. 874	15. 2054	19. 81
4. 1372	8. 1064	12. 1739	16. 1444	20. 3481

Chapter 26 Angles

Exercise 26a Page 220

1. 47°	3. 145°	5. 232°	7. 87°	9. 43°
2. 22°	4. 8°	6. 23° (22.5°)	8. 38°	10. 153°

Exercise 26c Page 221

1. Acute   3. Obtuse   5. Reflex   7. Acute   9. Acute
2. Acute   4. Acute   6. Acute   8. Acute   10. Obtuse

Exercise 26d Page 222

1. 40°   3. 150°   5. 120°   7. 37°   9. 44°
2. 150°   4. 125°   6. 75°   8. 24°   10. 61°

Exercise 26e Page 223

1. 40°   3. 38°   5. 94°   7. 117°   9. 45°
2. 155°   4. 145°   6. 92°   8. 28°   10. 20°

Exercise 26f Page 225

1. $a = \angle$PQR   3. $p = \angle$BAD or $\angle$CAD   5. $e = \angle$QPR
   $b = \angle$QRP $q = \angle$ADB $f = \angle$SPR
   $c = \angle$RPQ $r = \angle$BDC $g = \angle$QSR
                             $s = \angle$ABD $h = \angle$SQR

2. $a = \angle$CAB or $\angle$DAB $t = \angle$BCD or $\angle$ACD
   $b = \angle$ABC   6. $d = \angle$UTS or $\angle$UTX
   $c = \angle$BCE $e = \angle$WTV
   $d = \angle$DCE   4. $u = \angle$JLN $f = \angle$VTS or $\angle$VTX
                            $v = \angle$JLM $g = \angle$TSZ or $\angle$WSZ
                            $w = \angle$NLK $h = \angle$XSZ

Chapter 27   Practice and Revision 3

Exercise 27a Page 226

1. 77620   8. 1018072   15. $\frac{2}{3}$ 22. 2:3
2. 225646   9. 985036   16. 50 min   23. $2\frac{7}{20}$
3. £77.17   10. 134/11   17. $\frac{29}{35}$ 24. $9\frac{5}{24}$
4. £391.33   11. 4.64   18. $\frac{1}{2}$ 25. $5a$
5. £341.10   12. 1.835   19. 114/73   26. $8x + 3y$
6. £3.69   13. 0.26   20. 4   27. $15a - 6b$
7. 19152   14. 40, 42   21. 48   28. $x = 5$

Exercise 27b Page 227

1. 8
2. 12
3. £12.50
4. 4
5. 37, 41
6. 45p

7. E.g. $\frac{4}{10}$ $\frac{6}{15}$ $\frac{8}{20}$
8. £1925
9. 15
10. 16.94
11. 42.21
12. 7.55

13. $2\frac{5}{8}$
14. $\frac{9}{20}$
15. 0.75
16. 1×36
   2×18
   3×12
   4×9
   6×6

17. 4756 m^2
18. 60 mph
19. 1.8 m
20. £1.50
21. $x = 13$
22. (a) 1
   (b) 52

23. $2\frac{3}{10}$
24. $\frac{1}{2}$
25. $7\frac{1}{2}$
26. $\frac{43}{8}$

Exercise 27c Page 228

1. 32.583 ft
2. Parallel

3. Radius
   Diameter

5. (a) 117°
   (b) Obtuse

7. 126 cm^2
8. 75 in
9. 96 cm^2

10. (a) 38 cm
   (b) 72 cm^2

Exercise 27d Page 229

1. 1.15 kg
2. 1 hr 35 min
3. 41 240 ml

4. £51.60
5. £531.25

6. (a) 4575 acres
   (b) 7625 acres
   (c) £22,875,000
7. 50

8. 320
9. 75
10. £518.40
11. £16

12. £1.99
13. 5.4 km/h
14. (a) £59.90
   (b) 10p

Exercise 27e Page 230

1. $\frac{8}{9}$
2. $1\frac{3}{8}$
3. $1\frac{11}{24}$
4. $5\frac{5}{16}$
5. $8\frac{7}{40}$
6. $9\frac{13}{14}$
7. $1\frac{1}{3}$

8. $\frac{13}{24}$
9. $\frac{11}{16}$
10. $3\frac{1}{6}$
11. $10\frac{11}{24}$
12. $1\frac{1}{3}$
13. $\frac{1}{9}$
14. $\frac{5}{12}$

15. $\frac{5}{11}$
16. 24
17. 2
18. $3\frac{7}{9}$
19. $1\frac{1}{9}$
20. $\frac{5}{8}$
21. $16\frac{1}{2}$

22. $\frac{2}{9}$
23. $3\frac{3}{20}$
24. $4\frac{3}{8}$
25. $7\frac{9}{10}$
26. $\frac{5}{12}$
27. 2
28. $\frac{1}{5}$

29. $\frac{1}{5}$
30. $\frac{7}{16}$. 112
31. $\frac{1}{9}$ $\frac{1}{7}$ $\frac{1}{5}$ $\frac{1}{3}$
   $\frac{2}{9}$
32. 99p
33. 11.25 m
34. $3\frac{37}{42}$

35. £51.20
36. 3.75 kg
37. £11.20
38. $\frac{1}{25}$